A History of Popular Music
Before Rock Music

*

Blues, Country, Cabaret, Ragtime, Film Music, Soul,
European, Latin, Jamaican, African, Arab, Indian...

*

Piero Scaruffi

Scaruffi, Piero
A Brief History of Popular Music before Rock Music
All Rights Reserved © 2007 by Piero Scaruffi

ISBN-10: 0-9765531-2-0
ISBN-13: 978-0-9765531-2-0

Blues, Country, Cabaret, Ragtime, Film, Soul, Latin, Ska, African music

For information: www.scaruffi.com

Printed and published in the USA

Photo credits: Piero Scaruffi (photo of Wahd Dahr, Yemen, 2003)

Contents

Preface

Having written a book on rock music and a book on jazz music, and being in the process of writing a book on the classical music of the 20th century, I felt the need to put somewhere the many musical genres and movements that do not quite fit either of these categories. I also felt that I needed to research the beginning of the industry of popular music in Western Europe and the USA in order to better understand the dynamics of the jazz and rock music industry. I also felt that "ethnic" music (notably from Africa and Latin America) has become so pervasive that one should trace its parallel development next to Western European and US musical genres. This book aims at filling all these gaps. I did my best to give it an organic feeling, although it is obvious that musicians from such diverse regions of the world had very little in common. Only after the synthesis of the 1970s can we talk of a global history of popular music. This book is about the foundations of that synthesis.

It was not terribly difficult to decide how to separate jazz music from pop music. It was much more difficult to decide how to separate rock music from the rest of popular music, because rock music has absorbed just about everything. Bits and pieces of this book were originally written for my 2003 book on rock music. The borderline is really more temporal than stylistic. Anything that happened after the 1960s is or will be in the book on rock music. Thus reggae and salsa are not in this book, nor is country music of the 1970s. The idea is that you should read this book before you move on to read the history of jazz music and the history of rock music.

Thanks to Chris Ford for proof-reading the text.

piero scaruffi, January 2007

A Preface To All Histories

All histories are interesting, but the history of popular music is particularly interesting. The 20th century witnessed the rise of a new form of art that is still frantically evolving and far from stabilizing.

Four factors were instrumental in bringing this about. The first one was the rise of a new cultural power, the USA, that was largely indifferent to the dogmas of European culture. The USA adopted European culture, but then introduced all sorts of "barbaric" variations into that culture. It is not surprising that it was in the USA that popular music underwent a rapid and dramatic change.

The second factor was capitalism, which prospered particularly in the USA. Capitalism had always existed, since ancient Sumerian times, but it was in the USA that it wed populism and reached its ultimate scope: consumerism. US capitalism targeted the middle class, the ordinary family, the individual, and, eventually, even the non-working young individual. It was in the USA that capitalists understood that there was money to be made not in selling expensive goods/services to wealthy people at a hefty profit but in selling cheap goods/services to poor people for a meager margin multiplied by numbers: quantity matters. If you make a cent per item but sell millions of items, you make millions. Thus the USA introduced scheduled ships to Britain at a price affordable for middle-class families, and it introduced newspapers that targeted the ordinary urban citizen at a price that the ordinary urban citizen could afford. Entertainment was one of the most obvious fields of application for this theory. Music publishing became a big industry and helped define popular music as a separate business (if not art).

The third factor was the record. Before the invention of the record the vast majority of "composers" of popular music did not know how to write music. Therefore popular music could spread only orally, which greatly limited its geographic area and duration over time. When the record was invented, suddenly popular music could be spread without any need to write it down. It took a while to understand the power of the new invention (and to get rid of the cumbersome cylinder), but eventually the industry started recording just about anything, not just the music that was already published by the publishing companies. One of the consequences, for example, was to deliver the first recordings of blues and country music, and thus help popularize them outside their area of origin.

The fourth factor to decisively shape 20th century popular music was "youth culture". It is not easy to pinpoint the exact decade in which the youth of the USA became a major factor. It is likely that young people were already among the main consumers of the dance crazes of the 1920s, although they were officially limited to expensive clubs that did not admit teenagers anyway. There may have been countless places where young people were able to play those dances outside the clubs that popularized them. For sure, the youth in the USA was the main factor behind the extraordinary success of Benny Goodman's concert in Los Angeles of august 1935. The people who went crazy over swing music were mostly teenagers. There was a new segment of the market that was made of non-working young people who got money from their parents to spend on entertainment. That market segment became a social class distinct from the others, with its own features, rules and needs. It helped establish the vogue of the romantic singers after World War II (Frank Sinatra and the like) and eventually erupted in 1955 when the Elvis Presley phenomenon basically brought all the threads together: the US culture, capitalism for the masses, the record and youth culture. The youth culture remained dormant for a while, but it was growing through its less publicized aspects of rebellion against the "American way of life". The Vietnam war and the civil-rights movement transformed the explosion of youth culture into a major sociopolitical phenomenon. At that point popular music also acquired an ideological identity, well beyond its humble origins of entertainment for the masses. It became an international koine.

EUROPEAN BEGINNINGS

Musical entertainment for the masses

Musical entertainment was born as a reflection of the relationship between humans and nature. The first disconnects between these two entities occurred with courtly music and religious music, that reflected not humans in their natural environment but humans in artificial environments such as the court and the monastery. This branch of music eventually evolved into what we call "classical music".

It is likely that musical entertainment for the poor masses remained roughly the same over many centuries, because their lifestyle did not change all that much.

But the second major disconnect affected precisely these classes of people. It took place after the industrial revolution, when reckless urbanization and factory life dramatically altered the soundscape of the lower classes. Musical entertainment for the masses became a completely different phenomenon, although still derived from the market fair and the itinerant circus. It also coincided with the renewed vogue for the theater and with the booming capitalist attitude. In the USA it was further affected by the melting pot of immigrants (including slaves), by the vast linguistically-uniform territory and by the process of colonization of new lands. Musical entertainment for the masses in industrial society was to be quite different from anything that had gone before.

First of all, it became a commodity, just like many other things (from long-distance transportation to newspapers) were becoming commodities. An entire industry was born to profit from it and to fuel its growth. The tension between its social roots and the industry that turned it into a mass product was going to remain the fundamental theme of its history.

Secondly, it introduced a new way to experience musical entertainment by separating the stage and the audience in a way that did not exist in folk music (although it already existed in courtly music). Indirectly this led to the birth of the "auteur" also in popular music, not only in classical music.

Thirdly, it became the soundtrack of the middle class. As the middle class was being created in the big cities of Europe and the

US, musical entertainment reflected its hedonistic, social, political, economic urges.

Finally, it created a whole new spectrum of professions (the owner of the theater, the performer, the publisher, etc).

Napoli: the Aria

Pop music was born in Napoli, Italy, in 1679, when Alessandro Scarlatti composed his first opera, or even earlier, when Francesco Provenzale coined the musical language that Scarlatti popularized: light, lively and catchy. They placed the emphasis on arias, clearly separated from the "recitativo", and grounded the arias on a strong sense of rhythm and melody. The Neapolitan passion for melodic singing, as defined by Alessandro Scarlatti's **Griselda** (1721), Giovanni Pergolesi's **La Serva Padrona** (1733), Giovannni Paisiello's **Nina pazza per amore** (1789), Domenico Cimarosa's **Il Matrimonio Segreto** (1792), dominated Western Europe for at least a century. Thanks to them, the opera became a simpler, funny, popular form of entertainment, and the style of singing evolved into a refined art of its own, the "bel canto". The Italian audience loved to sing the arias of Gioacchino Rossini's **Il Barbiere di Siviglia** (1816), Vincenzo Bellini's **Norma** (1831), Gaetano Doninzetti's **Lucia di Lammermoor** (1835). Few people could afford to go to the opera, but many people would hum and whistle and mimick the great opera singers. Even Giuseppe Verdi, not exactly the lightest of composers, was sung at barber shops and wedding parties. More arias were added to the repertory by Pietro Mascagni's **Cavalleria Rusticana** (1890), Ruggero Leoncavallo's "I Pagliacci" (1892), Giacomo Puccini's **Madame Butterfly** (1904). The opera was a complex work of art, but their catchy arias served the less "sophisticated" taste of the masses as well as any folk dance.

An early example of how the aria of the opera transferred to popular music is Eduardo Di Capua's *O Sole Mio* (1898), one of the most recorded songs of all times.

Vienna: the Waltz

Following the social upheavals caused by the industrial revolution and by the US and French revolutions, the 19th century witnessed two major revolutions that were both social and cultural in nature: the rise of the bourgeoisie and romanticism. They both emphasized the "popular" element, a fact that did not take long to affect instrumental music.

The social dance of the Western aristocracy (since 1650) had been the minuet. The new social order required a new social dance, a "popular" one. The waltz, derived around 1800 from an Austrian folk dance (the laendler), as well as the mazurka from Poland and the polka from Bohemia, proved to be a good match for the new social mood. The first dance hall for waltzing opened in Germany in 1754, but the waltz came into its own when it took Vienna by storm at the turn of the century thanks to dance halls such as "Zum Sperl" (1807) and "Apollo" (1808). These dances were much more vibrant than the old minuet. They allowed for more creativity. And they were more "erotic" because they were "couple-oriented" dances and the dancers were facing each other and embracing each other. Where the minuet emphasized the collective pattern, the waltz emphasized the man-woman interaction, and left the couple free to interact or not interact with the other couples on the dance floor. From the Middle Ages on, the Church had discouraged this kind of "pagan" folk dance, considering it too suggestive and too disorderly. The age of romanticism rediscovered the jovial spirit of the folk dance, although it recast it into the cold, disciplined realm of uniformed officials and long lady dresses. Replacing the peasant combo with an orchestra helped make the folk dance palatable to the aristocracy. The *An der Schoenen Blauen Donau* (1867), composed by Austrian composer Johann Strauss Junior, marked the apogee of the phenomenon.

Paris, Vienna, London: the Operetta

"Opera-Comique", the theater founded in Paris in 1715 to stage popular forms of entertainment such as comedy, dance and music shows, descendants of the light entertainment provided by itinerant troupes at medieval fairs, eventually gave the name to a musical genre, the "opera-comique". They were related to the opera only insomuch as they borrowed the new styles made popular in Napoli, but their fragmented structure betrayed their origin as, basically, a "variety show".

Jacques Offenbach created the "opera bouffe", such as **Orphee Aux Enfers** (1858), as an extension of the same concept. The songs were meant to be simple and catchy, the rhythm engaging, the tone light and humurous, the theme farcical.

The Viennese operetta, pioneered by Franz von Suppe in the 1860s and popularized, once again, by Johann Strauss Junior's **Die Fledermaus** (1874) and Franz Lehar's **Die Lustige Witwe/ The Merry Widow** (1905), did something similar with the "singspiel".

The English operetta was significantly different from the operetta of Paris and Vienna. It descended from the "ballad opera" a` la John Gay's **The Beggar's Opera** (1728), a cycle of songs to accompany a an operatic parody. It was, generally speaking, far less provocative. The prototype was Henry Bishop's **Clari or the Maid of Milan** (1823), which contained one of the most popular songs of the century, *Home Sweet Home*. The genre peaked with the works of composer Arthur Sullivan and librettist William Gilbert: **The Sorcerer** (1877), **H.M.S. Pinafore** (1878), one of the most popular (*Farewell My Own*), **The Pirates of Penzance** (1880), premiered simultaneously in London and New York, **Iolanthe** (1882), the first operetta staged at D'Oyly Carte's super-modern "Savoy" theatre (the first "electrical" theater in the world), **Princess Ida** (1884), and **The Mikado** (1885), influenced by the Japanese craze of the time and probably their masterpiece (*Tit Willow*, *Three Little Maids*), one of the first to be recorded (with a cast that included the most famous pop stars of Britain, such as Peter Dawson and Stanley Kirkby). Sullivan proved to be one of the most versatile composers of his age, running the gamut from waltzes to quotations from Wagner's operas, from military marches to medieval madrigals. His style was, de facto, an exuberant parody of the entire body of western music. Gilbert, meanwhile, painted a social universe of declining aristocracy, revered royalty and proud imperial ambitions that "satirized" but did not "criticize". In fact, it was largely devoid of the social and political anxieties of those decades.

So popular were Gilbert and Sullivan's operettas that impresario Richard D'Oyly Carte built two theaters for them, the "Savoy" (1881) and the "Royal English Opera House" (1891).

His rival impresario George Edwardes, headquartered at the "Gaiety" theater, responded with Alfred Cellier's **Dorothy** (1886), including the hit *Queen of My Heart*, and Sidney Jones' **The Gaiety Girl** (1893), featuring the "Gaiety Girls", by far the greatest attraction of the decade.

While mostly ignored (or despised) in the Continent, the English operetta with its brisk pace, delirious wit and popular melodies was highly successful in the USA.

Leslie Stuart's **Floradora** (1899), instead, belonged to the genre of the musical comedy.

Paris: the Cabaret

After the Terror and the Napoleonic wars, the cafes that sprouted all over Paris became a symbol of a more relaxed (public as well as private) life. After the last major crisis, the German invasion of 1870, was over, an event immortalized by Pierre Degeyter's "L'International" (1888), Paris began craving for entertainment after decades of intolerance and wars. The cafes served alcohol, food and fun. One particular kind was the cafe-concert.

The theater was where the operas were performed with solemn pomp, but the "cafe-concert" was the place that offered a more casual environment for the bourgeoisie to listen to the same arias while drinking a liqueur and chatting with a friend at a table. Its performers were often amateurs, but devoted ones, who could approximate the styles of the opera. Most cafe-concert would also offer other forms of entertainment, such as comedians. Eventually, the singers of the cafe-concert began to write their own material, and sing it in more regular tones (not the tenors and the baritones of the operas). Since their audience was the bourgeoisie, they addressed issues that their audience could identify with, such as satirical accounts of celebrated events. The success of the operettas influenced a parallel evolution in the music, that became more lively, hummable and rhythmic, with an emphasis on a refrain that people could easily memorize. The "chanson" was born. The genre and the locale helped each other: people went to the cafe-concert to listen to the chansonniers, but they also listened to the chansonniers because they were meeting friends at the cafe-concert. The cafe-concert was also one of the few places where the politically-motivated intellectuals could hear political talk. It was the ideal place for the artists to meet and exchanged ideas. The cafe-concert soon became a reference point for the entire cultural life of Paris. The cafe-concert was the place where the social classes mingled: for the first time in French history, the aristocracy and the lower classes shared the same venue.

During those years, the star of the theater was Sarah Bernhardt, an actress who became a myth, an "immoral" woman who was one of the first feminists, jealous of her independence and indifferent to traditional family roles. Public opinion was against her when she ended her tenure at the "Odeon" in 1872, but her cult was just starting.

Around the same time, the circus was becoming more than just trained animals and pretty riders. Following the British example, each French circus was adding acrobats, clowns and singers to its parade of sensations. The result was a more exhilarating experience that drew bigger and bigger crowds.

The cabaret (originally the term for liquor stores) was born in 1881 in Paris when Rudolphe Salis opened "Le Chat Noir" in the Monmartre district, catering to a colorful crowd of writers, artists and musicians. It was the natural evolution of the cafe-concert, away from the opera and towards the young decadents. The cabaret was born for the artists to exhibit themselves: poets, comedians, musicians shared the stage. The satirical element (both of the politics and the customs of the day, and sometimes of the intellectuals themselves) was much stronger. It soon began to copy the format of the circus, adding acrobats and clowns to its program.

Two of the early chansonniers created the two archetypical styles. Aristide Bruant borrowed from folk music a plain tone that fit his stories of the lower classes. Yvette Guilbert, instead, the prototype of the "chanteuse", adopted a melodramatic, half-spoken style that was more influenced by Sarah Bernhardt than by folk singing. The former and his disciples were much more successful among the general audience.

The first music hall of Paris had been opened by Joseph Oller in 1875 (the "Fantasies Oller"), who also opened the most famous, the "Olympia", in 1888, on Boulevard des Capucines. In the following decade many more opened, mostly in Montmartre, including the "Folies-Bergere", mostly in the area around Boulevard de Strasbourg and the Porte St Denis.

Jeanne Bourgeois, better known as "Mistinguette", ruled the stage of the Parisian music halls when recordings made its stars famous world-wide: "Mon Homme," "La Rumba d'Amour", "Ca C'est Paris" and especially "Mon Homme" (1920) were her "hits". She is credited with pioneering the entrance from the top of a spectacular staircase and the fanciful exotic costumes that would become novelties around the world.

In 1909 during her legendary tenure at the "Folies Bergere" (established in 1869), Mistinguette discovered Maurice Chevalier, a young singer (13 years younger than her) who went on to become the most popular French entertainer between the two wars, and the quintessence of the French seducer for the rest of the world, with songs such as *Mimi, Louise, Dans la Vie Faut Pas s'en Faire* (1921), *Valentine* (1924), *Prosper* (1935), *Ma Pomme* (1936), *Ca Fait d'Excellents Francais* (1939). After the "Great War" (in which he served and was wounded), he became the star of the "Casino de Paris", where he entertained a crowd of US soldiers. Thanks to that connection, Chevalier became instrumental in bridging the world of the French cabaret and the world of African-American music (jazz, ragtime). He staged his first Broadway musical in 1922 and became the first foreign singer to star in a Hollywood musical in 1929.

The first dance halls, such as the "Moulin de la Galette", were simply venues for people to enjoy the music and also dance to it. But dancing soon took on a life of its own, and a lifestyle of its own. The "Moulin Rouge", opened in 1889 by Charles Zidler and Joseph Oller, was a dance hall that offered a wild and sumptuous environment for the wealthy male audience to forget their families and their work. There prevailed an explicit erotic element, both in the attire of the singers/dancers and in the themes of their songs. Fundamentally, it was a bigger and more ambitious (and more dissolute) form of cabaret, mixing music (played by a full orchestra) and dance (choreographed like a ballet) in elaborate shows. The rhythm was frantic, as epitomized by the "can can" that became the soundtrack of this era.

The prostitutes that used to hang out at the "brasseries" (sort of restaurant-brothels) became the stars of the cabarets. In fact, one could claim that the cabaret turned prostitution into a form of art. Their fans ranged from aristocrats to working-class students. The cabaret provided the first public arena for social and sexual promiscuity.

All in all, la "belle epoque" (Paris between 1890 and World War I) created the modern idea of entertainment. Those were also the years of the first films, of the Art Nouveau, of Impressionism, of Debussy, of the "Tour Eiffel" (1889). The cabaret was where people celebrated the "belle epoque". But the celebration ended in a massacre: World War I.

Nonetheless, the "Olympia" continued to dominate the night life till 1928 (when it turned into a movie theater). The main show was now starring the sexy and exotic African-American entertainer Josephine Baker, who had arrived in Paris with the "Revue Negre" in 1925 and became famous wearing only a costume of bananas.

Berlin: the Cabaret

The French cabaret spread to Berlin. While it already produced influential songs, such as Ernst von Wolzogen's *Madame Adele* (1901), the prototype of the prostitute song, cabaret music became a musical genre in its own right only during the 1920s, under the Weimar Republic, where it was closely related to the decadent atmosphere of night clubs as well as to expressionist culture (Frank Wedekind's "Lulu" or Josef von Sternberg's **Der Blaue Engel**). Unlike Paris, where Bruant's mellow, melodious style was always more popular, Berlin's cabaret music tended to follow the melodramatic style of Yvette Guilbert.

Cabaret music helped a repressed generation vent their frustration through erotic themes and political satire. The stars were almost always women, such as Marlene Dietrich, Margo Lion, Zarah Leander, Fritzi Massary, Kate Kuhl, Lotte Lenya, Lore Lorentz, Gisela May, Tatjana Sais, Helen Vita, Voli Geiler, Ursula Herking, Trude Hesterberg, Greta Keller, Hildegard Knef, Grete Weiser, Hanne Wieder, etc. The figure of the fatalist "chanteuse" came into its own in Berlin, not Paris.

In 1927 the classical composer Kurt Weill began a collaboration with the playwright Bertolt Brecht, incorporating jazz, folk and pop elements (probably the first time that the three genres had been merged) in the satirical-didactic musical dramas **Die Dreigroschenoper/ The Three-Penny Opera** (1928), based on John Gay's **The Beggar's Opera** (1728), containing the swinging theme of *Mack The Knife*, and **Aufstieg und Fall der Stadt Mahagonny/ Rise and Fall of the City of Mahagonny** (1929).

German cabaret died in 1933 with the advent of Hitler: the Nazis did not like the display of German decadence.

Ironically, the most typical song of the German cabaret will be Norbert Schultze's *Lili Marlene* (1939), sung in German by Danish cabaret chanteuse Lale Andersen, a tune that many interpreted as an anti-war song.

Britain: the Music Hall

The equestrian circus (which had nothing in common with the original "circus" of the Romans) was invented in London in 1768 by Philip Astley. It later came to include other trained animals besides horses. In 1859 it added the flying trapeze to its repertoire of acts. Soon, it also listed jugglers, acrobats, magicians and clowns. Popular music was for taverns. Comic plays were for the theaters. During the second half of the 19th century these three worlds started catering to the same audience. It was inevitable for them to merge.

British "music hall" was a genre, not a place. Charles Morton is credited with being the first entrepreneur who, in 1840, added a saloon for entertainment next to his restaurant, "St George's Tavern", in Pimlico. The idea quickly spread to other parts of London, as the lower classes liked the combination of food, beer and performers. Unlike the French music hall, that catered to all social classes and whose main patrons were from the aristocracy, the British music hall was very much a rowdy, lewd, unsophisticated low-class form of mass entertainment. A respectable gentleman would not set foot in a music hall, and a respectable performer would not perform on the stage of a music hall. So a new kind of performer was born, that harked back to the medieval fairs and to the circus, and a new kind of audience was born, one that appreciated a quick laugh and detested the pomp of literature and classical music. Morton admitted women to his new "Canterbury Hall" (1852), and soon other music halls sprouted all over London. By the end of the century, there were literally hundreds of them. The demand for songs grew exponentially and fueled a boom in songwriters. These songwriters were in charge of producing songs that were catchy, rhythmic, worked in loud environments and invited audience participation. The main inspiration came from the popular dances, whether jigs or polkas, but the melodies often mimicked folk ballads. The song had to be easy to learn, because the audience was expecting to sing along. The most famous song of the beginnings was probably *Champagne Charlie* (1854), but the first notable songwriter of the music hall was George LeBrunn, who wrote *Oh Mr Porter* (1893), *It's a Great Big Shame* (1894) *The*

Houses in Between (1894). Stars of the music hall included Marie Lloyd (1890s), Gus Elen (1890s), Larry Lauder (1900s), and Harry Champion (1900s), the author of *I'm Henry the Eighth I Am* (1911), each of them identified with a routine of sketches and songs.

A law meant to protect theaters forbade music halls from presenting theatrical plays, so they had to limit themselves to musical sketches (mainly sing-along routines). In 1907 the law was relaxed and the music halls began to stage comic sketches as well. It still kept its identity, though: the audience sat at tables, eating and drinking, while the shows were performed on stage. The popularity of these venues was such that in 1912 a revue took place in front of the king himself at the "Palace" theater. The music hall became more respectable (especially after the prohibition of alcohol in 1909 and of food in 1914) and found a new market: the middle class. It also expanded its horizons, becoming more similar to French-style variety shows that mixed acrobats, comedians, singers and clowns.

The music hall had survived the competition of the cinema, but did not survive the competition of the "British Broadcasting Company" (BBC) that began broadcasting in 1922.

Just a few months earlier, the French cabaret had taken London by storm.

Roma: the Canzonetta

The cafe-concert arrived in Italy already in 1890, when the "Salone Margherita" opened in Napoli, the capital of Italian pop music. It displayed the two elements that would remain typical of Italian variety shows: foreign singers marketed as "world stars" (although often totally unknown in their country of origin) and Neapolitan melody. The cafe-concert attracted classical composers and poets, but never truly represented the spirit of the Italian people.

Both in the north and in the south, Italian pop music of the beginning of the century was a music of poverty, not a music of entertainment. *Bandiera Rossa* (189#), the communist anthem of the workers, *Mamma Mia Dammi Cento Lire*, the lament of the emigrant, *Leggenda del Piave* (1918), a song of soldiers, *Stamattina mi Sono Alzata* (1918), which became famous during the following world war as the partisan anthem *Bella Ciao*, were the real soundtrack of ordinary lives. Mussolini erased the collective unconscious of these poor emigrants and replaced it with triumphal songs like *Giovinezza* (1926), the fascist anthem, and Mario Ruccione's *Faccetta Nera* (1935), composed to celebrate Italy's invasion of Ethiopia. Italian songwriters were only free to sing romantic love. Thus it is not surprising that the 1930s were the years of romantic songs such as Andrea Bixio's *Parlami d'Amore Mariu`* (1932), sung by one of Italy's most famous entertainers, Vittorio deSica. No matter what the purpose was, the Italian song remained fundamentally anchored to the format of Napoli's "canzone", in turn derived from the arias of the opera.

Even Mussolini could not fend the influence of the USA. In the age of Swing Jazz, the rhythm of many Italian hits betrayed its African-American roots: Pippo Barzizza's *Quel Motivetto che mi Piace Tanto*, Carlo Innocenzi and Alessandro Sopranzi's *Mille Lire al Mese* (1939), sung by Gilberto Mazzi, Luigi Astore and Riccardo Morbelli's *Ba-ba-baciami Piccina* (1940), sung by Alberto Rabagliati, Gorni Kramer's *Ho un Sassolino nella Scarpa* (1943), sung by Natalino Otto. The Trio Lescano (three ordinary-looking young Dutch women in long skirts) were the main hit makers of the fascist era: *Signorine Grandi Firme*, *Ma le Gambe* (1938), *Tulipan* (1938), Gorni Kramer's *Pippo Non lo Sa* (1939), Mario Panzeri's *Maramao Perche' Sei Morto* (1939). Eugenio De Curtis' *Non Ti Scordar di Me* (1935) and Odoardo Spadaro's *Porta Un Bacione a Firenze* (1938) were in the traditional melodic style. The fascist era was symbolically closed by Eros Sciorilli's melancholy *In Cerca di Te* (1945), sung by Nella Colombo.

THE USA UP TO WORLD WAR II

New York: Tin Pan Alley

The early British colonists of North America brought with them three kinds of music: religious music, folk dances and nursery rhymes. The function of religious music was amplified by the "camp meetings" that started in 1801 in Kentucky and rapidly spread throughout the Southeast. Thousands of people would gather to listen to Presbyterian, Baptist and Methodist preachers and to worship God with psalms that were descendants of the old Calvinist canon.

The first lay songs were patriotic in nature: *Yankee Doodle* (1780s), a rewrite of the Dutch folk song "Yanker Dudel", Philip Phile's *Hail Columbia* (1798), John Newton's *Amazing Grace* (1779), based on an anonymous folk melody, Francis Scott Key's *The Star Spangled Banner* (1814) Samuel Smith's *America* (1831), based on a German folk song, *The Yellow Rose of Texas* (1858), by an unknown author, *John Brown's Body* (1861), a variant on William Steffe's camp-meeting hymn *Say Brothers Will You Meet Us On Canaan's Happy Shore?* (1856), Patrick Sarsfield Gilmore's *When Johnny Comes Marching Home Again* (1863), Samuel Ward's *America The Beautiful* (1882), all the way to Carrie Jacobs Bond's *Oh Shenandoah* (1901).

In Pennsylvania, Stephen Foster's songs, such as *Oh Susanna* (1848), was initially composed for a "minstrel show" but soon became the anthem of California's gold rush, *Old Uncle Ned* (1848), the first song by Foster to display the influence of black folklore, *Camptown Races* (1850), *Old Folks at Home* (1851), *Massa's in de Cold Ground* (1852), another sketch of black life, *My Old Kentucky Home* (1853), *Jeanie with the Light Brown Hair* (1854), *Old Black Joe* (1860) and *Beautiful Dreamer* (1864) introduced a paradigm that would rule America's popular music for a century: a combination of Anglo-Irish narrative structures, black rhythms and Italian operatic melody.

But the pop stars of the 19th century were Italian opera singers. In fact, the Italian "bel canto" style would remain the dominant style of singing in US pop music. Most of the sheet music sold in the 19th century was opera, followed by minstrel shows.

John Philip Sousa, the leader of the most popular "marching band", ruled the early charts with *Washington Post March* (1889) and *Semper Fidelis* (1890), besides composing *Stars and Stripes Forever* (1897) and recording George Evans' *In The Good Old Summertime* (1903), as well as composing the operetta **El Capitan** (1896).

Paul Dresser's nostalgic stories, such as *The Letter That Never Came* (1884), *On The Banks of the Wabash* (1897), *Just Tell Them That You Saw Me* (1895) and *My Gal Sal* (1905), seemed to presage the dramatic changes that lay ahead (for both the industry and the nation).

Charles Harris' *After the Ball* (1892) was the first music sheet that sold one million copies. Its success is normally credited with starting the commercial exploitation of popular music, and thus the music industry itself. Other influential or popular songs of the era include: George Washington Johnson's *Laughing Song* (1891), whose recorded version (the cylinder, not just the music sheet) was probably the best seller of the cylinder era, Henry Sayers' *Ta-Ra-Ra-Boom-Der-E* (1891), Percy Gaunt's *The Bowery* (1892), Harry Dacre's *Daisy Bell* (1892), James Blake's *Sidewalks Of New York* (1894), Charles Ward's *The Band Played On* (1895), Theo Metz's *A Hot Time In The Old Town* (1896), Gussie Davis' *In The Baggage Coach Ahead* (1896), the first hit by a black songwriter, James Thornton's *When You Were Sweet Sixteen* (1898), Will Cobb's *Good Bye Dolly Gray* (1900), George Evans' *In The Good Old Summertime* (1902), Kerry Mills' *Meet Me In St Louis* (1904), Alex Rogers' *Nobody* (1905), Albert von Tilzer's *That's What The Daisy Said* (1903) and *Take Me Out To The Ballgame* (1908), Gus Edwards' *By The Light Of The Silvery Moon* (1909), Shelton Brooks' *Some Of These Days* (1910), Cecil Macklin's *Too Much Mustard* (1912), Lewis Muir's *Waiting For The Robert E. Lee* (1912), James Royce Shannon's *Too-ra-loo-ra-loo-ral* (1914).

Harry von Tilzer, brother of Albert, was one of the most popular songwriters at the turn of the century, thanks to *I Love You Both* (1892), *My Old New Hampshire Home* (1898), *I'd Leave My Happy Home For You* (1899), *A Bird In A Gilded Cage* (1900), *On A Sunday Afternoon* (1902), *Down Where The Wurzberger Flows* (1902), *Wait Till The Sun Shines Nellie* (1905), *I Want A Girl Just Like The Girl That Married Dear Old Dad* (1911).

Victor Herbert was the first classical composer to create pop music, for example *Gypsy Love Song* (1898), *Kiss Me Again* (1905), *Because You're You* (1906).

Theodore Morse composed *Dear Old Girl* (1903), *Oysters And Clams* (1904), *Keep On the Sunny Side* (1906), *Make Believe* (1907), *M-O-T-H-E-R* (1915), and two songs that started a "monkey" craze: *In Monkey Land* (1907) and *Down In Jungle Town* (1908).

New York music publishers started renting offices around 28th Street (between Sixth Avenue and Broadway), next to the vaudeville theaters of 27th Street, an area that soon came to be known as "Tin Pan Alley". Sheet music was the primary "product" of popular music and the industry was dominated by music publishing houses.

A technological innovation changed the format, if not the beneficiaries, of popular music. The first sound recording was made in 1860 by the French inventor Eduard-Leon Scott, who used his "phonautograph" to make visual recordings of sound, but the father of the recording industry is the US inventor Thomas Edison, who built the first "phonograph" (a musical cylinder). In 1887, Emile Berliner built the first gramophone, that played sound recorded at 78 RPM on a flat record (as opposed to Edison's cylinder) made of shellac. The new device proved to be popular with the masses who were ever so eager to listen to the voices of the famous opera stars, starting with Ferruccio Giannini singing Giuseppe Verdi's *La Donna E` Mobile* (1896). Millions of gramophones were sold in the first decade of the 20th century. It made the fortune of Italian tenor Enrico Caruso, whose *Vesti la Giubba* (1902) became the first record (not sheet or cylinder) to sell a million copies. In fact, it was his success that turned the gramophone into an indispensable appliance. It also turned countless furniture stores (the place where gramophones were sold) into recording studios for local musicians. Fred Gaisberg (the same man who had recorded Giannini, Caruso and Beniamino Gigli) opened the first recording studio, in Philadelphia, and traveled around the world to make the first "field recordings" of ethnic music (originally meant as marketing stunts to promote the gramophone all over the world). Edward Easton had already founded in 1889 the first record label, Columbia, that in 1891 had a catalog of 200 cylinders, and in 1898 began pressing discs. In 1901, Emile Berliner himself founded the record label

Victor Talking Machines, specifically for discs. In 1894 the weekly Billboard magazine began publication, offering "charts" of music sales. In 1898 the Gramophone Company or HMV (His Master's Voice) bought the European rights to Emile Berliner's gramophone, and soon became the largest record company in the world.

Len Spencer was probably the first singer to realize that there was a market for recording other people's music. His *Arkansas Traveler* (1900) was also a best-seller (perhaps touching million) and was followed by a string of popular songs, from James Bland's *Carry Me Back to Ole Virginny* to George Cohan's *I Guess I'll Have To Telegraph My Baby*, as well as countless "coon songs". Irish tenor John McCormack imitated both Caruso and Spencer, recording both popular music (mostly for the British audience, starting in 1906) and operatic arias (mostly for the USA audience, from 1910) and went on to sell 200 million records.

Henry Burr, launched by *Come Down Ma Evening Star* (1903) and *In The Shade Of The Old Apple Tree* (1905), and Bill Murray, who sang most of George Cohan's compositions, became the most famous singers of the early decades of recording (Ada Jones was the most popular among women). Besides solo singers, the other popular format was the vocal quartet, for example the Hayden Quartet and the Empire City Quartet, both of which recorded *Sweet Adeline* (1904).

Now music had a voice and a name (of the singer), not just a song title and a song composer.

Indirectly, that invention helped establish both white and black rural music, because black music was oriented towards the performer, not the sheet. The first jazz record was cut in New York in 1917. The first records of "hillbilly music" were also cut at this time.

Tin Pan Alley's golden years were the "Roaring Twenties". By 1921, 106 million records were sold yearly in the USA, mostly published on "Tin Pan Alley", but control of the market was already shifting towards the record companies. In 1925 a technical innovation made it even easier to cut records: the electrical recording process was commercially introduced, quickly replacing the old mechanical one. Then the speed of 78.26 RPM became the standard because it was the easiest to obtain using the standard 3600-rpm motor and 46-tooth gear (78.26 = 3600/46). Thus 1926 and 1927 witnessed a boom in recording (particularly of classical music). In october 1926, the first major magazine devoted to recorded music, the "Phonograph Monthly Review" began publication.

It is not a coincidence that, at about this time, new record companies were created that were to last for a century. In 1921 General Electric acquired the US branch of Marconi Wireless Telegraph and renamed it "Radio Corporation of America" (RCA). In 1924 the Music Corporation of America (MCA) was founded in Chicago as a talent agency, and the German record company Deutsche Grammophon (DG) opened the Polydor company to distribute records abroad. In 1929 Decca was founded in Britain by Edward Lewis, and RCA purchased the glorious Victor Talking Machines. In 1931 EMI (Electrical and Musical Industries), formed by the merger of Gramophone (HMV) and the British subsidiary of Columbia, by far the largest record label in the world (a position it was to maintain for the next 50 years), opened the largest recording studio in the world at Abbey Road in London.

Record companies soon realized that the support was not adequate for a mass market. In 1926 Vitaphone introduced 16-inch acetate-coated shellac discs playing at 33 1/3 RPM (a size and speed calculated to be the equivalent of a reel of film because they were originally meant for the soundtrack of Alan Crosland's **Don Juan**). But they were hardly noticed. This "long playing" format came to be called "album" because, before its invention, long recordings used to be packaged in "albums" of several 78-RPM records.

Another innovation was crucial to the dissemination of music. In 1895 Italian inventor Guglielmo Marconi had invented radio broadcasting, but it took a while for people to realize that it could be used beyond the maritime realm (initially, for about 20 years, it was mainly used by ships). When the USA entered World War I, the government decided that radio broadcasting was a strategic technology and helped perfect it to the point that, at the end of the war, in 1920, Westinghouse Electric established a commercial radio station, "KDKA". It also played records. In 1921 a radio station made the first broadcast of a sporting event (a boxing match). In 1926 General Electric started the "National Broadcasting Company" (NBC), run by David Sarnoff, and in 1928 the United Independent Broadcasters (later renamed Columbia Broadcasting System, or

CBS), run by William Paley, was created by 47 affiliate stations. These US pioneers thought that the money was not to be made by selling the programs (that remained free in the USA), but by selling radios. In 1922 there were only 60,000 radios in the USA, but in 1929 there were more than 10 million. (It was only later that they also started making money with advertising). In Europe, owners of radio had to pay a fee to the government. In the USA, the number of radio stations increased dramatically, whereas in Europe governments controlled radio broadcasting. That was one of the reasons that popular music developed in such different ways in the USA and in Europe.

The effect of the new media and the new distribution channels was dramatic. Tin Pan Alley's music was changing rapidly.

Richard Whiting interpreted the new business mood with his popular tunes: *Till We Meet Again* (1918), one of the biggest hits of the era, *The Japanese Sandman* (1920), *Ain't We Got Fun* (1921), *Sleepy Time Gal* (1926), *Louise* (1929).

Influenced by jazz, pianist and singer Hoagy Carmichael was perhaps the first great songwriter of the century (and the prototype of the "singer-songwriter"), as attested by songs such as *Free Wheelin'* (1924), a "hot jazz" piece (recorded by Bix Beiderbecke as *Riverboat Shuffle*), *Washboard Blues* (may 1925), *Stardust* (october 1927), styled as a ragtime and reminiscent of Louis Armstrong's *Potato Head Blues* (1927), *Rockin's Chair* (december 1929), a duet with Armstrong, *Georgia on My Mind* (september 1930), recorded with Bix Beiderbecke, Bud Freeman, Joe Venuti, Eddie Lang, Jimmy Dorsey and Gene Kupra, *Lazy River* (november 1930), with a similar cast, and *Lazy Bones* (september 1933), but much of published music still served the Broadway stages. He was also one of the first white musicians to truly "understand" the rhythm of black music.

Walter Donaldson had some of the greatest hits of the era: *My Mammy* (1918) for Al Jolson, *Yes Sir That's My Baby* (1925), *My Blue Heaven* (1927), that, recorded by Gene Austin, would remain the all-time best-seller for two decades, *At Sundown* (1927), *Love Me Or Leave Me* (1928), that turned Ruth Etting into a star, *Making Whoopee* (1929), *My Baby Just Cares for Me* (1930).

Fred Ahlert composed *I'll Get By* (1928), *Mean To me* (1929), *I Don't Know Why* (1931), *Where The Blue of the Night Meets The*

Gold of the Day (1931). Jose Padilla's *La Violetera* (1923) was one of the earliest Latin hits. Other hits between the first world war and the Depression were: Vincent Rose's *Whispering* (1920) and *Avalon* (1920), Guy Massey's *The Prisoner's Song* (1924) and Herman Hupfeld's *As Time Goes By* (1931).

Johnny Black's *Dardanella* (1920), sung by Ben Selvin, was the first massive hit by a dance song.

Radio shows and vaudeville shows often presented "blues singers", who were simply white ladies from the South singing melancholy tunes. The Boswell Sisters were a piano-cello-violin trio from New Orleans, who started recording in 1925 but became famous in New York in the 1930s with orchestral numbers, including Sammy Fain's *When I Take My Sugar to Tea* (1931) and one titled *Rock And Roll* (1934), a black euphemism for the sexual act.

Sammy Fain, who had already composed *Let A Smile Be Your Umbrella* (1927) and *Wedding Bells Are Breaking Up That Old Gang Of Mine* (1929), became one of the first to specialize in songs for films: *You Brought A New Kind of Love To Me* (1930) for Maurice Chevalier, *When I Take My Sugar to Tea* (1931) for the Boswell Sisters, *I Can Dream Can't I* (1938), *I'll Be Seeing You* (1938), *Dear Hearts And Gentle People* (1949) for Bing Crosby, *Secret Love* (1953) for Doris Day, *Love Is A Many-Splendored Thing* (1955) for the Four Aces, *April Love* (1957) for Pat Boone, *A Certain Smile* (1958) for Johnny Mathis.

Bing Crosby, who debuted in 1926 with Paul Whiteman's big band in Los Angeles, featuring Bix Beiderbecke on cornet, was the best-selling singer of the first half of the 20th century, and one of the most popular radio stars of all times (on the "Kraft Music Hall" show since 1935). Crosby's style of singing de facto invented the "crooning" style in opposition to Al Jolson's shouting style. Crooning was derived from the "bel canto" of the Italian opera but focused on nuances rather than power (a fact also due to the electrical microphone, that allowed singers to care about pathos instead of volume). He became a star, suddenly, in 1931, at the age of 28, when he started recording on his own but his repertory was mainly covers such as Al Hoffman's *I Apologize* (1931), Jay Gorney's *Brother Can You Spare a Dime?* (1932), Harry Warren's *You're Getting to Be a Habit With Me* (1933), *Silent Night Holy*

Night (1934), the English version of Austrian church organist Franz Gruber's *Stille Nacht Heilige Nacht* (1818) of a century earlier, that became a Christmas classic. His vocal skills increased steadily through classics *Pennies from Heaven* (1936), that remained ten weeks at the top of the charts, Harry Warren's *Remember Me* (1937) and *You Must Have Been a Beautiful Baby* (1938), James Monaco's *I've Got A Pocketful Of Dreams* (1938) and *Only Forever* (1940), Irving Berlin's *White Christmas* (1941), Jimmy Van Heusen's *Swinging On a Star* (1944), Sammy Fain's *I'll Be Seeing You* (1944) etc. Much credit for their success went to his arranger, John Scott Trotter, and his orchestra.

The term "crooner" (thanks to a vocal effect produced via a megaphone) was actually first used to refer to Rudy Vallee, who was the most celebrated star of the 1930s (the first pop singer to cause mass hysteria), although *The Vagabond Lover* (1929), *My Time Is Your Time* (1929), *Betty Co-Ed* (1931) and Herman Hupfield's *As Time Goes By* (1931).

The first Italian-American stars were Russ Columbo, who became famous in the 1930s with Fred Ahlert's *I Don't Know Why* (1931) and the first recording of Leo Robin's *Prisoner Of Love* (1931), and Jimmy Durante, whose many hits included *Inka Dinka Do* (1934) and *The Guy Who Found The Lost Chord* (1947).

The biggest hit of the 1930s came from Britain, Jack Strachey's *These Foolish Things* (1936), originally written for a revue.

Two instruments debuted that were to become the staple of rock bands: Adolph Rickenbacker invented (1931) the electric guitar and Laurens Hammond invented (1933) the Hammond organ. Also important for the future of rock media, in 1930 the first "fanzines" debuted: these were science fiction pulp magazines ("Comet" and "Time Traveller") that allowed sci-fi fans to communicate. They created an "underground" community.

The market for records collapsed during the Great Depression (in 1933 only six million records were sold in the USA). The recovery was slow, but in 1935 the radio program "Hit Parade" was launched, a clear sign of life, and and in 1937 records by the "big bands" rejuvenated the scene.

At the end of the Depression, technological progress also resumed. In 1939 the Panoram visual jukebox was invented, a device that played short films of records, i.e. the first music videos, an idea that would be shelved for about 40 years. In 1940 Disney's "Fantasia" introduced stereo sound.

New York: the Minstrel Show

The minstrel show was staged by itinerant troupes of white actors, mimes and musicians who painted their face black. It became popular during the first half of the 19th century, and assumed a definitive format in 1843 with the New York-based Virginia Minstrels, a quartet of musicians (banjo, tambourine, castanets, fiddle). The minstrel show resembled the Italian "commedia dell'arte" in that the shows gravitated around a number of easily-recognized stereotyped characters: the elderly crippled black slave Jim Crow (created in 1828 by Thomas "Daddy" Rice with the song *Jim Crow* that became the first international "hit" song ever), the ever-smiling black fool Sambo, the elegant black playboy Dandy Jim aping the manners of a European gentleman. The Christy Minstrels developed the comic routine of Mr Tambo, Mr Bones and Mr Interlocutor, which became a much imitated standard. The minstrel show became a carefully staged event in two or three parts, obeying a canonic sequence of acts, a popular form of entertainment in the city, hosted by several theaters every week. One of the standard routines was the "cakewalk", in which the blackface actors walked around parodying the way the slaves of the plantations walked during formal occasions (the "cake" being the prize awarded by the plantation owner to the slaves who learned to walk more elegantly). It eventually developed into a dance step. The "olio" was the part of the show in which each of the "minstrels" performed its specialty, whether music or comedy. The songs were often "coon songs", racial jokes about blacks (plantation slaves were nicknamed "coons" because they were said to like the meat of racoons) set to the melodies of popular tunes and to a syncopated rhythm. The syncopated rhythm was probably meant to make them even funnier, but ended up being the first exposure of the white audience to syncopation and influenced the entire evolution of black music in the USA.

Daniel Emmett, the fiddler of the Virginia Minstrels who called himself the "Ethiopian minstrel" (and started a whole craze of Ethiopian bands and musicians, all of them white) was the author of their most notorious numbers, *Old Dan Tucker* (1830) and *Dixie's*

Land (1859), that during the Civil War became an anthem for the Confederates.

Many of the minstrel songs had originated in the southern plantations, but they came to be known by the name of the white minstrel who performed them. The notable exception was James Bland, a Washington minstrel who was truly black, the first major black songwriter, who went on to compose over 700 songs, such as *Carry Me Back to Ole Virginny* (1873), *In The Evening By The Moonlight* (1879) and *Oh Dem Golden Slippers* (1879), mostly set in the plantations. Gussie Lord Davis' *Goodnight Irene* (1886) was also originally composed for a minstrel show.

The Georgia Minstrels were the first black minstrel troupe (formed in 1865), and remained the exception until the last decade of the century. Only in the 1890s did the demand for black musicians increase rapidly, and minstrel shows became launching pads for the careers of several black singers and actors.

Towards the end of the century, the minstrel show became more and more extravagant, competing with the circus and variety shows. In fact, the elaborate productions of Haverly's Mastodon Minstrels and Lew Dockstader's Minstrels had few precedents outside of Paris.

At the same time, minstrel shows moved away from the fragmented structure of the early days and towards a more organic presentation, a "plot". **The Creole Show** (1890) and **The Octoroons** (1895) were more than minstrel shows: they were musical comedies, whose routines were organized along a storyline. The "narrative" minstrel show peaked with **Black Patti's Troubadours** (1896), mostly scored by black songwriter Bob Cole.

The music of minstrel shows was based on the banjo, and basically retained the fundamental characteristic of black banjo playing: strumming the chords with the nails. Until the invention of minstrelsy, the banjo had been an exclusively black instrument. Minstrel shows were instrumental in popularizing the banjo among white audiences. In fact, the instrument generated a bit of a craze during the 1880s, thanks to manufacturers such as Samuel Swain Stewart that promoted it actively and tried to emancipate it from its African heritage. The result was that the banjo became less of a percussive instrument and more of a guitar-like melodic instrument.

The minstrel shows also fostered the development of tap dancing, that was originally performed with wooden soles (adopting metal plates in the 1920s) and wed Irish step dance and black dance, a confluence that may have happened on the Mississippi steamboats, a stage that minstrel shows shared with troupes of Irish dancers.

New York: the Revue

Not long after the end of the Civil War, the USA experienced a dramatic process of population growth and territorial expansion. Millions of Europeans emigrated to the USA and thousands of Easterners moved West. Cities became metropolises and became cosmopolitan. The USA became the "land of opportunities": cheap labor and capital allowed anyone with a good idea to become a millionaire. One of the obvious opportunities was to entertain those cosmopolitan masses, and the inspiration usually came from Europe. New York was the quintessence of the social phenomenon that was changing the face of the USA, so it is no surprise that the new forms of entertainment were first experimented in New York. The city worked as a laboratory of a Darwinian evolution of ideas.

Theaters were still the places where literary works were being performed. Some of them were musical in nature, but the music followed the story. Before the Civil War, theaters were by far the main source of entertainment for the urban population.

Just before the Civil War erupted, actress Laura Keene, who had already staged several successful musical comedies at her Broadway theater, conceived **Seven Sisters** (1860), a show that was a mixture of farce and opera, loosely based on Wilhelm Friedrich's play **Die Toechter Luzifers** (1846) and scored by composer Thomas Baker. Its 253 performances set a new record for US theater. Keene had created a truly US version of the British "ballad opera", and the New York audience loved it. (Ironically, Abraham Lincoln was assassinated while he was watching one of Keene's musical plays).

Right after the Civil War, in 1866, William Wheatley, owner of the "Niblo's Garden", one of the largest New York theaters, that could seat over three thousand spectators, followed Keene's intuition for a new kind of drama, one that mixed a literary text, dance, music, but that relied on spectacular stage effects more than anything else: **The Black Crook**. It was based on a mediocre play by a Charles Barras, but it was transformed by Wheatley into a five-hour "extravaganza" (the term that came to define this kind of show) featuring prominently a scantily-dressed Parisian ballet troupe that was touring the USA.

The "burlesque" was an exaggeration of the least sophisticated elements of the minstrel show. It was born around the time when the minstrel show became a respectable form of entertainment (the 1860s) but it was not particularly popular, catering mostly to a male audience of the very low classes. In the Broadway theaters, the burlesques was mainly a parody of the opera, and it was popular with a literate audience that could relate to the operas and poems that were being spoofed. As Edward Rice put it, the burlesque "burlesqued" something. The first major success on Broadway was Lydia Thompson's **Ixion** (1868), another hit of "Niblo's Garden" whose main feature was the almost naked dancers (all girls who played both male and female roles). Edward Rice scored two of the biggest burlesque musical extravaganzas, as usual staged at "Niblo's Garden" with the usual lavish scenography: **Evangeline** (1874) and **Adonis** (1884).

At about the same time, the USA improved on the British circus by introducing a multitude of rings. The large, lavish, boisterous circus was the invention of Phineas-Taylor Barnum, the owner of the "American Museum" of New York that exhibited midgets and Siamese twins to a morbid audience: in 1871 he opened a mobile circus based in Brooklyn and marketed it as "the Greatest Show on Earth". Within a decade it had become just that, touring all over Europe. In 1884 the five "Ringling Brothers" organized their first circus, soon to become a colossal business enterprise.

In 1884 also the first rollercoaster, built by Lemarcus Thompson, opened at the Coney Island amusement park of New York. In 1897 George Cornelius Tilyou transformed the area into "Steeplechase Park", a large ensemble of rides and attractions, that soon drew millions of visitors each year (twenty million in 1909).

The vaudeville was basically the US version of the British music hall (rowdy entertainment for the uneducated masses) although it probably evolved from the "olio" of the minstrel shows. The "Fourteenth Street Theater", opened in 1881 by impresario Tony Pastor, was the first major venue in New York, but the vaudeville spread throughout America when (1885) Benjamin Franklin Keith and Edward Franklin Albee II partnered in Boston to set up a nation-wide chain of vaudeville theaters. It was probably the first infusion of capitalism into mass entertainment. Starting in 1902 out of Seattle, Greek-born impresario Pericles "Alexander" Pantages built a circuit of vaudeville theatres across the western United States and Canada. In 1905 Austrian-born Martin Beck obtained control of the Orpheum Circuit and proceeded to expand it from its base of San Francisco to Chicago. (When in 1928 the Orpheum and the Keith-Albee circuits united, they formed the Keith-Albee-Orpheum Circuit, or KAO, the progenitor of Radio Keith Orpheum, or RKO). In 1907 Fred Barrasso, based in Memphis, created a chain of vaudeville theaters under what became the Theater Owners's Booking Association (TOBA) that was influential in bringing black music to a white audience, such as proto-blues musicians Baby Seals, the composer of *Shake, Rattle and Roll*, and pianist Butler "String Beans" May, perhaps the first major black star of the vaudeville, famous for his *Titanic Blues* (1913).

George Lederer upped the ante by staging his **Passing Show** (1894) at the "Casino Theater" (opened by producer Rudolph Aronson in 1882), a French-style revue that set the traditional vaudeville acts against the background of a fanciful and lavish scenography, as well as wrapping the characters into fantastic costumes.

Florenz Ziegfeld, who had been produced musical shows for French cabaret star Anna Held starting with **A Parlor Match** (1896), took Lederer's intuition literally and set out to create the US equivalent of the "Folies Bergere", focusing on scantily-clad feminine beauty rather than on vaudeville characters. His new show, the "Ziegfeld Follies" debuted in 1907 at the "New York Theater", producing popular songs such as Nora Bayes' *Shine on Harvest Moon* (1908), Irving Berlin's *Woodman Spare That Tree* (1911), Henry Marshall's *Be My Little Baby Bumble Bee* (1912), Leo Edwards' "Isle D'Amour" (1913), Dave Stamper's *A Pretty Girl Is Like A Melody* (1919) and James Hanley's *Rose of Washington Square* (1920), while launching new stars such as Fanny Brice (1910) and Eddie "Cantor" Iskowitz (*That's The Kind Of A Baby For Me*, 1917). In 1910 Ziegfeld let a black actor, singer and songwriter, Bert Williams, the author of *Nobody* (1905), *Let It Alone* (1906) and *That's A Plenty* (1909), be the protagonist of The "Follies", the first time such an honor was bestowed on a black artist in a white show. One of the greatest songwriters of the era, Louis Hirsch, was employed by Ziegfeld in 1914 and delivered *Sweet Kentucky Lady* (1914), *Hello Frisco* (1915), *Going Up* (1917) and *Love Nest* (1920), besides being the brain behind many of the storylines and concepts. From 1912 on, Gene Buck was the main lyricist for the Follies. It was probably during the 1913 Ziegfeld Follies that a comedian, Harry Fox, invented a frenetic dance step called "fox-trot" (at the breakneck pace of 160 beats per minute).

A popular star of the Ziegfeld Folies was Russian-born Sophie Tucker (Kalish), the former "voice" of ragtime in blackface make-up (or, better, of "coon songs"), and one of the first openly sexual personas, who scored massive hits with Shelton Brooks' *Some of These Days* (1911), Ted Shapiro's *Red-Hot Mama* (1924), Jack Yellen's *My Yiddishe Mama* (1928).

Among the stars of the vaudeville, Marie Dressler (Leila Marie Koerber) was unique in being a fat woman. The character she inaugurated with **Tillie's Nightmare** (1909), based on the play by Edgar Smith and scored by Alfred Baldwin Sloane (who in 1903 had scored most of the children's book **Wizard of Oz**), became so popular that Mack Sennett used it (as well as Dressler) for **Tillie's Punctured Romance** (1913), the first full-length comedy in the history of US cinema.

The lush, extravagant revue of the USA was exported back to Europe by a French producer, Andre Charlot, in 1912, who then developed a personal touch, most evident in **London Calling** (1923).

Lee and Jacob Shubert, two Polish Jews, started their business empire in New York by acquiring in 1900 the "Herald Square" theater, where, incidentally, they staged Augustus Thomas' play **Arizona** (1899), considered the first western. In 1906 they built the "Hippodrome" theater, a better venue to stage extravaganzas, and then the "Winter Garden", where they staged **La Belle Paree** (1911). Between 1913 and 1924, the "Winter Garden" became the preferred venue for the most famous of the Shubert revues, the "Passing Show", a lavish spectacle that had few artistic merits but an obsession for sexy chorus girls. The "Passing Show" featured all sorts of vaudeville artists (including the debut of singer Marilyn Miller and the second appearance of dancer Fred Astaire). This series was followed by an even more explicit one, "Artists and Models" (1923), whose only attraction was the half-naked girls. The

Shubert musical comedies were mostly scored by Sigmund Romberg: **The Blue Paradise** (1915), with *Auf Wiedersehen*, **Maytime** (1917), with *Will You Remember*, by far the most popular, **Blossom Time** (1921), based on Franz Schubert's melodies, **The Student Prince in Heidelberg** (1924), with *The Drinking Song*.

However, the Shuberts' greatest invention was Al Jolson (Asa Yoelson), a Lithuanian Jew who was a veteran of the minstrel show and the vaudeville. Introduced by **La Belle Paree** (1911), his first recording was George Cohan's *That Haunting Melody* (1911). He introduced Gus, the blackface character that he had developed during from his years in minstrel shows, in **The Whirl of Society** (1912), the first of many highly successful revues. He was as successful in selling records, especially Lewis Muir's *Ragging the Baby to Sleep* (1912), James Monaco's romantic ballad *You Made Me Love You* (1913), Jean Schwartz's *Back to the Carolina You Love* (1914). **Robinson Crusoe Jr** (1916) spawned George Meyer's *Where Did Robinson Crusoe Go With Friday On Saturday Night* and Pete Wendling's *Yaacka Hula Hickey Dula*. At the peak of his fame, Jolson debuted at the "Winter Garden" the classic trilogy of Gus: **Sinbad** (1918), that spawned two hit songs, Ray Henderson's *Rock-a-Bye Your Baby With a Dixie Melody* and Walter Donaldson's *My Mammy*, Al Jolson's signature song, **Bombo** (1921) and **Big Boy** (1924), including Ray Henderson's *It All Depends on You*. His hits, that always featured in his revues, included Jean Schwartz's *Hello Central Give Me No-Man's Land* (1918), *Rock-A-Bye Your Baby With a Dixie Melody* (1918) and *I'm All Bound 'Round With the Mason-Dixon Line* (1919), Walter Donaldson's *My Mammy* (1918), Gus Kahn's *I'll Say She Does* (1918), George Gershwin's *Swanee* (1919), Vincent Rose's *Avalon* (1920), Louis Silvers' *April Showers* (1921), Abner Silver's *Angel Child* (1922), Gus Kahn's *Toot Toot Tootsie* (1922), Joseph Meyer's *California Here I Come* (1924), Milton Ager's *I Wonder What's Become Of Sally* (1924), John McCormack's *All Alone* (1925), Ray Henderson's *I'm Sitting on Top of the World* (1925), Harry Woods' *When The Red Red Robin Comes Bob Bob Bobbin' Along* (1926). Jolson appeared in Alan Crosland's **The Jazz Singer** (1927), the first major "talking" film and largely his own biography. Its follow-up, Lloyd Bacon's **The Singing Fool** (1928), that included Dave Dreyer's *There's a Rainbow Round My Shoulder* and Ray Henderson's *Sonny Boy*, remained the all-time best-seller of cinema for eleven years. Henderson's *Little Pal* (1929) was his last major hit. Starting in 1932, he became a radio entertainer. Jolson had the unique honor of being a star in all forms of entertainment: minstrel show, vaudeville, revue, record, cinema and radio.

In the meantime, the Shuberts kept acquiring and building theaters so that in 1924 they controlled more than half of all theatres in the USA. And they were among the few impresarios to survive the Great Depression. In fact, they would eventually stage the most successful revue of all times, **Hellzapoppin** (1938), scripted by two veterans of the vaudeville, Ole Olsen and Chic Johnson, and scored by Sammy Fain, a wild merry-go-round of irreverent sketches and specialty acts in the old tradition.

The Shuberts were not the only low point in taste and morals: George White's "Scandals" (from 1919 till 1939) and Earl Carroll's "Vanities" (from 1923) catered to the same audience of peeping toms. The great composer of George White's "Scandals" was Ray Henderson, who penned *Birth Of The Blues* (1926) and *Black Bottom* (1926), *The Thrill Is Gone* (1931) and *Life Is Just A Bowl Of Cherries* (1931).

At the other end of the spectrum, the "Palace Theater", that had been opened in 1913 by Martin Beck, debuting Ed Wynn and Ethel Barrymore in that year, represented the top tier of vaudeville entertainment, hosting daily shows that featured the famous European stars (such as Sarah Bernhardt) as well as the New York regulars (Eddie Cantor, Fanny Brice). John Murray Anderson's "Greenwich Village Follies" (from 1919 till 1928) was the most sophisticated of the revues.

Producer Lew Leslie staged his **Blackbirds Revue** (1926) at the "Liberty" theater. It featured an all-black cast (notably singer Ethel Waters and dancer Bill "Bojangles" Robinson) but it was created by an all-white team, notably composer Jimmy McHugh (*I Can't Give You Anything But Love* in 1928, *Doin' the New Low Down, On The Sunny Side of the Street* in 1930, and later the author of *I'm in the Mood for Love* in 1935 and *Have I Told You Lately that I Love You* in 1947). In the **Blackbirds of 1928**, another black revue for white audiences, Leslie introduced Bill "Bojangles" Robinson, who had been tap-dancing for black audiences all his life, and finally had a chance to infect white performers with his mesmerizing style.

Chicago-based white vaudeville singer Cliff "Ukulele Ike" Edwards was a humble comedian, but introduced one of the most influential inventions of the era: "scat" singing (wordless vocalizing), first documented in his version of James Johnson's *Old Fashioned Love* (1923). It came as an evolution of the vocal improvisations that he had pioneered, with which he was basically trying to imitate a jazz trumpet. That is how he injected life into pop material such as Fred Meinken's *Virginia Blues* (february 1922), Edwin Weber's *Nobody Lied* (june 1922), Irving Berlin's *Homesick* (september 1922), etc. This kind of vocal imitation of improvised instrumental music was already popular among white vaudeville performers before the first recordings of jazz, as proven by Gene Greene's hit *King of the Bungaloos* (1911), one decade before Ukulele Ike.

In the 1920s the vaudeville was still very popular, but was beginning to share the theaters with movies, and by 1930 even the "Palace" had dropped vaudeville altogether and become a movie-only venue. Many of the vaudeville comedians such as Buster Keaton and the Marx Brothers simply continued their routines in cinema. Other stars of the vaudeville, such as Bob Hope and George Burns, migrated to the radio and then to the television. Others, such as Jimmy Durante and Sophie Tucker, migrated to the cabarets.

When the popularity of the vaudeville began to decline, the burlesque became more popular because it basically had no competition. Cinema and the radio were now providing entertainment for the masses, but not strip teases and obscene comedy: one could see and hear them only at the burlesque. The music was now merely used to introduce the acts and as accompaniment for the strip-tease.

New York: the Night Club

The other form of entertainment that survived because of its "forbidden" nature was the cabaret. New York's first cabaret, "Sans-Souci" on 42nd Street, was opened in 1915 by Vernon and Irene Castle, a popular duo of dancers. Condemned by the moral establishment, the cabaret nonetheless attracted a colorful crowd of professionals, businessmen, artists, mingling with prostitutes and black performers. When, in 1918, the USA banned alcohol, the cabaret simply went underground. Its golden age (the "age of jazz") came later. The "Cotton Club" opened in Harlem in 1923 and featured only black entertainers, catering to a white-only audience. The program was scored by professional musicians such as Harold Arlen, the author of the club's biggest hits (some of them originally written for Hollywood movies): *Get Happy* (1930), *Between the Devil and the Deep Blue Sea* (1931), *I've Got the World on a String* (1932), *Let's Fall in Love* (1933), *Stormy Weather* (1932), for black singer Ethel Waters and Duke Ellington's orchestra, *It's Only a Paper Moon* (1932), *Ill Wind* (1934).

The masses that could not afford to pay the ticket of these clubs had to content themselves with the "speakeasies", the illegal bars (mostly run by organized crime) that defied the law in countless basements and backrooms around the country. The speakeasies resurrected the chanteuse of the original French cabaret, except that they tended to specialize in torch ballads, notably among them Helen Morgan and Texas Guinan.

The "Prohibition" (which ended officially in 1933) was followed by the "Great Depression", during which the cabaret split between the large and expensive halls such as the "Copacabana", opened in 1940 by a former speakeasy operator, Jules Podell, and the smaller and cheaper "supper clubs", basically bars that were forced by the law to also serve some food. The former could afford an orchestra behind the singer, whereas the latter were mostly limited to piano and voice. Max Gordon opened the "Village Vanguard" in 1935, located in the Greenwich Village. One of the most creative night-clubs of the era was "Spivy's Roof", opened in 1940 by the notorious lesbian actress "Madame Spivy", a club that performed works such as **A Sentimental Playlet** (1946), a puppet play written by Charles Henri Ford, a surrealist poet living in Paris, scored by expatriate novelist Paul Bowles and featuring puppets by Swiss surrealist artist Kurt Seligmann.

For black musicians, the most important theater to open in those years was the "Apollo" (1934), located in the heart of New York's Harlem district, a venue soon to become the testing ground for any new black genre (harmony quartets, gospel, soul).

St Louis: Ragtime

During the 1870s the piano became one of the most popular instruments, and many dancehalls replaced the string orchestra with a piano player. By the end of the century, pianos had become so cheap that there was virtually no home without a piano. The passion for playing music caused a boom in music publishing. Not only was sheet music available even in the small towns of the Far West, but the player piano had been invented in 1863 by Henri Fourneaux in France, but had remained a curio. In 1897 Edwin Scott Votey developed his "Pianola", the first mass-produced player piano, and in 1901 Melville Clark built the first full 88-key player piano. That invention changed the way music was consumed. It introduced the concept of "music on demand", music that did not depend on the performer to be physically present. By 1910, the industry was producing 350,000 pianos per year, many of them equipped to play "player-piano rolls". Before World War I, the piano was by far the main form of popular entertainment. Whether the house had a pianist who used sheet music or a player piano that used rolls, the family could enjoy music produced in cities far away.

Needless to say, most black musicians did not know how to read music (the European way of playing piano). They simply adapted the piano to their African traditions.

At the turn of the 19th century, the process of urbanization within the province stimulated the rapid diffusion of casual forms of entertainment, affordable for the local clubs (which usually could not afford professional musicians) and still enjoyable for an audience that was mainly accustomed to folk music. The saloons became the stage for a generation of itinerant pianists who traveled with a heterogeneous repertory of folk songs, marches and opera arias.

The most famous of the marches were John Philip Sousa's *Washington Post March* (1889) and *Semper Fidelis* (1890), and Sousa's band was easily the most popular of the marching bands. Sometime before World War I, a new style evolved from the march (2/4 tempo) and the "cakewalk" that was syncopated like jazz music: the left hand would play a fast and monotonous march, while the right hand would play syncopated melodic figures, often derived from the style of banjo players.

The "coon songs" of the minstrel shows and the cakewalk dance were the first examples of syncopated melodies that became popular among whites.

"Ragtime" was a term derived from "rag" music, the music played by blacks to entertain blacks. By the end of the 19th century, the piano had become an immensely popular instrument (100,000 pianos were sold in 1890) and had replaced the fiddle as the main instrument for such entertainment. Initially, "ragtime" and "coon song" were interchangeable terms. Eventually, the "rag" came to represent the piano arrangement of a coon song, or the setting to syncopated piano of an existing tune. Eventually, "rag" came to refer specifically to syncopated piano instrumentals. Soon pianists were producing syncopated versions even of classical music and opera melodies.

In a sense, ragtime transferred the syncopation of minstrel shows from a naive rural environment to a more sophisticated, decadent and intellectual urban environment.

Just like in Sousa's marching band, the ragtime piece (in 16 or 32 measures) relied on a rhythmic contrast between the two hands of the pianist: the left hand provided a steady beat, while the right hand played the syncopated melody.

The first ragtime to be published was Ben Harney's *You've Been a Good Old Wagon* (1895), but ragtime pianists were probably already an attraction in Chicago during the World's Fair of 1893. In 1896 Harney relocated from Louisville (Kentucky) to New York City, and in a few years Tin Pan Alley began to exploit commercially this style and marketed it as "ragtime". The hit *All Coons Look Alike to Me* (1896), composed by black minstrel songwriter Ernest Hogan, showed the link with the "coons" of the minstrel shows and was responsible for the brief popularity of syncopated "coon songs". The first published rag, William Krell's *Mississippi Rag* (1897), was orchestral (and Krell was white); but Tom Turpin's *Harlem Rag* (1892), published in 1897, was finally an authentic black piece (the first piano rag published by a black songwriter), and started Turpin's string of hits: *Bowery Buck* (1899), *A Ragtime Nightmare* (1900), *St Louis Rag* (1900), *Buffalo Rag* (1904).

Despite the fact that it was clearly African in nature, ragtime appealed to a white audience that was willing to experiment with "decadent" entertainment, just like it was willing to attend minstrel shows and all-black Broadway musicals.

If Chicago was where ragtime became a sensation, it was in Missouri (in the red-light districts of St Louis and Sedalia) that ragtime became big business, thanks to entrepreneurs such as Sedalia's John Stark (who published the bulk of classic rags and soon opened offices also in St Louis and New York) and entertainers such as Tom Turpin. Sedalia's saloon "Maple Leaf" was one of the earliest venues, immortalized by Scott Joplin's *Maple Leaf Rag* (1899). St Louis (where Joplin himself relocated) soon became the capital of ragtime, challenged only by Kansas City, where another black pianist, James Scott, ruled with *Frog Legs Rag* (1906), *Kansas City Rag* (1907), *Quality* (1911), *Climax Rag* (1914), *Pegasus* (1920), *Broadway Rag* (1922). Joe Jordan, who crafted *Nappy Lee* (1903) and *Pekin Rag* (1904), was one of the black purists who moved from St Louis to Chicago.

Other significant pieces were Joseph-Francis Lamb's *American Beauty Rag* (1913), Euday Bowman's *Twelfth Street Rag* (1914), and Artie Matthews's *Pastime Rag No 1-5* (1913-20).

Ragtime was the first major example of the black culture assimilating white technology (the piano) and white musical styles (such as marches and waltzes) to its syncopated rhythms.

Unlike jazz, ragtime was always a "composed" (not improvised) form of music. It was also meant to be played solo (not by a band) and at the piano. Nonetheless, the border between ragtime and jazz was blurred. For example, James Johnson's second recording of *Carolina Shout* (1921) is ragtime, but boasts a piano solo that is already jazz. In fact, the term "jazz" was used for the first time in the song *Uncle Josh in Society*, but it referred to ragtime, and for a decade white people thought of jazz as merely a kind of ragtime.

Scott Joplin, the author of the driving *Maple Leaf Rag* (1897), *The Entertainer* (1902) and *The Cascade* (1904), had started his career in the traditional style of marches. His ragtime pieces were actually slow and rather delicate compared with the stereotypes of Tin Pan Alley (or, better, of the coin-operated player pianos that played them at breakneck speed). However, Joplin's repertory already spanned a broad range of styles: the syncopated waltz *Behena* (1905), the neoclassical *Euphonic Sounds* (1909), the Mexican-tango serenade *Solace* (1909), etc. At the peak of ragtime's popularity, Joplin, who had been raised on European classical music and probably didn't feel at home in the dives where ragtime was usually performed, even wrote a 20-minute *Ragtime Dance* (1902) and two "ragtime operas", **The Ragtime Dance** (1899), that he presented on a 1903 tour,

Treemonisha (1911), a colossal work that was only remotely related to ragtime. His last composition, *Magnetic Rag* (1914), embodied his classical ambitions.

But the composer who convinced Tin Pan Alley was white, Kerry Mills, whose *Rastus On Parade* (1893) was the first cakewalk ever published, and who created popular ragtime pieces for mass consumption such as: *At a Georgia Campmeeting* (1897), *Mr Rufus* (1899), *Meet Me in St Louis* (1904), *Redwing* (1907), *Ragtime Dance* (1909).

Ragtime was often arranged for string bands, typically clarinet, trumpet, trombone, piano, bass and drums. Well connected with Joplin was William Spiller's band, that was actually directed by his wife Isabele Spiller (perhaps the first black female arranger) and that toured the vaudeville circuit in the 1910s (it also exported ragtime to Britain in 1912). In fact, ragtime pianists may have invented ragtime by trying to imitate on the piano the string bands of the plantations (Stark used to advertise Joplin's rags as "banjo imitations").

Then Tin Pan Alley's publishing industry began flooding the country with ragtime tunes. Ragtime was mainly sold as tapes for player pianos. The first recordings of black artists (1917) came too late to document the original ragtime style.

Such was the popularity of ragtime that all sorts of composers and songwriters started using the term "ragtime" (e.g., Irving Berlin's celebrated *Alexander's Ragtime Band* of 1911, which is not ragtime at all).

Eubie Blake, a veteran pianist of Baltimore's vaudeville/minstrel-show circuit, penned the *Charleston Rag*, published in 1919 but originally composed in 1899 (and featuring left-hand figures that predated boogie-woogie), *Baltimore Todolo* (1909), *Troublesome Ivories* (1911), *Chevy Chase* (1914).

There were also white composers of ragtime music, although none was of the same caliber as Joplin and Blake. Ragtime songs were sung by the pop stars of the time: Billy Murray (whose *Grand Old Rag* of 1906 was perhaps the genre's greatest hit), Al Jolson and Sophie Tucker.

The fad spread to Europe and thus ragtime became the first international musical genre to originate from the USA. *My Ragtime Baby* (1898) had been the first international hit of black music. It was, in a sense, the first demonstration of the enormous power of black music, a sign of what was to come for the rest of the century.

USA: Ballroom Dancing

Ballrooms played an important social role in mass entertainment before radio and television were invented.

The "cakewalk", a very syncopated dance for couples, was perhaps the first dance craze. It had existed for decades within the routines of the minstrel shows (so called because the best dancer would be awarded a cake) and was already used in many Broadway revues, but it became popular with the white masses only around 1900. It was the first black dance to be adopted by the white masses. Its first recording was probably *Rastus On Parade* (1893) by white songwriter Kerry Mills. It was exported to Britain in 1903 by Will-Marion Cook's musical revue **In Dahomey**.

The foxtrot, probably invented at the Ziegfeld Follies in 1913, became a sort of generational anthem, a symbol of rebellion against the formal dances of the previous century.

The "Charleston", a black dance that had evolved in the South Carolina port town of Charleston, was the next dance craze. It was popularized on Broadway by ragtime pianist James Johnson's musical **Runnin' Wild** (1923), containing the song *Charleston*, and in Paris by the black cabaret star Josephine Baker. It was even wilder than the fox-trot (up to 240 beats per minute), the dancers looking positively possessed.

These dances represented a significant shift in popular taste. At the beginning of the music industry (end of the 19th century), the middle class was buying music sheets in order to play a song on the piano at home and sing it along. In the 1910s, the middle class did not want to sing: they wanted to dance. Instead of buying sheets, many preferred to spend their money in a dance club. Black musicians were the main beneficiaries of this new trend. Not a coincidence: the transition from playing a song on the piano to dancing a song in a dancehall was, de facto, a transition from European-style music consumption to African-style music consumption.

Black syncopated orchestras (usually string orchestras sometimes augmented with a piano) became increasingly popular in the "Black Bohemia" (Manhattan's 53rd Street, around the "Marshall Hotel").

To serve this growing market, Ernest Hogan created a black "orchestra", the Memphis Students, that debuted in 1905 on Broadway, with music composed by James Europe and Joe Jordan. This orchestra dispensed with the strings and the woodwinds of the traditional orchestra, replacing them with folk instruments such as guitar, mandolin and banjo. It introduced the saxophone, that had not been used extensively in traditional orchestras. Because of its success, it was the first show to publicize the syncopated music of southern blacks. With the conductor dancing at the rhythm of the music and the drummer entertaining the audience with acrobatic moves, the orchestra introduced the music of the blacks to a wider white audience. The Memphis Students were also the first "singing band" (the musicians sang while they played), and their favorite format of singing was four-part harmony (the style that came to be known as "barber-shop harmony"). Finally, their music was meant for dancing (not enjoyment of the melody), for which it relied on the syncopated rhythms. The result was that syncopated orchestras soon flourished in most cities.

Dance songs composed by blacks sold well in the 1910s and 1920s: Shelton Brooks' instrumental *Walkin' The Dog* (1916) and *Darktown Strutters Ball* (1917), John Turner Layton's *After You've Gone* (1918), *Strut Miss Lizzie* (1921) and *Way Down Yonder in New Orleans* (1922). The most successful dance orchestra was led by Ford Dabney, the (black) composer of *That's Why They Call me Shine* (1910) and *Castle Walk* (1914), the title of another dance craze (after the name of the inventors, Vernon and Irene Castle).

Several of the dances (including the fox-trot) were invented or, at least, popularized by another famous black bandleader and songwriter, James Europe, who founded the "Clef Club" in 1909 (an orchestra of rotating black musicians that even performed at Carnegie Hall) and who exported black music to Europe when he organized an orchestra, the Hellfighters, to play for the US soldiers at the end of World War I (1918). In 1916 a string band of black musicians from the "Clef Club" (Ciro's Club Coon Orchestra) recorded in Britain songs such as *My Foxtrot Wedding Day* and *Yacka Hula Hickey Dula* that even sounded like jazz. Another influential black syncopated orchestra was conducted by Will-Marion Cook, the composer of the black musicals **Clorindy the Origin of the Cakewalk** (1898) and **In Dahomey** (1902), and of syncopated songs such as *Lover's Lane* (1900). Both Europe's Hellfighters (that played in France in 1918) and Will-Marion Cook's syncopated orchestra (that played for British king George V in 1919) exported black music (including jazz) to Europe.

New York was the main center for the dance crazes. Harlem even boasted an all-women orchestra, the Famous Ladies Orchestra, conducted by Marie Lucas. Unlike blues musicians, that at the beginning of the century only catered to the underworld of brothels and vaudeville theaters, black syncopated orchestras reached a more "respectable" audience.

The market for dances boomed before World War I. Dancers such as Vernon and Irene Castle were international stars (they even wrote a manual of the legitimate dance steps, "Modern Dancing", in 1914). They hired both Ford Dabney and James Europe to write original dances for them.

Art Hickman, from San Francisco, is credited as being the first bandleader to arrange music for saxophones, adding a saxophone section to the traditional brass section of syncopated orchestras. The most successful dance band of the Roaring Twenties was the one formed (also in San Francisco) by Paul Whiteman, marketed as a jazz band.

Bennie Moten in Kansas City, Ben Pollack in Chicago, Jean Goldkette in Detroit (in which several white jazz stars cut their teeth), and Ted Weems in Philadelphia were other popular leaders of dance bands of the 1920s. The dance craze that originated in Chicago was spread around the USA mainly by "territory bands" that traveled the circuit of vaudeville theaters and other improvised dancehalls.

Big-band swing jazz became popular towards the end of the Roaring Twenties. In the dance halls that featured that music a new syncopated dance for couples appeared, the "jitterbug", that involved more movement (sometimes acrobatic movement) and the usual black music's ebullience. During World War II it spread to Europe.

Memphis: Jug music

The medicine shows of Memphis spawned a kind of band that became popular throughout the South: the "jug" band (the jug being a poor man's version of the tuba, played by blowing into an empty jug). Typically, around the bass sound of the jug, these bands featured banjo, guitar, mandolin, the "kazoo" (another toy instrument, similar to a comb, that was played by humming into it), the "washboard", and the "bull-fiddle" (a contrabass made of a garbage can, a broom stick and a string). Popular imagination made up for the lack of money.

Whether the craze started in Memphis or Louisville, the most popular jug bands of the 1920s were based in Memphis: Will Shade's Memphis Jug Band (*Cocaine Habit Blues*, 1930), Jack Kelly's South Memphis Jug Band, Jed Davenport's Beale Street Jug Band, and especially Gus Cannon's Jug Stompers (that also featured, besides Cannon's ferocious banjo, Noah Lewis's harmonica and Ashley Thompson's guitar). The latter's *Minglewood Blues* (1928) was probably the first nationwide hit, followed by *Viola Lee Blues* (1928).

New Orleans: Spasm

"Spasm" was a euphoric kind of black music that originated from New Orleans, and another instance in which poor blacks built their own instruments (banjos made from cigar boxes, percussions made of bones, the "Brownie" bass, built out of a tub by inserting a wire into the metallic pipe, cowbells, coffeepots, and so forth). The line-up of a spasm band, such as the Razzy Dazzy Spasm Band, was an ingenious assortment of home-made instruments.

Lafayette: Cajun

Louisiana, and particularly its "bayou country" around Lafayette, inhabited by the "cajuns" (a slang term for the French "acadiens" or "people of Acadie", Acadie being Nova Scotia, the original settlement of the French colonists who during the Seven-Years war made it to Louisiana) was the site of a unique phenomenon. The French aristocracy that had relocated here after the French revolution brought with them the "contredanse" (or "square dance"), the cotillions, the waltz, the mazurka, that, mixing with Anglosaxon, African and Caribbean influences, evolved into "fais-do-do" street dancing and, once transferred to the dance halls (especially after the oil boom of 1901), finally into cajun music. Joseph Falcon, an accordionist, recorded the first cajun single, *Allons a Lafayette*, in 1928. Fiddle (pioneered in the 1930s by Dennis McGee) and accordion (pioneered in the 1920s by Amedee Ardoin, a black musician) became the basic instruments of cajun music. Lyrics in French and stomping rhythm were the other common elements. The 1930s were dominated by the Hackberry Ramblers and fiddler Leo Soileau. The revival of the post-war period yielded hits that crossed the borders of Louisiana: fiddler Harry Choates' *Jole Blon* (1946), accordionist Nathan Abshire's *Pine Grove Blues* (1948), accordionist Ivy Lejeune's *Love Bridge Waltz* (1951). The 1960s were dominated by accordionist Belton Richard and especially virtuoso fiddler Doug Kershaw, author of *Lousiana Man* (1960). Zydeco was a blues-based variant of cajun music for French-speaking black musicians (the "creoles"), best represented by accordionist Clifton Chenier in the decade between *Squeeze Box Boogie* (1955) and *Ai Ai Ai* (1964), and later by Chenier's former organist Stanley "Buckwheat Zydeco" Dural. Cajun music did not change much over the decades until, starting with **Bayou des Mysteres** (1976), Zachary Richard successfully blended it with rock, blues and funk.

Texas: tex-mex

The Mexican-Americans of Texas (the "chicanos") retained their musical traditions and developed their unique sound: the brass-driven "mariachi" music (coined in the 1920s) and the accordion-driven polka-waltz bands ("conjuntos") of the 1930s (pioneered by accordionists Santiago Jimenez and Narciso Martinez, popularized for the Anglosaxon audience by accordionist Flaco Jimenez, Santiago's son). Lydia Mendoza, immortalized by *Mal Hombre* (1934), was the first star of tex-mex music.

London: Mood music

Instrumental pop music had existed from the beginning of Tin Pan Alley, but it was in Britain that it developed into an independent genre.

British composer Albert Ketelbey was one of the first purveyors of "exotica" with his instrumental "mood music": *In A Monastery Garden* (1915), *In A Persian Market* (1920), *In A Chinese Temple Garden* (1925), *By The Blue Hawaian Waters* (1927), *In The Mystic Land of Egypt* (1931), *From A Japanese Screen* (1934).

In Europe and in its colonies, the vogue of the 1920s was "hotel orchestras" that performed sprightly light music in hotel halls. The most famous in Britain was the Max Jaffa Saloon Orchestra, first broadcast on the radio in 1929.

Ray Noble's orchestra played mellow swing-infected melodies, basically a crossbreeding of the hotel orchestra and the swing orchestra, and conquered the USA with an endless waterfall of hits, mostly composed by him: *Goodnight Sweetheart* (1931), *Love Is The Sweetest Thing* (1932), Billy Hill's *The Old Spinning Wheel In The Parlor* (1933), *The Very Thought Of You* (1934), Will Grosz's *Isle Of Capri* (1934), *Paris In The Spring* (1935), *The Touch Of Your Lips* (1936), *Why The Stars Come Out Tonight* (1936), *I Hadn't Anyone Till You* (1938), *Cherokee* (1938), Gus Edwards' *By The Light Of The Silvery Moon* (1941), Jack Lawrence's *Linda* (1947).

Also in Britain, Eric Coates coined the term "light music" ("musica leggera" in Italian) for the kind of mellow melodic instrumental music that he went on to produce for many years with impeccable taste and sense of orchestration: *Four Ways Suite* (1925), *By A Sleepy Lagoon* (1930), *Knightsbridge* (1933), *London Suite* (1933), *Saxo-Rhapsody* (1936), *Springtime Suite* (1937), *Calling All Workers* (1940), *The Three Elizabeths* (1944), and the theme for *Desert Island Discs* (1948).

The first international star of mood music was Italian-born Annunzio-Paolo Mantovani, also the first British artist to become a star in the USA (Wilhelm Grosz's *Red Sails In The Sunset*, 1935; Luigi Cherubini's *Serenade In The Night*, 1936), one of the first artists to prefer the album to the single, and the first artist to sell one million stereo albums. He started in the 1930s conducting his small orchestra (with vocalist) in hotel halls. By the 1950s, he had refined his style of "cascading strings", that led to all-instrumental collections such as **Immortal Classics** (1954).

In Germany, Burt Kaempfert composed *Morgen* (1959), *Wunderland bei Nacht* (1960), *Moon Over Naples* (1964), and *Strangers In The Night* (1966),

Orchestral music of the depression

Guy Lombardo's band, from Canada, pioneered the instrumental medley of hits, besides introducing smooth, saxophone-driven songs such as *Sweethearts on Parade* (1928), *A Sailboat in The Moonlight* (1937), *Powder Your Face with Sunshine* (1949). He sold more than 100 million records.

Perhaps the most popular dance band during the dark years of the "New Deal" was Sammy Kaye's (*Rosalie*, 1937; *Love Walked In*, 1938; *Dream Valley*, 1940), followed by Hal Kemp's (*Got A Date With An Angel*, 1937).

New York's 1939 World Fair is credited with importing Latin American music into the USA. Soon, the USA were dancing to the sound of rumba, mambo, samba, cha cha, calypso, etc. Their steps were much more sensual than anything the USA had inherited from the blacks. (In practice, rock'n'roll dancing would adopt and exaggerate the body language of Latin dances). Xavier Cugat's orchestra was responsible for popularizing many of these dances, as well as Latin-American tunes such as Alberto Dominguez's *Perfidia* (1939).

In the 1940s, the scene of orchestral pop music was dominated by David Rose, who composed *Holiday for Strings* (1944), *Calypso Melody* (1957), *The Stripper* (1958).

Canadian-born Robert Farnon, one of pop music's most influential arrangers, created mini-suites inspired by classical music such as *Jumping Bean* (1948) and *Westminster Waltz* (1956).

Percy Faith's orchestra was the leader in popular instrumental music from *Delicado* (1952) till *Maybe September* (1966). But the leadership sort of moved to France, where Raymond Lefevre, Franck Pourcel and Paul Mauriat competed for the easy-listening market. One of the most successful composers was Andre Popp, the author of *Les Lavandieres du Portugal* (1954) and especially *L'amour Est Bleu* (1967), which sold more than 100 million copies in dozens of different versions. Popp also released the madcap collection of **Delirium in Hi-Fi** (1957), under the moniker Elsa Popping And Her Pixie Landers.

USA: TV Variety Show

In 1927 Philo Farnsworth invented the television set, the last step of a series of innovations that had made possible the broadcasting of images. The following year General Electric started building television receivers for homes ("tv sets"). But the first public broadcast took place in London, where Marconi-EMI's system was chosen as the British standard. Television broadcast began in 1939 in the USA, but World War II caused a six-year hiatus. At that point there were about seven thousand tv sets in the USA, served by nine stations (four in New York, two each in Chicago and Los Angeles, one in Philadelphia). At the end of the war, television broadcast resumed and, finally, tv sets could be sold by the millions. In 1943 RCA had been forced by the government to divest itself of part of its broadcasting business, and in 1945 that part became a separate broadcasting network, the "ABC" network. Thus there were now three national networks: CBS, NBC and ABC. In 1947 "Kraft Television Theatre" brought Broadway theater into the average home. In 1948 Ed Sullivan started a variety show, "Toast of the Town" (later renamed "Ed Sullivan Show"), followed by the "Perry Como Show" (1948), while the "Arthur Godfrey's Talent Scouts" was transferred from radio to television, and Milton Berle hosted the "Texaco Star Theater" (1948), that soon became the most popular show in the country. These tv variety shows were, de facto, resurrecting the vaudeville for an audience that was no longer local but global. In 1949 a new kind of star was born when an ordinary girl by the name of Betty Furness was featured in commercial spots for Westinghouse refrigerators: she became as popular as comedians and singers. She was one of the reasons that advertisers left the radio and poured into television: the audience was captivated by the live demonstration of a product more than by the traditional "commercial jingle" of the radio. "Your Hit Parade" (1950) and the "Jack Benny Show" (1950) were instrumental in promoting, respectively, music and comedy on television.

The popularity of comic strips had prompted radio stations to create "situation comedies" (or "sitcoms"), that were basically the equivalent of a recurring comic strip without the pictures. The first one aired in 1926 in Chicago. They became very popular thanks to the skills of the comedians who ran them, but they found their ideal medium with television. "Mary Kay and Johnny" (1947) and "The Goldbergs" (1949) were the first sitcoms on tv. In 1950 the "Colgate Comedy Hour" was born, which went down in history as the first show to telecast in color (1953). "I Love Lucy" debuted in 1951. The "Bob Hope Show" moved from radio to television in 1952.

In 1952 Dave Garroway launched the "Today" show, the first early-morning show, and in 1954 comedian Steve Allen launched the "Tonight Show". George Burns and Bob Hope became the most famous comedians in the country thanks to their tv appearances, surpassing any Broadway or radio personality. There were now about 20 million tv sets in the USA. The Broadway revue had simply migrated to the small screen, that could reach millions of people around the country. In the process, it had been forced to downplay the choreography and to emphasize the star (whether comedian or singer or host). Rock'n'roll changed television broadcasting too: in 1957 Ed Sullivan passed all the other shows in popularity.

USA: the Soap Opera

During the 1920s several radio stations began broadcasting daytime serial dramas that were aimed at an audience of housewives (the audience listening to the radio during daytime hours). These dramas were therefore sponsored by advertisers who targeted housewives marketing products such as soap. These dramas came to be known as "soap operas". They migrated to television almost immediately, "The Guiding Light" (inaugurated on radio in 1937) being the archetype of all future soap operas (it migrated to tv in 1952), and "Faraway Hill" (1946) being the first one specifically designed for television, followed by "Search for Tomorrow" (1951), "Love of Life" (1951) and, in Britain, by the BBC serial "Archers" (1951). Their episodes lasted about 15 minutes. It was only in 1956 that soap operas assumed the classic half-hour structure. Like their radio ancestors, they had a soundtrack that was performed by an organist, drawing from a wealth of melodramatic melodies. Given their target audience, these soap operas indulged in endless intricate adventures, usually of a romantic nature. The goal of each episode was to set the foundations for future episodes, not to reach closure. Many soap operas were telecast for decades, some for more than 30 years. "Peyton Place" (1964) was the first prime-time soap opera (thus targeting a broader audience than just housewives). By that time, soap operas had become part of the collective subconscious of the national youth.

USA: Remaking the Music Business

Founded in 1912, the American Society for Composers (ASCAP) was a union for songwriters. It soon became a monopoly that controlled the radio broadcasts of music. Radio broadcasters fought a battle against ASCAP by establishing their own "union", the Broadcast Music Inc (BMI) that assembled mainly singers. Needless to say, radio stations were more motivated to play the music of singers (who were members of the BMI) than instrumental music (almost entirely controlled by the ASCAP). Even after 1941 (when the dispute was solved), singers maintained a grip on the recording industry that they had never had before. Founded in 1896, the American Federation of Musicians had become a powerful union precisely because the recording industry had become such a huge industry. This union claimed that instrumentalists were hurt by recordings, though. If their music could be reproduced at will by radios and jukeboxes, then there was less need of their physical presence. The union demanded that artists be payed royalties not only for each record sold but also for radio broadcasts and use in jukeboxes. The record labels refused. In august 1942 the AFM banned all recordings of instrumental music, whether classical or jazz. The three major labels (Decca, Victor, Columbia) gave in only in november 1944. Thus for two years virtually no jazz instrumentalist could cut a commercial record. There were two exceptions to the ban. The first one was for vocals-only recordings: singers were not members of the union. Thus the ban helped a-cappella groups get established nation-wide, and, generally speaking, contributed to pop music's bias towards vocal music that would remain in place throughout the century. The second exception was made for the V-Discs. These were records cut by the government for the troops that were fighting in World War II. They introduced a new format: the 12" vinyl 78 RPM that could fit almost seven minutes of music (as opposed to the three minutes of the traditional 10" record). People got used to hearing an extended performance. It took only three years from the end of the war for Columbia to introduce (in 1948) the 12-inch 33-1/3 RPM long-playing vinyl record (the LP), that allowed recordings of more than twenty minutes per side. At the same time, Nazi Germany had been developing the portable electromagnetic recorder because Adolf Hitler loved to be able to speak to every town without having to physically travel to each one. In 1934 AEG introduced the "magnetophone" that recorded on tapes and the technology was rapidly improved for high fidelity during the war. At the end of the war a USA engineer copied the German invention and turned it into Ampex's first tape recorder (first used in august 1947 to record Bing Crosby). It was now possible to tape lengthy performances of music at an affordable cost. Both the LP and the tape made the old cumbersome "album" (the set of several 78 RPM records) obsolete. This was yet another step in the process that made the live performance less and less essential (after the sheet music, the piano roll, the radio and the 78 RPM record). Each step in this process distancing the listening experience from the actual performance had caused a commercial revolution and further increased the business of music, and the innovations of 1947-48 turned out to be no exception to the rule.

The Origins of the American Domination

Record labels per se had only limited power to create new demand. They had to rely on radio and tv stations (or musicals or films) to publicize their "products" (artists and songs). That is where the dynamics of the European and US systems diverged dramatically.

European television was controlled by bureaucrats with little motivation to change format or content. US television was controlled by businessmen with strong motivation to continuously try new formats and content. In the USA, competition led to innovation. Each radio and tv station had to do something different in order to beat the other stations. They were constantly looking for something   new.

In Europe, bureaucracy led, at best, to imitation. European radio and television stations, run by the State, kept showing the same kind of programs over and over again, mostly derived from the theaters. In Europe, innovation did not come from the bureaucrats who ran the stations, but from the actors and musicians who visited the USA and brought back new ideas: innovation was bottom-up. In the USA, innovation was top-down, driven by the very management of the stations on the basis of elementary market competition. The press played the same role in Europe and in the USA, except that in the USA it had a lot more to write about. Because of the language, and of a vibrant underground scene, Britain was faster to absorb US innovations, but, again, the innovation came from US stations, not from the BBC. It may well be that US music would have dominated the western world anyway because of its unique black element, but the very way in which music was channeled to the consumer gave US music an advantage.

Transience

- When Gilbert Seldes wrote the first comprehensive treatise on US pop culture, "The Seven Lively Arts" (1924), that examined the features shared by comics, movies, vaudeville and pop music, it was already clear to him that their essential quality was transience. Pop culture in the USA (unlike pop culture in Europe) was very much the product of unrestrained capitalism, that demanded continuous competition. These "lively" arts shared the unremitting pressure to change. And it wasn't gradual change either: success came with quantum jumps, not gradual change. Thus artists and entrepreneurs are constantly in search of revolutionary ideas. Whereas Bach is "cool" even centuries later, the pop artist is "cool" only for a few years, after which she or he rapidly becomes outdated. Thus the system was set in motion that would yield a century of permanent artistic revolution.

THE MUSICAL

New York: the Musical

A significant break with the formats of the vaudeville and the burlesque had been represented by the musical farce **The Mulligan Guard Picnic** (1878), scored by David Braham and starring comedians Edward Harrigan and Tony Hart, an evolution of the "Mulligan Shows" that Harrigan and Hart had performed around the country for years. Harrigan was the genius behind the storyline and the dialogues, which were taken mostly from everyday life. This time the audience was laughing at itself, because Harrigan's focus was on ordinary lives. Both the vaudeville and the burlesque had required minimal linguistic skills in the audience, being mostly "physical" (singalong melodies, body movement, facial expressions, stereotyped characters, imitation and parody) while Harrigan's farces represented a significant step towards a more literate form. Ditto for the singers, who were sopranos (Edna May, Lillian Russell, Vivienne Segal) and contraltos (Fay Templeton), not prostitutes turned chanteuses.

Charles Hoyt's **A Trip To Chinatown** (1891), that included the tune *After the Ball*, and **Whoop-Dee-Doo** (1904), the vehicle for comedians Joe Weber and Lew Fields (still in the style of the burlesque), were some of the musical farces that were able to compete against Gilbert and Sullivan's operettas, the real hits of the 1890s, imitated in New York by productions such as Reginald deKoven's **Robin Hood** (1891), John Philip Sousa's **El Capitan** (1896), Leslie Stuart's **Florodora** (1900), whose six female stars (the "Florodora girls") became instant celebrities, Howard Talbot's **A Chinese Honeymoon** (1901).

Bob Cole's **A Trip to Coontown** (1898) was the first musical comedy entirely produced and performed by blacks in a Broadway theater (largely inspired to the routines of the minstrel show), followed by Will-Marion Cook's ragtime-tinged **Clorindy the Origin of the Cakewalk** (1898), staged at the "Casino Theatre", and the highly successful **In Dahomey** (1902), that turned Antigua-born comedian Bert "Mr Nobody" Williams and minstrel George Walker into influential models for all black entertainers.

The European operetta was transplanted to New York by works such as Reginald de Koven's **Robin Hood** (1890), Victor Herbert's **Babes in Toyland** (1903) and **Naughty Marietta** (1910), with *Sweet Mysterty of Life*, Rudolf Friml's **The Firefly** (1912), mostly composed by immigrants.

The first complete artist of the musical comedy was George Cohan, a veteran vaudeville performer and successful songwriter (*I Guess I'll Have To Telegraph My Baby*, 1898), who composed the lavishly-choreographed musical melodrama **Little Johnny Jones** (1904), that, like its predecessor **The Governor's Son** (1901), shunned the random, implausible plots of the musical comedies for a coherent and cohesive storyline. It included the classics *Yankee Doodle Dandy* and *Give My Regards to Broadway*, and was blessed with unprecedented success, repeated by **45 Minutes From Broadway** (1906), with *Mary's a Grand Old Name*, **George Washington Jr** (1906), with *You're a Grand Old Flag*, and several more. He also wrote *That Haunting Melody* for **Vera Violetta** (1911).

Cohan's equivalent in Britain was Lionel Monckton, who created the first British musical in which the songs "were" the plot (rather than the musical being a mere parade of mostly unrelated songs): **The Arcadians** (1909).

Russian-born Irving Berlin (Israel Baline), a former singing waiter, fused the worlds of Stephen Foster, Tin Pan Alley and Broadway in his simple, unpretentious hit songs: *Alexander's Ragtime Band* (1911), that sounded more like a military march than a ragtime, *Everybody's Doing It* (1911) for Eddie Cantor, *Play a Simple Melody* and *Syncopated Walk*, off his first musical, **Watch Your Step** (1914), influenced by ragtime, composed for dancers Vernon and Irene Castle, *God Bless America* (1917) and *Oh How I Hate to Get Up in the Morning* (1918), off the musical **Yip Yip Yaphank** (1918), *A Pretty Girl is Like a Melody* (1919), the signature song of the Ziegfeld follies. Their exuberance became the soundtrack of the Broadway musical in its infancy, merging syncopation (the craze of Tin Pan Alley) and melodrama. Later, Berlin continued to compose songs that defined their era: *Mandy* (1919), *All Alone* (1924), *Blue Skies* (1927), *Marie* (1929), *Easter Parade* (1933), *White Christmas* (1942). His best musical was perhaps **Annie Get Your Gun** (1946), that contained *There's No Business Like Show Business* and *Anything you Can Do.*

Jerome Kern's melodies highlighted musicals, staged in humble venues, such as **Sally** (1920) that were relatively humble and ordinary compared with the opulence of the extravaganzas that were being staged by the larger theaters. Jerome Kern had re-invented the "musical" by integrating music and story in everyday settings (not the fantasy lands of the operettas), thus wedding Sullivan's aesthetics and Cohan's aesthetics. He then began a collaboration with lyricist Oscar Hammerstein II that peaked with **Show Boat** (1927), his masterpiece, based on the novel by Edna Ferber, a realistic saga produced by Ziegfeld that included several moments of high pathos (the spiritual *Ol' Man River*, *Make Believe*, *You Are Love*, the cakewalk *Can't Help Lovin' That Man* and *Bill*, the latter two the songs that turned Helen Morgan into a star). Kern then scored **Roberta** (1933), with *Smoke Gets in Your Eyes*, and *Yesterdays*, Mark Sandrich's film **Top Hat** (1935), with *The Piccolino, Isn't This A Lovely Day, Cheek to Cheek* and *Top Hat White Tie and Tails*, **Swing Time** (1936), with *The Way You Look Tonight*, the ambitious and experimental **High Wide And Handsome** (1937), with *The Folks Who Live On The Hill*, **Lady Be Good** (1941), with *The Last Time I Saw Paris*, etc.

George Gershwin's songs, versified mostly by his brother Ira Gershwin, represented a step forward in rhythm and sophistication, because Gershwin was fluent in both pop, jazz and classical music, a fact best represented by the jazz opera **Blue Monday Blues** (1922), the main attraction of George White's "Scandals" in 1922, the symphonic **Rhapsody in Blue** (1924) and the folk opera **Porgy and Bess** (1935), containing *Summertime*. After writing an Al Jolson hit, *Swanee* (1919), Gershwin entered the arena of Broadway musicals with **Lady Be Good** (1924), that launched the career of dancer Fred Astaire and established the trend of having the title-song as one of the main hits. Other musicals included *Someone To Watch Over Me* (1926), *S'Wonderful* (1927), the ballet *An American in Paris* (1929), *I've Got a Crush on You* (1930), *I Got Rhythm* (1930), that launched the careet of Ethel Merman (the band included Benny Goodman, Jimmy Dorsey, Glenn Miller, Jack Teargarden, Gene Krupa), and a political satire, **Of Thee I Sing** (1931) that became the biggest hit of the decade. His *Cuban Overture* (1932) was one of the first Latin pieces to become popular in the USA.

Shuffle Along (1921) was entirely produced and performed by blacks (including the still unknown Josephine Baker and Paul Robeson). The music, including the hits *Love Will Find a Way* and *I'm Just Wild About Harry*, was scored by a veteran of the vaudeville and the minstrel-shows, Eubie Blake, who had already scored several ragtime hits. But, more importantly, it introduced white audiences to a wealth of black dance styles, from tap dancing to jazz dancing, that had been developing in the clubs of Harlem. The success of that musical allowed Blake to score **The Chocolate Dandies** (1924), another showcase for black dances that turned Josephine Baker into a star. Blake also crafted hits such as *You Were Meant For Me* (1923), *Dixie Moon* (1924) and "Memories of You" (1930). In the meantime another black composer, jazz pianist James Price Johnson, had scored **Runnin' Wild** (1923), whose main hit, *Charleston*, launched the biggest dance craze of the decade.

Ray Henderson, one of the most successful Tin Pan Alley composers, as proven by *Rock-a-Bye Your Baby With a Dixie Melody* (1918), *Georgette* (1922), *That Old Gang Of Mine* (1923), *It All Depends on You* (1924), *Bye Bye Blackbird* (1925), *Alabama Bound* (1925), *I'm Sitting on Top of the World* (1925), *The Thrill Is Gone* (1931), *Life Is Just A Bowl Of Cherries* (1931), teamed up with lyricists Lew Brown and Buddy George de Sylva, a trio that became a legend. They wrote *Birth of the Blues* and *Black Bottom* for George White's **Scandals of 1925**. Their youthful, exuberant **Good News** (1927) started the trend of satires of college life and incorporated most dancing styles of the time, such as the Charleston (*The Varsity Drag*), besides their hit *The Best Things in Life Are Free*. Their musicals were not particularly original but always contained a hit song or two: *You're The Cream in my Coffee* in **Hold Everything** (1928), *Button Up Your Overcoat* and *You Are My Lucky Star* in **Follow Through** (1929). They also composed *Sonny Boy* for Lloyd Bacon's film **The Singing Fool** (1928) and *Keep Your Sunny Side Up* and *If I Had A Talking Picture of You* for their own film **Sunnyside Up** (1929), one of the most innovative of the early musicals, as well as music for their sci-fi fantasy film **Just Imagine** (1930).

In the years after World War I, the musical became New York's premier form of entertainment. Harry Tierney's **Irene** (1919) and Vincent Youmans' **No No Nanette** (1925), the epitome of the "Roaring Twenties", with *Tea For Two* and *I Want To Be Happy*, were the most influential Broadway musicals, while Youmans' **Wildflower** (1923), with *Bambolina*, Czech-born Rudolf Friml's **Rose Marie** (1924) and **The Vagabond King** (1925), with *Only a Rose*, and Hungarian-born Sigmund Romberg's **Student Prince** (1924), with *Gaudeamus Igitur* and *The Drinking Song*, **The Desert Song** (1926) and **The New Moon** (1928), with *Lover Come Back to Me*, were still in the old format of the operetta. Will Ortman's **Holka-Polka** (1925) is only important because it marked Busby Berkeley's debut and his first experiment with eccentric choreography.

Bert Kalamar and Harry Rubenstein, who had already composed *Who's Sorry Now* (1923) and *I Wanna Be Loved By You* (1928), scored the Marx Brothers' **Animal Crackers** (1928), **Horse Feathers** (1932) and **Duck Soup** (1933).

London's main novelty at the time was Noel Coward, the new talent that made a splash with his first musicals: **This Year of Grace** (1928), that included *A Room With a View* and *Dance Little Lady*, and **Bitter Sweet** (1929), including *I'll See You Again* and *If Love Were All*, **The Third Little Show** (1931), with *Mad Dogs and Englishmen*, plus the revue **Cavalcade** (1931), with *Twentieth Century Blues*.

His competitors in Britain were Noel Gay (Richard Armitage), whose fortune peaked with **Me And My Girl** (1937), that included *The Lambeth Walk*, and Ivor Novello (David Davies), whose main musicals were **Crest Of A Wave** (1937), with *Rose Of England*, and **Perchance To Dream** (1945), with *We'll Gather Lilacs*

Richard Rodgers was the next giant of US pop music after Irving Berlin. With lyricist Lorenz Hart he composed a number of Broadway hits that already included some of Rodgers' memorable melodies: *Manhattan* (1925), *My Heart Stood Still* (1927), *With A Song In My Heart* (1929), *Blue Moon* (1934), *The Most Beautiful Girl in the World* (1935). This phase peaked with **Babes In Arms** (1937), the musical with *My Funny Valentine*, *Johnny One Note* and *The Lady is a Tramp*, and **Pal Joey** (1940), one of his most innovative works (considered the first musical about an anti-hero).

Having refined the craft, Rodgers proceeded to revolutionize it after he partnered with Oscar Hammerstein II with **Oklahoma** (1944), a daring work that did not rely on gags or girls or catchy melodies but on a "dramatic" story and "dramatic" characters (the songs were monologues and dialogues, not just lyrics), a musical that employed avantgarde dancers (choreographed by Agnes de Mille) instead of chorus girls (and whose dancing numbers were about the story and not mere stage effects). It was also the first musical ever recorded in its entirety on an LP. Rodgers' most experimental work was **Allegro** (1947), a melodic fantasia rather than a simple sequence of songs. Along the way they charmed the audience with immensely popular tunes such as *You'll Never Walk Alone* (1945), *The Gentleman Is A Dope* (1947), *Some Enchanted Evening* (1949), **South Pacific** (1949), *Whistle a Happy Tune* (1951). The album of **The Sound of Music** (1959) charted for seven years. Rodgers' and Hammerstein's musicals crystallized a view of the world, that relied on traditional moral values and faith in the USA as a paradise on Earth.

The Great Depression and the talking movie were supposed to bury the Broadway musical, but, instead, the 1930s turned out to be its golden age. In a sense, the Broadway musical cannibalized both its enemies: it turned the Great Depression and its mood into an epic theme, and it turned the talking movie into a vehicle to perpetuate the musical itself. The big losers were the erotic revues (Ziegfeld's "Follies", White's "Scandals" and Carroll's "Vanities") that looked antiquated and definitely out of touch with the zeitgeist of the Great Depression.

Arthur Schwartz's **Three's A Crowd** (1930) and especially **The Band Wagon** (1931), the ultimate "backstage" musical, scripted by playwright George Kaufman and containing *Dancing In The Dark*, and Harold Rome's **Pins and Needles** (1937) were musicals that reflected their times. So was Vernon Duke's all-black allegory **Cabin In The Sky** (1940), that made vocalist Lena Horne's fortune (but, despite the cast of black stars, it contained no black music but melodic ditties such as *Takin' A Chance on Love*). Russian-born Vernon Duke (Vladimir Dukelsky) also composed *April In Paris* (1932), *Autumn in New York* (1934) and *I Can't Get Started Without You* (1936) for other revues. Expelled from Germany, Kurt Weill also analyzed US society in **Knickerbocker Holiday** (1938), the psychoanalytical thriller **Lady in the Dark** (1941) and **Lost in the**

Stars (1949), scripted by Maxwell Anderson. Not so in London, where the hits were Ivor Novello's **The Dancing Years** (1939) and Noel Gay's **Me and My Girl** (1937), two rather shallow works.

However, the real genius of the decade was Cole Porter, the first New York songwriter who was not afraid to talk about sex, as he proved in **Paris** (1928), **Fifty Million Frenchmen** (1929) and **The Gay Divorcee** (1932), as well as in tunes such as *I'm In Love Again* (1924), *What Is This Thing Called Love?* (1929) and *Love for Sale* (1930). His melodic craft reached its zenith with **Anything Goes** (1934), followed by several other top-notch musicals and by tunes such as *I've Got You Under My Skin* (1936), *In The Still of the Night* (1937), *My Heart Belongs to Daddy* (1938), etc. His greatest triumph came with the "backstage" musical **Kiss Me Kate** (1948), based on William Shakespeare's **Taming of the Shrew**, followed by **Can-Can** (1953) and the jazzy soundtrack for Charles Walters' film **High Society** (1956), featuring Louis Armstrong, Frank Sinatra and Bing Crosby.

Hollywood: the Musical Films

Music had been part of cinema since its inception, but the musical score was neither controlled by the film producer nor the same for each projection: it was up to the theater to decide which musicians to hire (usually only one per projection, an organist) and it was largely up to the musician to write or improvise the music for the film. Rudolph Valentino popularized the tango in Rex Ingram's **The Four Horsemen of the Apocalypse** (1921), but it was the dance, not the music, that caught the imagination of world audiences. Many of Valentino's fans had no idea what a tango sounded like.

Occasionally the studio would provide the theaters with "suggestions" on what kind of music to play. D.W.Griffith's **The Birth of a Nation** (1915) first came with an orchestral "soundtrack" prepared by Joseph-Carl Briel that featured music by Liszt, Verdi, Beethoven, Wagner and Tchaikovsky, then came with an original score composed by Victor Herbert. Classical composers were frequently asked to work on such film scores. In France, Arthur Honegger composed the music for Abel Gance's **La Roue** (1923) and **Napoleon** (1927), while Erik Satie composed music for Rene' Clair's **Entr'acte** (1924). In Russia, Edmund Meisel composed the music for Sergei Eisenstein's masterpiece **Potemkin** (1926), an even more sensational and organic piece of music. Several more classical composers scored the music for important silent films. For the theaters that could not afford an orchestra, the American Photoplayer Company introduced a seven-meter long player-piano, the "Fotoplayer Style", that could play orchestral music as well as sound effects, so that each theater could customize its own sountrack (about 10,000 were built between 1910 and 1928). And it was for a film, Alan Crosland's **Don Juan** (1926), that 16-inch 33 1/3 RPM records were introduced (a size and a speed determined by the size and speed of a reel of film).

What studios did provide was "theme" songs, that usually accompanied the movie: *Charmaine*, composed by Erno Rapee for Raoul Walsh's **What Price Glory** (1926), based on a Hungarian waltz from 1913, *Diane*, composed again by Erno Rapee for Frank Borzage's **Seventh Heaven** (1927), *Ramona*, another waltz, composed by Mabel Wayne for Edwin Carewe's **Ramona** (1928), etc

In 1926 Alan Crosland's **Don Juan** was released with a musical soundtrack prepared by the studio. The evening opened with a short musical film in which movement and sound were synchronized, the first public demonstration of Lee Forest's "Vitaphone". Another short musical film was made in 1927 of Xavier Cugart's tango orchestra.

The "talking" movies were officially born with Alan Crosland's **The Jazz Singer** (1927), a musical adaptation of Samson Raphaelson's **The Day of Atonement** (1926), already staged on Broadway, but turned by the Warner studios into a suite of melodies from disparate sources (Tchaikowsky, Hebrew folk music, Irving Berlin's *Blue Skies*) and a vehicle for pop star Al Jolson. This film was, actually, mostly silent. Lloyd Bacon's **The Singing Fool** (1928) was more of the same, but Ray Henderson's *Sonny Boy* became a nation-wide hit (the soundtrack included several older Henderson-Brown-da Sylva songs), and caused an avalanche: the Hollywood studios started hiring Broadway stars (Fanny Brice, Sophie Tucker, Marilyn Miller) as well as foreign stars (Maurice Chevalier) and providing them with vehicles for their debut on the big screen. Charles Reisner directed the **Hollywood Revue** (1929), which was really a Broadway revue starring Marie Dressler next to Hollywood comedians such as Buster Keaton, Stan Laurel and Oliver Hardy, and that included Nacio Herb Brown's *Singin' in The Rain* and *You Were Meant for Me*. The "Ziegfeld Follies" were immortalized in Thornton Freeland's musical film **Whoopee** (1930), that included Walter Donaldson's *Making Whoopee* and *My Baby Just Cares for Me*, was choreographed by Busby Berkeley, and turned Eddie Cantor into a star. The studios also began transposing Broadway hits to the big screen, and one of them, Roy Del Ruth's 1929 version of Sigmund Romberg's **The Desert Song** (1926), is credited with being the first fully musical operetta of cinema, followed by an adaptation of Irving Berlin's **The Cocoanuts** (1925) for the Marx Brothers, and by Harry Pollard's version of Jerome Kern's **Show Boat** (1927), all of them in 1929.

After these tentative marriages of picture and sound came the first serious talking movies: King Vidor's **Halleluja** (1929) was the first musical drama, dedicated to black music (mostly spirituals plus Irving Berlin's *Waiting At The End Of The Road*), Ernst Lubitsch's **The Love Parade** (1929) was the first musical comedy (protagonist Maurice Chevalier), scored by Victor Schertzinger (*Dream Lover*, *March of the Grenadiers*), Rouben Mamoulian's **Applause** (1929) was the first "backstage" musical, starring Helen Morgan and including Jay Gorney's *What I Wouldn't Do For That Man?*. But perhaps the first real musical should be considered **The Broadway Melody** (1929), scored by Nacio Herb Brown and directed by Harry Beaumont, the composer being much more important than the director (*Wedding of the Painted Doll, You Were Meant for Me*).

Nacio Herb Brown was a towering figure of the era, crafting (besides those 1929 hits): the instrumental *Doll Dance* (1921), *Singin' in The Rain* (1929), *Pagan Love Song* (1929), *The Broadway Melody* (1930), *Paradise* (1932), *Eadie Was A Lady* (1932), *Beautiful Girl* (1933), *Temptation* (1933), *All I Do Is Dream of You* (1934), *You Are My Lucky Star* (1936), *I've Got a Feelin' You're Foolin'* (1936), *Good Morning* (1939), *I'm Feelin' Like a Million* (1938), *Alone* (1940), *Make 'Em Laugh* (1952), all of them created for movie soundtracks.

After one year, the novelty was already old news, and the cinematic musical seemed dead. Instead, along came choreographer Busby Berkeley and composer Harry Warren (real name Salvatore Guaragna), already the author of *Rose Of The Rio Grande* (1922), *I Found a Million-Dollar Baby* (1930) and *You're My Everything*

(1931), a couple that crafted Lloyd Bacon's **42nd Street** (1933), with *Lullaby of Broadway*, *Shuffle Off to Buffalo*, *You're Getting To Be A Habit With Me* and *42nd Street*, Mervin LeRoy's **Gold Diggers of 1933** (1933), with *High Life*, *I've Got To Sing A Torch Song*, *Pettin' In The Park*, *Remember My Forgotten Man*, *Shadow Waltz*, especially *The Gold Diggers' Song/ We're In The Money*, and Lloyd Bacon's **Footlight Parade** (1933), with *Honeymoon Hotel* and *Shanghai Lil*. Berkeley redefined the musical as a visual and dynamic show in which the opulence is not due to the stage effects but to the colorful and geometric patterns created by the dancers. Thus 1933 became a watershed year. The golden age of the Hollywood musical had just begun.

Warren's later hits (written for a variety of films) included: *I Found a Million Dollar Baby* (1931), *You're My Everything* (1931), *I Only Have Eyes For You* (1934), *The Girl At The Ironing Board* (1934), *The Boulevard of Broken Dreams* (1934), *Lulu's Back In Town* (1935), *September In The Rain* (1937), *You Must Have Been a Beautiful Baby* (1938), *Daydreaming* (1938), *Jeepers Creepers* (1938), *Chattanooga Choo Choo* (1940), *There Will Never Be Another You* (1942), *You'll Never Know* (1943), *On the Atchison Topeka and the Santa Fe* (1945), *The More I See You* (1945). He wrote more than 900 songs. The soundtracks and the songs make Warren one of the most influential composers of both Hollywood and Broadway of all times.

Broadway veteran Vincent Youmans scored the hits (*Carioca*, *Flying Down To Rio*) of Thornton Freeland's **Flying Down To Rio** (1933), another important step in the development of the cinematic musical because it inaugurated the legendary dancing/singing couple of Fred Astaire and Ginger Rogers. They were the stars of Mark Sandrich's 1934 version of Cole Porter's **The Gay Divorcee**, that included only one Porter original and a set of new songs (notably Con Conrad's *The Continental* and *Needle in a Haystack*), William Seiter's 1934 version of Kern's **Roberta** and, finally, their quintessential musical, Mark Sandrich's **Top Hat** (1935), scored by Irving Berlin.

Harold Arlen, the veteran of the "Cotton Club", was called in to score Victor Fleming's **Wizard of Oz** (1939), the musical that turned Judy Garland into a star, and Arlen delivered one of most famous ballads of all times, *Somewhere Over the Rainbow*. Arlen's other Hollywood hits were: *Last Night When We Were Young* (1935), *Lydia the Tatoo'd Lady* (1939), *Blues in the Night* (1941), perhaps his artistic peak, *That Old Black Magic* (1942), *Happiness is a Thing Called Joe* (1943), *Ac-Cent-Tchu-Ate the Positive* (1944), *Any Place I Hang My Hat Is Home* (1946). He wrote more than 400 songs.

Two important "musicals" of the age did not follow the Hollywood dogmas: Sergey Eisenstein's **Alexander Nevsky** (1938), scored by classical composer Sergey Prokofiev, and Walt Disney's **Fantasia** (1940), a cartoon that introduced stereo sound. Also notable was Michael Curtiz's **Yankee Doodle Dandy** (1942), a musical biography of George Cohan.

Bing Crosby and Bob Hope starred in a series of musical comedies, starting with Victor Schertzinger's **The Road To Singapore** (1940) and ending 22 years later. Both became enormously popular. Bob Hope's signature song was Leo Robin's *Thanks For The Memory* (1938).

FILM MUSIC

Hollywood: Film Music

Charlie Chaplin composed his own music for **City Lights** (1931), **Modern Times** (1936) and **Limelight** (1952). That was the exception, and few film-makers would imitate him. He wasn't clear at all whose job was to score the soundtracks.

German cabaret pianist Friedrich Hollaender scored Josef von Sternberg's **Der Blaue Engel/ The Blue Angel** (1930), which included Marlene Dietrich's signature tune *Ich bin von Kopf bis Fuss auf Liebe Eingestellt/ Falling In Love Again*. Von Sternberg kept changing musicians: Karl Hajos scored **Morocco** (1930) and Franke Harling **Shangai Express** (1932) and **The Scarlet Empress** (1934).

In the 1930s, after a few years of experimentation, scoring film soundtracks became an art in earnest thanks to a small group of foreign-born musicians, first and foremost two Austrian-born and classically-trained composers. Erich-Wolfgang Korngold's coined a lush, overwhelming, operatic style with Michael Curtiz's **Captain Blood** (1935) and especially **The Adventures of Robin Hood** (1938) and **The Sea Hawk** (1940), as well as Charles Gerhardt's **Anthony Adverse** (1936) and Sam Wood's **Kings Row** (1942).

Max Steiner explored many different moods, sensational in Ernest Schoedsack's **King Kong** (1933), one of the first soundtracks to rely heavily on sound effects, pathetic in Victor Fleming's **Gone With The Wind** (1939), including *Tara* and countless references to traditional songs, exotic in Michael Curtiz's **Casablanca** (1942), melodramatic in Irving Rapper's **Now Voyager** (1942), gloomy in John Huston's **The Treasure of the Sierra Madre** (1948), epic in John Ford's **The Searchers** (1956), romantic in Delmer Daves' **A Summer Place** (1959), whose instrumental theme was a massive hit for Percy Faith's orchestra, etc. He also scored Howard Hawks' **The Big Sleep** (1946), John Huston's **Key Largo** (1948), Raoul Walsh's **White Heat** (1949).

Roy Webb (the New Yorker among all these foreigners) invented the musical language for the light comedy with the soundtracks to George Cukor's **Sylvia Scarlett** (1935), Howard Hawks' **Bringing Up Baby** (1938) and Rene` Clair's **I Married A Witch** (1942). Then he turned to Jacques Tourneur's horror movies, such as **Cat**

People (1942), **I Walked With A Zombie** (1943) and **Out Of The Past** (1947), and to psychological thrillers such as Don Siegel's **Invasion of the Body Snatchers** (1956), Robert Siodmak's **Spiral Staircase** (1946) and Alfred Hitchcock's **Notorious** (1946).

The master of horror was Austrian organist Hans Salter who developed a new language for trivial suspense vehicles such as Frank Skinner's **The Son of Frankenstein** (1939), Christy Cabanne's **The Mummy's Hand** (1940), George Waggner's **The Wolf Man** (1941). The soundtracks for Jack Arnold's **The Creature from the Black Lagoon** (1954) and **The Incredible Shrinking Man** (1957) were more accomplished but simply recycled the vocabulary he had devised in the 1940s.

A master in the grand lush orchestral style, and a veteran vaudeville pianist and conductor of Broadway musicals, Alfred Newman scored jazz-tinged and classical-tinged soundtracks for King Vidor's **Street Scene** (1931) and William Wyler's **Wuthering Heights** (1939). His frequently colorful and exuberant scores taught a whole generation how to write music for films: John Cromwell's **The Prisoner of Zenda** (1937), William Dieterle's **The Hunchback of Notre Dame** (1939), William Wyler's **Wuthering Heights** (1939). The success of his score for Henry King's **The Song Of Bernadette** (1943) convinced the record labels that soundtracks were a viable product (until then, very few scores had been released on record). He then scored some classics such as Joseph Mankiewicz's **All About Eve** (1950), Henry Koster's **The Robe** (1953), the first Cinemascope film, Jean Negulesco's **How To Marry A Millionaire** (1953), Billy Wilder's **The Seven Year Itch** (1955), and went on to compose *Love Is a Many Splendored Thing* (1955),

The western movie developed its own musical language, thanks to Ukrainian-born Dmitri Tiomkin. After working on magniloquent music for Frank Capra's **Lost Horizon** (1937), **Mr Smith Goes to Washington** (1939), **Meet John Doe** (1941) and **It's A Wonderful Life** (1946), as well as for Alfred Hitchcock's **Shadow of a Doubt**(1943) and **Dial M For Murder** (1954), Tiomkin focused on the western in a series of breathtaking scores: King Vidor's **Duel in the Sun** (1946), Howard Hawks' **Red River** (1948) and **Big Sky** (1952), Fred Zinnemann's **High Noon** (1952), the first movie to be promoted by its theme song (originally titled *Do Not Forsake Me*) rather than viceversa, and George Stevens' **Giant** (1956). Having become the darling of Hollywood producers, he applied his hit-oriented language to John Sturges' **Gunfight at the OK Corral** (1957) and Howard Hawks' **Rio Bravo** (1959), but also to the tv themes *Rawhide* (1959) and *Gunslinger* (1961), as well as to Alfred Hitchcock's **I Confess** (1953) and **Dial M for murder** (1954). Each of them contains at least a song that was meant to be just that, a song, and a catchy one, as opposed to music that underpins the story.

Hungarian-born Miklos Rozsa helped develop the musical language of the film noir with his ominous scores for Zoltan Korda's **Jungle Book** (1942), which was re-recorded with a symphonic orchestra and issued on a three-record album, Billy Wilder's **Double Indemnity** (1944) and **The Lost Weekend** (1945), Alfred Hitchcock's **Spellbound** (1945), Robert Siodmak's **The Killers** (1946), whose theme song became the theme for the tv series **Dragnet**, scores that sometimes utilized the theremin (for the first time in **Lost Weekend**, played by Sam Hoffman); Vincent Minnelli's **Madame Bovary** (1949), the first film soundtrack (other than cartoons and musicals) to be released in its original format on record; and the epics of Mervin LeRoy's **Quo Vadis** (1951) and William Wyler's **Ben Hur** (1959).

Another poet of the film noir was German-born Franz Waxman, who scored Alfred Hitchcock's **Rebecca** (1940), **Suspicion** (1941) and **Rear Window** (1954), as well as Billy Wilder's **Sunset Boulevard** (1950) and George Cukor's **The Philadelphia Story** (1940).

Austrian cabaret composer Anton Karas (basically an amateur) ended up composing one of the most famous themes, the one for Carol Reed's **The Third Man** (1949), containing *Harry Lime Theme*.

Hugo Friedhofer, who had assisted Korngold and Steiner, applied their late-romantic lesson in his moving and nostalgic soundtrack for William Wyler's **The Best Years of Our Lives** (1946).

The prolific Adolph Deutsch scored several of cinema's masterpieces: Raoul Walsh's **High Sierra** (1941), John Huston's **The Maltese Falcon** (1941), Billy Wilder's **Some Like It Hot** (1959) and **The Apartment** (1960).

Joseph Kosma, who set Prevert (*Les Feuilles Mortes, Barbara, En Sortant de l'Ecole, Les Enfants qui s'aiment, La Peche A la Baleine,*

Inventaire, 1956) and other French poets to music, was the musical hero of French cinema before World War II: Jean Renoir's **Le Crime de M Lange** (1936), **La Grande Illusion** (1937), **La Bete Humaine** (1938), **La Regle du Jeu** (1939), as well as Marcel Carne's **Les Enfants du Paradis** (1945).

The most important, and most prolific, of the classical composers who wrote for the cinema was Dmitri Shostakovich, who scored 34 films. They are mostly bombastic and celebratory, for example: Grigori Kozintsev's and Leonid Trauberg's **Novyj Vavilon/ The New Babylon** (1929), **Odna** (1931), **Maxim** (1935), **The Tale of the Priest and His Servant Balda** (1936) and **Vyborg District** (1938), Sergei Yutkevich's **Zlatyye Gory/ Golden Mountains** (1931) and **Vstrechnyj/ Counterplan** (1932), Lev Arnstam's **Zoya** (1944), Aleksandr Dovzhenko's **Michurin** (1949), Mikhail Chiaureli's **Fall of Berlin** (1949), Alexander Faintsimmer's **The Gadfly** (1955), Grigorii Roshal's **God Kak Zhizn/ A Year Is Like A Lifetime** (1965). Shostakovich found a more personal cinematic language for Grigori Kozintsev's **Hamlet** (1964) and **Korol Lir/ King Lear** (1969).

French composer Georges Auric employed classical melody in a slightly oneiric way for Jean Cocteau's cinematic poems **Le Sang d'un Poète** (1930) and **La Belle et la Bète** (1946), Henry Clouzot's **Le Salaire De La Peur** (1953), Otto Preminger's **Bonjour Tristesse** (1957), Jack Clayton's **The Innocents** (1961), and with a light touch for British comedies such as Henry Cornelius' **Passport to Pimlico** (1949) and Charles Crichton's **The Lavender Hill Mob** (1951).

British classical composer Arthur Bliss crafted one of the most original of the early soundtracks, for Alexander Korda's science-fiction movie **Things to Come** (1935).

The scores of Armenian classical composer Aram Khachaturian for Amo Bek-Nazarov's **Pepo** (1935) and **Zanzegur** (1936) were among the most celebrated of Soviet cinema.

Among the most popular scores of the 1930s were the soundtracks for Walt Disney's series of **Silly Symphonies**, shown between 1929 and 1939. These included Frank Churchill's *Who's Afraid of the Big Bad Wolf?*, off **Three Little Pigs** (1933), *Lullaby Land of Nowhere* (1933) and *Somebody Rubbed Out My Robin* (1935), as well as Leigh Harline's *Help Me Plant My Corn* (1934) and *The Penguin Is a Very Funny Creature* (1934). Walt Disney's **Snow White and The**

Seven Dwarfs (1937), whose best numbers (*I'm Wishing, Whistle While You Work, Heigh Ho, Some Day My Prince Will Come*) were composed by Frank Churchill, was even more important, both because the songs were an organic whole and because, for the first time, a label (Victor) released original soundtrack music (not the same songs interpreted by other musicians) as a an "album" of three 78 RPM records (of which at least two, *Whistle While you Work* and *Heigh Ho*, became extremely popular). By the same token, **Pinocchio** (1939) featured one of the era's most famous songs, *When You Wish Upon A Star*, again by Leigh Harline. Walt Disney's films turned the animated cartoon into a musical. They also legitimized the soundtrack as a commercial product. In fact the expression "original sound track" was coined by the Disney studios for the release of music from **Pinocchio** as a three-record album in 1940.

But the first truly original composer of cartoon music was Carl Stalling, who, after scoring Walt Disney's **The Skeleton Dance** (1929), composed soundtracks for the cartoons of "Bugs Bunny", "Daffy Duck", "Tweety", "Sylvester" and many more from 1930 till 1958. He was given access to a vast library of recorded music and took full advantage of it. He was, in fact, the first composer to rely on the recorded works of other composers. His scores were frenetic collages of jazz (especially Raymond Scott's instrumentals), folk, pop, classical music and commercial jingles, as well as his own music. They indulged in fractured rhythms, truncated melodies, dissonant orchestration, demented timbres, hysterical tempos and distorted instruments.

Harline's hit, outside the Disney cartoons, was Hal Walker's **Road to Utopia** (1945), a very popular musical comedy for Bob Hope and Bing Crosby.

In Italy, Alessandro Cicognini scored several classics of Neorealism, such as Alessandro Blasetti's **Quattro Passi Fra le Nuvole** (1942), Vittorio de Sica's masterpieces **Sciuscia** (1946), **Il Ladri Biciclette** (1947), **Umberto D** (1955) and **Miracolo a Milano** (1951), but also comedies such as Mario Camerini's **Grandi Magazzini** (1939) and Mario Monicelli's **Guardie e Ladri** (1951).

The US composer Aaron Copland scored a few films in his typical orchestral style overflowing with references to the national tradition, notably Lewis Milestone's **The Red Pony** (1949) and William Wyler's **The Heiress** (1949).

Allan Gray (born Joseph Zmigrod in Poland) was one of the main British composers of soundtracks, and also scored John Huston's **The African Queen** (1951).

Alex North wrote some memorable melodies, such as *Unchained Melody* (1955), sung by gospel singer Roy Hamilton for Hall Bartlett's **Unchained** (1955), as well as disturbing "mood music", such as the soundtracks for Elia Kazan's cinematic adaptation of Tennesse Williams' **A Streetcar Named Desire** (1951), the first major score to be based on jazz, Kazan's **Viva Zapata** (1952), almost a medley of Mexican folk songs, John Huston's **The Misfits** (1961), and John Ford's **Cheyenne Autumn** (1964), one of the first subdued scores for western films, and the unreleased score for Stanley Kubrick's **2001 A Space Odyssey** (1968), possibly his technical peak.

David Raksin created a score for Otto Preminger's **Laura** (1944) that kept repeating the same theme whenever the title character was referred to (the theme was going to be recorded by more than 400 artists). A more elaborate score met Otto Preminger's **Forever Amber** (1947), and probably remained his best one. After these two milestones, his most original soundtracks were Abraham Polonsky's **Force Of Evil** (1948), Vincent Minnelli's **The Bad And The Beautiful** (1952) and John Cassavetes' **Too Late Blues** (1962), each in its own style.

Bernard Herrmann, perhaps the most celebrated of the "symphonic" composers of soundtracks, revealed his subtle psychological talent with Orson Welles' **Citizen Kane** (1941) and **The Magnificent Ambersons** (1942), as well as John Brahm's **Hangover Square** (1945), basically a pretext to write his own piano concerto, Robert Wise's **The Day the Earth Stood Still** (1951), built around the sound of two theremins juxtaposed to electric instruments, and went on to become the quintessential Hitchcock composer, penning the surrealistic scores for **The Man Who Knew Too Much** (1956), **The Trouble With Harry** (1956), **North By Northwest** (1959), permeated by the rhythm of fandango, **Psycho** (1960), one of the most famous of all times, a cubist clockwork of deconstructed string-based melodies and sound effects, **Vertigo** (1958), perhaps his tour de force, **The Birds** (1963), with its harrowing orchestration of dissonance (mainly created by Oskar Sala's "trautonium"), these three being the most original ones, and

Marnie (1964), soundtracks that rely on strident passages as metaphors for the horror of the scenes. The music for Martin Scorsese's **Taxi Driver** (1976) was existential noir at its best. His soundtracks sounded violent because they indulged in sudden contrasts as opposed to smooth melodic flows. Herrmann did not write leitmotifs, he toyed with them as if engaging in a slow, endless semiotic torture.

By the mid-1940s, those who composed for the movies fell into a well-established category, many of them churning out dozens of soundtracks per year. Nonetheless, only Walt Disney had released "original soundtracks" (not modified for the phonographic medium). The first non-Disney album of original soundtrack music was the musical Richard Whorf's **Till the Clouds Roll By** (1946), based on standards by Jerome Kern, but it was essentially a parade of stars singing Kern's hits. "Tribute" musicals of this kind followed, such as Vincent Minnelli's **The Pirate** (1948), a tribute to Cole Porter, and were released unadulterated on album.

The style of western soundtracks crystallized with Richard Hageman's scores for John Ford's **Fort Apache** (1948) and **She Wore A Yellow Ribbon** (1949), and with Victor Young's scores for John Ford's **Rio Grande**(1950) and George Stevens' **Shane** (1953). Young's opulent and romantic style, best represented by **For Whom The Bell Tolls** (1944), was the quintessential Hollywood style of the era. Young also composed songs such as *Stella by Starlight* (1947) and *My Foolish Heart* (1950).

Another master of the western soundtrack was Elmer Bernstein, who scored John Sturges' **The Magnificent Seven** (1960), the quintessential western soundtrack before Morricone, Henry Hathaway's **True Grit** (1968) and Don Siegel's **The Shootist** (1976), but who was also a master of highlighting neurotic characters, such as in Otto Preminger's **The Man with the Golden Arm** (1955), for jazz band and orchestra, and in Robert Mulligan's **To Kill A Mockingbird** (1962), a powerful suite of roots-inspired music for chamber ensemble, and a master of creating claustrophobic atmospheres, as he proved with Vincent Minnelli's **Some Came Running** (1958). Other jazzy scores of his include Alexander MacKendrick's **Sweet Smell of Success** (1957) and Edward Dmytryk's **Walk on the Wild Side** (1962).

The other great western soundtrack of the Fifties was composed by Jerome Moross for William Wyler's **The Big Country** (1958).

Jerry Fielding had a long career crowned by two sensational soundtracks, Howard Hawks's **The Big Sleep** (1946) and especially Sam Peckinpah's **The Wild Bunch** (1969), an abullient western and Latin score, as well as Sam Peckinpah's **Straw Dogs** (1971) and Michael Winner's **The Mechanic** (1972), two scores that flirt with avantgarde music.

Kenyon Hopkins scored Elia Kazan's **Baby Doll**(1956) and **Wild River/ Fango sulle Stelle** (1960), as well as Robert Rossen's **The Hustler** (1961).

Daniele Amfitheatrof (the son of a Russian composer) scored Max Ophuls' **Letter From an Unknown Woman** (1948) and Fritz Lang's **The Big Heat** (1953).

A passion for lushly-orchestral neoclassical melodies is also found in British composer Malcolm Arnold, whose main achievements were David Lean's **The Bridge on the River Kwai** (1957), with a main theme derived from the traditional *Colonel Bogey*, Mark Robson's **Inn of the Sixth Happiness** (1958), with *Children's Marching Song*, and Bryan Forbes' **Whistle Down the Wind** (1962).

Classical music conductor Andre Previn composed the eclectic and exuberant soundtrack for Richard Brooks' **Elmer Gantry** (1960) and recreated the sounds of Paris for Billy Wilder's **Irma La Douce** (1963).

Legendary conductor Leonard Bernstein scored Elia Kazan's films **On The Waterfront** (1954) and **East of Eden** (1954).

Johnny Mandel wrote one of the three or four best jazz scores of the 1950s, for Robert Wise's **I Want to Live** (1958), and the suspenseful score for John Boorman's **Point Blank** (1967), as well as hits such as *The Shadow of Your Smile*, from Vincent Minnelli's **The Sandpiper** (1965), and the theme song *Suicide is Painless*, from Robert Altman's **M.A.S.H.** (1970).

The event that symbolically closed the age of classic Hollywood soundtracks was Vincent Minnelli's **The Cobweb** (1955), scored by Leonard Rosenman, who had debuted on Elia Kazan's **East of Eden** (1955): it was harsh, dissonant, unnerving music a` la Schoenberg, introducing avantgarde music to the movie-going crowd. Rosenman's psychological and non-melodic approach yielded the music for Nicholas Ray's **Rebel Without a Cause** (1955), Richard Fleischer's **Fantastic Voyage** (1966) and Ted Post's **Beneath the Planet of the Apes** (1970).

Rock Around The Clock (1954), written in 1953 by James Myers and Max Freedman, was the first rock song used in a movie soundtrack, Richard Brooks' **Blackboard Jungle** (1955), and the movie turned it into a hit song. But Hollywood consciously capitalized on rock stars, and perfected the symbiosis between film and record, only with Elvis Presley's musicals. The soundtrack albums for the Presley vehicles that Norman Taurog directed, **G.I. Blues** (1960), **Blue Hawaii** (1961) and **Girls Girls Girls** (1962), were the best-selling albums of the early Sixties. The songs were both old and new, composed by a variety of white and black songwriters. Those films were terrible collections of stereotypes, both as cinema and music, but immensely successful. In a sense, they were the first "music videos", because the film per se was only a pretext: people watched the film to see Presley sing the song.

BLUES MUSIC

The South: Negro Music

While we will never know for sure, it is likely that music originally developed (thousands and thousands of years ago) as a means to coordinate and synchronize collective human movement, such as for hunting or farming. Even today, it comes natural to start singing a rhythmic song to accompany the activity of a group of people, whether hiking in the mountains or building a roof. Presumably, great singers held an important social status just like shamans or top hunters. Later, as percussion instruments developed to accompany music, individual percussionists may have also emerged. Then new kinds of instruments, not only percussive, emerged that further enabled virtuoso playing. Sometimes during the evolution of civilizations, "solo music" was invented so that the music of the best singers and instrumentalists could be admired and appreciated. It is likely that, initially, their performances were mainly for the aristocracy and were purely musical. At some point it came natural to merge solo music and solo poetry to entertain the aristocracy (and later the masses) with stories that people were familiar with. During the classic age of Greek theater, these stories became more abstract and metaphorical, and the music became less straightforward. Christianity further bent the purpose of music to sing the praise of the Lord and to call the faithful to prayer. Music, basically, became the vehicle for a message. The message (even when it was an epic) was not just a story, but a whole ideological system. At some point ordinary people started creating songs for their own consumption: these were what we call "folk" songs. These songs were not about heros or God, but about the joys and sorrows of rural life.

The music for the aristocracy became more and more sophisticated, both because it could buy the best instruments on the market and because it could hire the best singers and instrumentalists in the kingdom. It came to be called "classical" music. Through the invention of polyphony, it greatly reduced the emphasis on rhythm, which came to be considered a rather primitive and plebean element. On the contrary, folk music relied heavily on rhythm, both for dancing and for singing. Rhythm became the factor that came to differentiate between classical and folk music.

That was the situation when European music (both classical and folk) arrived in the Americas. In the melting pot of the Americas, Europeans were forced to admit for the first time that there were many different kinds of folk music. While the racial instinct was to separate the western European forms (and the Anglo-Saxons in particular) from the others, it was only a matter of centuries before the boundaries were blurred. The most traumatic confrontation for Europeans was the existence of African music. Long discarded as an oddity of the animal kingdom (pretty much like the sounds of animals), African music managed to coexist for two centuries next to European music before making inroads into white US society. During the 19th century several elements of African music began to percolate into white folk music. (This phenomenon took place in the Americas. No Afro-contamination took place in European society until much later).

Again, rhythm was the key differentiating factor. Rhythm was not an African invention, but certainly the African polyrhythms were wildly different from the linear rhythms of European folk music. The effect of African music on white music was initially barely felt, but it was going to become the main factor fueling innovation. In fact, European folk music had barely changed at all over the centuries, but was going to change dramatically and more rapidly once African-American music came to influence it.

The fusion of European folk music with African folk music was the most important source of innovation for music in the western world after the Ars Nova.

The status of European classical music remained a bit odd. It steadfastedly refused to accept African music (still regarded as some form of inferior animal expression) and all its mulatto offspring. Thus the gap between classical and folk music increased dramatically during the 19th century until the Sixties.

Negro Music: the African Perspective

"African" music is actually quite a pointless term. Music varies across Africa much more than it does across Europe (precisely because no single musical culture came to dominate and spread across the continent). Most slaves traded with the Americas came from West Africa, whose music was completely different from the music of other parts of Africa. It was also quite different from the way European music had developed since Greek times.

If the core of European music was to embellish a melody via the counterpoint of a number of melodic instruments, and incidentally set it to a rhythm (which was sometimes specified only in vague terms such as "adagio" or "allegro"), the core of West African music was to color a rhythm via the counterpoint of a number of rhythmic instruments, and incidentally dress it up with a melody. Thus the key elements of West African music were rhythm and timbre, not melody and harmony. Instead of melodic counterpoint, West African music was about rhythmic counterpoint.

Just like European melodism was an extension of the Indo-European language, West African percussionism turns out to be an extension of the West African languages, which are mostly based on timbre and rhythm. West African percussive music was nothing but a simulation of the spoken language. In a sense, West Africans learned how to play music (the music in which rhythmic and timbric subtleties play a key role) while they were learning to speak. West African percussive music had the same "semantic" value as European melodic music, except that the axis of meaning was perpendicular.

Initially the European colonists of the North America had no intention of converting the slaves to Christianity: the fact that the slaves were "pagans" was the moral justification for slavery. They were not "Christians", and in those days "Christian" meant "human". People who were not "Christian" were inferior beings. The Methodist and Baptist revival that started in 1734 with the "Great Awakening" of Massachusetts created a new ideology of slavery: slavery was justified because it was a means to save the pagans from certain damnation. Therefore the conversion of pagans was not only welcomed but even mandatory. Slavery came to be viewed (in fanatically religious quarters) as a crusade for saving souls. The "spirituals" (spiritual hymns) were the first original form of music created by the slaves of North America. The canon developed via the adaptation of African rituals to Christian rituals and via the adaptation of European liturgical music to the musical system of West Africa. Needless to say, the development of black spirituals picked up speed tremendously when the first black preachers started practicing, because then the preacher and its audience would simply turn their "call and response" relationship into musical interaction. Because blacks were segregated from whites, they had to be given their own preachers (often slaves themselves), who would preach to a black audience only. In the 1750s black preachers were already ubiquitous. Black congregations were formed in the 1770s.

A scale is the ordered sequence of notes used in a musical system. European music used the diatonic scale (divided into eight tones, the eighth being a repetition of the first tone an octave higher), or, better, its extension, the chromatic scale (twelve tones per octave). West African music used a pentatonic scale (that comprises only the first, second, third, fifth, and sixth tones of a diatonic scale). Two scales developed through the merger of European and African music: the deviant pentatonic scale of "spiritual" music and the expanded diatonic scale of "blues" music. All of black music in the USA would develop from these two fundamental scales. The black folk music that was more closely related to its West African roots was the work song.

In 1776 the USA declared their independence from Britain.

Negro Music: the European Perspective

The Atlantic slave trade, started by the Portuguese in the 16th century and turned into the engine of North American growth by the British in the 18th century, left the newly born USA with its most embarrassing legacy: one million slaves. By the time of the Civil War, they had increased to more than four million.

The African population posed a moral dilemma to the very religious crowds of European colonists: how to turn the African pagans into good Christians. The missionaries who took on that crucial task were the first white folks to realize the outstanding musical talent of the black race. Where they came from, music was a social phenomenon that accompanied every activity. The same was roughly true of white folk music, but that music survived mainly in poor rural communities. The rich white plantation owners had adopted the stifled musical habits of their European counterparts (music as a formal event), thus repudiating music as a commentary on daily life. The Africans of the plantations hung on to their traditions, and the missionaries found it convenient to adapt the Christian liturgy to the musical mind of the Africans. It became normal for black congregations to accompany sacred ceremonies with music that was, de facto, imported from Africa. For example, the polished, linear vocal harmonies of European singing were replaced by syncopated vocal harmonies with all sorts of rhythmic subtleties. This "spiritual" music was the first instance of African music adapted to the social environment of the New World (in this case, the church, something that did not exist in Africa, and the lyrics of the Gospels). It was not difficult for the individual slave to identify with the martyrdom of Jesus, and for the community as a whole to identify with the odyssey of the Jews.

The other kinds of musical expression, mainly work songs (by "hollers" and "arhoolies", i.e. cotton and wheat pickers) and party dances, were closer to the original music of Africa, because the same activities (work and party) existed in Africa. *Go Down Moses* is an example of "jubilee song", songs for the "jubilees", or plantation parties. "Hollers" and "arhoolies" (workers of, respectively, cotton and wheat plantations) developed work songs that were synchronized with the rhythm of work.

All three kinds of music (religious, work and party) shared the same characteristic: they were basically hypnotizing both the singer and the listeners. Whether ecstatic, mournful or exuberant, the music of the Africans tended to be repetitive, rhythmic and deeply felt. Its "hypnotic" effect perhaps expressed the resigned acceptance of a tragic destiny. At the same time, whether ecstatic (religious), mournful (work) or exuberant (party), it was much more emotional than white folk music; a fact that perhaps expressed the hope of a less tragic future. This emotion led to individual improvisation over collective themes. The combined effect of the hypnotic format and the emotional content created loose structures that could extend for indefinite periods of time, in a virtually endless alternation of repetition and improvisation.

Three more aspects of black music were innovative for the standards of white music. The rhythm was generally syncopated, and (at the beginning) only provided by hand clapping and foot stomping. The singer employed a broad vocal range and bridged notes in an acrobatic manner, thus introducing a freedom unknown to western harmony. The black equivalent of counterpoint was mostly implemented in the "call and response" format: a leader intoned a melody and a choir repeated it in a different register, and sometimes a different tempo, often bending the melody slightly. The role of spontaneous improvisation in black music clearly contrasted with the clockwork precision of western harmony. And the open-ended structure of black music contrasted with the linear progression of western music.

Originally, slave music was purely vocal. Many blacks of the plantations were skilled fiddlers, but that was a job they mostly performed for the white masters, not for their own community. They played music at the dancing parties of their masters.

The African heritage was mainly preserved in the South. The blacks of the North were much better integrated in white society in the 19th century. For example, the first black theater had opened in New York already in 1821 (the "African Grove", at the corner of Bleecker and Mercer, part of the Greenwich Village, which was then a bit outside New York proper). Francis Johnson was a respected composer of orchestral music in Philadelphia (he performed the first "concert à` la Musard" in the USA in 1838). And Elizabeth Greenfield, also in Philadelphia, became a respected concert vocalist in 1851. It was in the South that the blacks, barred from integrating in the white society, had to "content" themselves with their African traditions.

Theoretically, the civil war that ended in 1865 freed the African slaves, and, in fact, the first collection of black songs was published shortly afterwards, **Slave Songs of the United States** (1867). In practice, it did little to improve the condition of the black man: same job, same discrimination. Even for the blacks who left the Southern states, the cities of the North promised freedom, but mostly delivered a different kind of slavery. On the other hand, the end of slavery meant, to some extent, the dissolution of the two traditional meeting points for the African community: the plantation and the church.

Music remained the main vehicle to vent the frustration of a people, but the end of slavery introduced the individual: instead of being defined by a group (the faithful or the workers), the black singer was now free to and capable of defining himself as an individual. His words and mood still echoed the condition of an entire people, but solo singers represented a new take on that condition, the view of a man finally enabled to travel, and no longer a prisoner of his community, although, sometimes, more lonely. The songs of a black man were the diary of his life (road, train, prison, saloon, sex), often an itinerant life, as opposed to the diary of a community (plantation, church).

Solo singers needed instruments. The banjo, an African instrument ("banhjour"), came on the ships. The guitar and the harmonica were adopted from the whites. Eventually, the guitar came to be the second "voice" of the bluesman. Instead of addressing an audience in a church or plantation, and interacting with it, the black songster was interacting with his guitar. The blues became a dialogue between a human being and his guitar. The itinerant black "songsters" of the time of the Reconstruction, armed with the guitar, adapted the songs of the hollers to the narrative format of the British ballad (for example, *John Henry*).

Although they were similar in tone, the difference between black and white folk music was profound. They were both realist, but white folk music created "epics" out of ordinary events, while the "blues" was almost brutal in its depiction of real life. The landscape of the blues was one of prisons (*Midnight Special*) and dusty roads. "Love" was simply sex, not a romantic emotion. Death was a fact of life, not a step towards eternal life. On the other hand, the existential quality of the music was stronger in the blues. The blues was, first and foremost, a state of mind. No matter how direct, death and sex ultimately harked back to prisons and saloons, which in turn harked back to poverty and misery. The unbridled materialism of the blues was not self glorification but self pity. The blues was, fundamentally, the sense of an unavoidable fate (both individual and collective).

The quintessence of the blues was pain, but the art of the blues often consisted in bridging the chasm between tragedy and (broadly speaking) comedy.

Musically, blues music is twelve-bars long in 4/4 time (although this may have been a later development). Its melody is shaped by a scale that is an adaptation of the African five-note scale to the western seven-note scale. Blues music introduced two "flattened" notes, the "blue" notes.

Black music was originally meant as music for blacks only, not only ignored but often despised by the white community. The demographic movement of the economic boom that followed the reconstruction after the Civil War helped export black musicians and their music to white cities, and tear down some of the cultural walls between the two communities.

By far, the elements that sounded most outrageous to white ears were the obscenity of the lyrics and the indecent movements. Sex was the dominant theme of "negro" ballads, and the lyrics were often explicit. Black songsters liked to boast about their sexual performances. This was not so much an African tradition as a plantation tradition: the slave holders used to encourage extramarital intercourse among slaves. Thus black people came from environments in which sexual promiscuity was more than tolerated: it was ordinary life. The other "indecent" element was the Christian ceremonies that looked more like pagan ceremonies, in which loud and inebriating singing mixed with hysterical dancing and orgasmic howling. Black churches encouraged the exhibition of mystic fervor through savage body language, but white folks saw it as evidence that blacks were not civilized beings.

As blues music was heard and "consumed" by white folks, it became more aware of its own meaning. It also had to somehow "hide" the meaning (e.g., the sexual one), that was not compatible with the values of white society. Thus the bluesmen indulged in "double talk" to confront themes that white people shunned. The blues became more metaphorical and allegorical (*Bollweavil Blues, Stewball, Uncle Rabbitt, The Grey Goose*).

As ghettos sprouted up in all big cities, the topics of blues music adapted to the urban landscape, and began to depict life in the ghetto. But blues music was never meant to reflect the rhythm of urban life. As a matter of fact, the ghetto remained unsung till the 1970s, when rap was born.

The first venue for "negro" music was the "medicine show", the itinerant variety show that accompanied the "doctors" in their quest for gullable customers (thus the slang term "physick wagon"). The "doctors" used black musicians, actors and dancers as cheap entertainment to draw an audience to their sales pitches. Eventually, the "medicine show" became an art in itself, that toured several counties and even states, often augmented with magicians, acrobats, etc.

In Memphis in 1907 the first permanent theater for medicine shows was set up by Fred Barrasso. This led to the formation of the T.O.B.A. ("Theater Owners Booking Association"), a network of theaters specializing in "negro" shows. Those black musicians, abused and underpaid by their employers, were nonetheless the first black professional entertainers.

Minstrel shows, although run by white entertainers, began to hire black singers after the Civil War, and eventually became mainly black. White entrepreneur John Isham organized the first itinerant black revue (basically, a better organized minstrel show), "Jack's Creole Burlesque Company", in 1890. One such revue even toured Europe in 1897. These revues maintained the three-part format of the minstrel show (opening skit, specialty acts and finale), but were, for all practical purposes, variety shows with orchestras and choirs.

New York: the Birth of a Black Nation

The turmoil in music reflected the emergence of black intellectuals that challenged the stereotypes of white culture. At the end of the Civil War, the biggest problem faced by the USA was how to deal with the millions of uneducated blacks, who were still dependent on white people for their livelihood. For example, in 1867 a white abolitionist of Nashville (Tennessee), Clinton-Bowen Fisk, founded Fisk University with the aim of educating the former slaves and their children. After the death of Frederick Douglass, the only major black figure of the abolitionist era (an escaped slave who supported both John Brown and Abraham Lincoln), Booker-Taliaferro Washington, the son of a Virginia slave, became the leading black intellectual of the Reconstruction era. He believed that education would give blacks a chance in US society. In a 1895 speech, he called on blacks to accept segregation and to invest in their future, so that some day blacks would be equal to whites. But a decade later along came William-Edward-Burghardt DuBois, who instead organized the "Niagara Movement" in 1905 with the explicit aim of creating a platform to fight segregation. When, in 1909, several white and black activists founded the "National Association for the Advancement of Colored People" (NAACP). Du Bois became one of its leaders. The problems faced by the black community in those days were quite basic: white communities were expelling and lynching blacks by the hundreds (at the peak, in 1892, more than 200 blacks were lynched in one year). In 1916, Jamaica-born Marcus Garvey moved to New York and lauched a new black nationalist and separatist movement. Unlike his predecessors, he believed that black civilization was actually superior to white civilization, and that blacks should return to Africa.

Thanks to the efforts of the previous decades in educating blacks, the 1920s witnessed a "Harlem Renaissance", led by blacks such as poet Langston Hughes. Music was only one realm in which black culture was being accepted during the 1920s.

The commercial recording of black music was a direct consequence of this "black renaissance". Realizing that black artists were becoming a lucrative business (Scott Joplin in ragtime, William Handy in blues, Eubie Blake in pop, Louis Armstrong in jazz), and that record labels were still reluctant to let black artists make records, Atlanta's black songwriter Harry Pace (a former partner of William Handy) opened in Harlem his own label, "Pace Phonograph Company" (later "Black Swan Records"), in 1921, employing a young Fletcher Henderson as the studio pianist. Pace's success was such that white-owned labels such as Paramount (Alberta Hunter, Ida Cox, Charley Patton, Blind Lemon Jefferson) and Columbia (Bessie Smith, Ethel Waters) started competing fiercely for black recording artists. In 1924 Paramount bought the Black Swan catalog altogether. Black Swan's brief adventure legitimized the black recording artist, and opened the floodgates to the recording of black music throughout the country.

New Orleans, Kansas City, Memphis

The urban development of black music in the 20th century owed a lot to the sin cities of the south: New Orleans, Kansas City and Memphis. Their saloons, clubs, brothels, steamboats and speakeasies sponsored countless black musicians who migrated from the countryside.

New Orleans, at the mouth of the Mississippi river, the old French city that had exhibited an amoral opulence before the Civil War, was a melting pot with no equals in the south (Blacks, Italians, Caribbeans, French-speaking white and black Creoles, native Americans, Mexicans, and descendants of the Europeans). Its port was an infinite source of cultural exchanges with the rest of the world. Like most seaports, New Orleans boasted a colorful night life of prostitution, gambling and entertainment ("dixies"); and the "laissez faire" (laid-back) attitude of the Caribbean-French population made it even more tolerant than most seaports.

Untouched by the industrial revolution and less socially stressed than other plantation-oriented economies, New Orleans was able to retain the traditions of the various ethnic groups while they were rapidly being annihilated in the rest of the USA. Exoteric rituals, tribal dances, pagan festivals, funeral marches and all sorts of parties continued to exist well into the 20th century. Its "Mardi Gras" carnival was a hybrid musical celebration that mixed African, French and Native traditions in its colorful parades and marching bands. New Orleans, a commercial city, was more tolerant towards the blacks than the other southern cities. When the blacks were emancipated, it was a much friendlier place to be for a black musician than most of the South. In 1897 the puritan government of the city had created "Storyville", the red-light district, nicknamed after the politician who had the idea, a district that quickly became a city within the city. Since most establishments had a musician entertaining the customers, "Storyville" became the biggest employer of black musicians outside of Broadway. When "Storyville" was shut down in 1917, black musicians spread all over the country, bringing with them bits and pieces of New Orleans' sound. It was a New Orleans' band, the Original Creole Band, that exported a new kind of music that would be called "jazz".

Kansas City had experienced its first wave of black immigrants after the disputed presidential elections of 1877, that basically killed any remaining hopes of sincere black integration in the South. Blacks from states such as Louisiana and Mississippi emigrated by the thousands towards more tolerant places such as Kansas City.

During the corrupt reign of Tom Pendergast (from 1925 till 1939, when he was convicted of tax evasion), the illegal clubs of Kansas City flourished, virtually mocking the "Prohibition" of alcohol (1920-33). The booming industry of alcohol and gambling turned out to be a bonanza for black musicians, who became the backbone of the entertainment machine.

Memphis, an important inland port on the Mississipi and an important railway node between New York and Chicago, made wealthy by the cotton industry, was the natural link between the rural South and the industrial North. Memphis was often the first step on the way out of the plantations for the blacks who wanted to migrate north. Many of them ended up playing or singing on Beale Street, the center of the night life. When nylon replaced cotton,

Memphis began to decay, and blacks joined the mass migration towards Chicago, the next major stop on the railway.

The Delta: Blues Music

Blues music was the antithesis of city life, but the early recording of blues music was a New York affair.

Several blues stars (Bessie Smith, Ma Rainey, Ida "Cox" Prather) started out in minstrel shows, and then simply migrated from the itinerant shows of the South to the permanent vaudeville theaters of New York, where their songs were written specifically for a broader audience by professional black songwriters such as William Handy, based in Memphis, who "composed" (but maybe simply published) several of the early "classics": *Memphis Blues* (originally written in 1909 for a political campaign, but published only in 1912), *St Louis Blues* (1914), *Beale Street Blues* (1916), *Loveless Love* (1921), *Harlem Blues* (1923), *Careless Love Blues* (1925). Handy was fully aware that he had "invented" a new musical genre, as he wrote in 1916: "I have added another form to musical composition and to the world". He realized that the key feature of blues music that made it unique was that it was about sorrow, not about joy. Handy made his own recording of these compositions with his Memphis Blues Band between 1917 and 1923. The orchestra featured trombone, clarinet, alto sax, violins, piano, tuba, string bass, drums and xylophone. He had clearly introduced elements of western harmony in the original blues (for example, one can detect a sixteen-bar tango within *St Louis Blues*). Handy also recorded one of the first songs with "jazz" in the title: *Jazz Dance* (1917).

The twelve-bar structure that eventually became the standard was an invention of these urban songwriters: the original blues music was largely free form.

The blues singers bridged different realms of black music, bringing together the styles and practices of the minstrel shows, of the vaudeville theaters, of ragtime and of their native rural environments.

The first blues songs to be published, in 1912, were *Baby Seals Blues*, written by ragtime artist Artie Matthews, and *Dallas Blues*, written by white songwriter Hart Wand in Oklahoma. Several scores that mixed blues and ragtime had already been published, for example Chapman's and Smith's "One O' Those Things" (1904) and

Anthony Maggio's "I Got the Blues" (1908), the latter a hit in New Orleans.

Ohio-born Mamie Smith (not truly a blues singer, although black) sang two blues numbers written for her by black songwriter Perry Bradford: *That Thing Called Love* (february 1920), the first record by a black female artist, and *Crazy Blues* (august 1920), the first blues to become a nation-wide hit (with Willie Smith on piano). It sold 200,000 copies the first year. She was accompanied by the Jazz Hounds, that featured Memphis trumpeter Johnny Dunn, the first master of the plunger mute. Before Smith's hit, blues music only catered to the underworld of brothels and vaudeville theaters. Afterwards, blues music became as "respectable" as the black syncopated orchestras, despite the fact that it was a music about sorrow instead of joy. The idea of that record was largely due to its black producer, Alabama-born pianist Perry Bradford, a veteran of the minstrel-show circuit and now a songwriter, author of *Lonesome Blues* (1918), who had just composed the blues-based revue **Made in Harlem** (1918), that had starred Mamie Smith. He revised James Johnson's *Mama's And Papa's Blues* as *Crazy Blues*, architected the "respectable" sound of the record (different from the "wild" live sound of the Jazz Hounds) and convinced the label (Okeh) to release the first blues record by black musicians. In 1921 Okeh introduced a "Colored Catalog" targeting the black community, the first series of "race records".

Alberta Hunter, from Memphis, followed suit in 1921 with *How Long Sweet Daddy* and had a hit with *Gulf Coast Blues* (1922) before joining the jazz orchestras.

Bessie Smith, from Tennessee, made her first record in february 1923 (Alberta Hunter's *Down Hearted Blues* accompanied by Clarence Williams on piano and Williams' own *Gulf Coast Blues*), which became an instant hit, and in january 1925 she cut her version of *St Louis Blues* with Louis Armstrong on cornet. She was instrumental in both sculpting a powerful, emotional vocal style and in bridging the worlds of blues, pop and jazz. The musicians who played with her had to develop new styles of playing. Ted Wallace's *House Rent Blues* (july 1924) contrasted her with Fletcher Henderson's piano and Charlie Green's trombone. Pam Carter's *Weeping Willow Blues* (september 1924) featured piano, trombone and Joe Smith imitating Smith's vocals on cornet. William Handy's

Careless Love Blues (may 1925) relied on a dialogue with Louis Armstrong's cornet that seems to "sing" as much as the singer. Ragtime pianist James Johnson accompanied her in the 32-bar song *Preachin' The Blues* (february 1927) and especially in *Backwater Blues* (february 1927). Her interpretation of James Johnson's *Empty Bed Blues* (march 1928) lasted six minutes (two sides of a 78-RPM record) with accompaniment of piano and trombone. The filmed 17-minute version of *St Louis Blues* (1929), sung by Bessie Smith with Louis Armstrong on cornet and James Johnson on piano, with an all-black cast and directed by Dudley Murphy, who had directed **Le Ballet Mechanique** (1924), may be considered the first music video.

Gertrude "Ma" Rainey, from Georgia, debuted in 1923 and the following year delivered *Blame It On The Blues* and *Night Time Blues*, both written by pianist Thomas "Georgia Tom" Dorsey and accompanied by his Wildcats Jazz Band, and then *See See Rider* (recorded in october 1924 with Louis Armstrong on trumpet and Fletcher Henderson on piano). The first real star was perhaps Ethel Waters, from Los Angeles, who was first recorded in 1921 and featured in several musical comedies, and eventually obtained her own itinerant revue ("The Ethel Waters Vanities") and became a celebrity. All of them had moved to New York, and none of them was a real blues musician (an itinerant, street performer from the South). The "classic blues", as it came to be called, was not classic, and was not even blues. Alberta Hunter's most famous number, *Nobody Knows the Way I Feel This Mornin'* (1924), was a ballad backed by Louis Armstrong and Sidney Bechet, two jazz musicians. The bluesmen were starving in the South while the "classic" blues singers were getting rich in New York. These "classic" singers were almost all women, in the tradition of the old vaudeville shows. Their style was more polished, structured (twelve bars, no less and no more) and arranged (they fronted a band instead of playing the guitar).

The first records featuring a blues guitar were Sylvester Weaver's instrumentals *Guitar Blues/ Guitar Rag* (1923), although the B side was played on a guitar-banjo, recorded in Louisville (Kentucky), and Charlie Jackson's *Papa's Lawdy Lawdy Blues* (1924), recorded in Chicago. Charlie Jackson's *Shake That Thing* (1925) was the first hit by a self-accompanied bluesman. (Jackson actually played a six-string banjo).

One of the few female composers, Texas blueswoman Victoria Spivey recorded in St Louis, accompanying herself at the piano, her own *Blue Snake Blues* (1926), *Arkansas Road Blues* (1927), with Alonzo "Lonnie" Johnson on guitar, *Dope Head Blues* (1927), *T.B. Blues* (1927), *Toothache Blues* (1928), a duet with Johnson, and *Moaning Blues* (1929).

The country blues was initially heard in an "arranged" version, performed by "string bands" such as Bo Carter's. String bands had been common in plantations at the turn of the century for entertaining the masters. The popularity of the original bluesmen dates from much later.

In 1926 Blind Lemon Jefferson became the first real bluesman ("country" bluesman) to enter a major recording studio. It was the beginning of a trend: record labels would go and look for talents in the Mississippi Delta region, bring them to the city, dress them up and send them to stage backed by a jazz combo. The blues music that white audiences heard in those days bore little resemblance to the blues music that was heard by black audiences in the "barrelhouses" and "juke points" of the South. Their songs were curtailed to three minutes because the 78 RPM record could hold only that much music. Their lyrics were censored to avoid any reference to sex. Their performance was constrained to sound as close as possible to the style of white singers. The African elements (the polyrhythms, the antiphonal singing, the vocal range) were diluted or avoided altogether.

Many bluesmen of the South were too poor to buy instruments. They learned how to make music out of washboards, kazoos and jugs. **Hometown Skiffle** (1929), one of the earliest "samplers", coined the word "skiffle" to refer to such music.

The record labels found out that there existed a market for "race records" among the liberal white audiences and the small black middle-class of the big cities, particularly New York and Chicago.

The term "rock'n'roll" might be as old as any of these historical events. Trixie Smith cut *My Man Rocks Me With One Steady Roll* (1922) four years before Chuck Berry was born. In 1934 John Lomax and his son Alan began recording black music of the southern states, and discovered the gospel genre of "rocking and reeling" that had been around for years, if not decades.

Despite being much older, the country blues of the Mississippi Delta region, south of Memphis, was recorded after the classic blues had already become a sensation in the big cities of the north. The country-blues style had no jazz combo: only a guitar and a harmonica. The most influential in Mississippi were: Charley Patton, a werewolf-like vocalist and sophisticated slide guitarist (two gifts that made his style the most fluid vocal-guitar duet of blues music) who wrote the classics *High Water Everywhere* (october 1929), *Pony Blues* (june 1929), *Prayer of Death* (june 1929), *Moon Going Down* (june 1930); Eddie "Son" House, another powerful vocalist who in 1930 recorded, as two-sided 78 RPM records, lengthy ballads such as *Preachin' The Blues* and *My Black Mama*, With guitarist Willie Brown and pianist Louise Johnson; Tommy "Snake" Johnson, an acrobatic vocalist who wrote *Canned Heat Blues* (1928), *Big Road Blues*, *Cool Drink of Water Blues* and *Maggie Campbell* (all recorded between 1928 and 1929, his only recording dates); Nehemiah "Skip" James, who introduced a less rhythmic, folkish style in *Devil Got My Woman* (1931), learned from his guitar teacher, *I'm So Glad* (1931) and *Cypress Grove* (1931); and "Mississippi" John Hurt, one of the first to enter a recording studio, with *Avalon Blues* (1928) as well as his adaptations of *Candy Man Blues* (1928) and *Nobody's Dirty Business* (1928), and one of the most archaic in style, but then forgotten for 34 years.

St Louis' multi-instrumentalist Alonzo "Lonnie" Johnson, one of the first black instrumentalists to make a record, used the violin in *Falling Rain Blues* (1925), and occasionally played the piano, but made his name with the "singing" (vibrato-laden) guitar lines that accompanied most of his blues and gospel numbers, such as *Dark Was The Night Cold Was The Ground* (1925), *Woman Changed My Life* (1926), *You Don't See Into the Blues Like Me* (1926), *I Have No Sweet Woman Now* (1926), *Lonesome Jail Blues* (1926), *Love Story Blues* (1926), *Blue Ghost Blues* (1927), *Life Saver Blues* (1927), *Away Down In The Alley Blues* (1928), *Steppin' On The Blues* (1930), plus *Blue Blood Blues* (1929) and *Jet Black Blues* (1929) recorded with Eddie Lang. His style (and his collaborations with jazz guitarist Eddie Lang) was instrumental in bringing together blues, jazz and pop.

Memphis (Tennessee) had Walter "Furry" Lewis, one of the first to play the slide guitar with a bottleneck, whose *Mr Furry's Blues* (1927) and *Cannonball Blues* (1928) predated even Patton; and "Sleepy" John Estes, one of the most popular bluesmen since he debuted in 1929, his biggest success probably *Married Woman Blues* (1935).

Texas boasted Blind Lemon Jefferson, the most versatile interpreter, a master of both dramatic recitation and guitar accompaniment who penned *Bad Luck Blues* (1926), Spivey's *Black Snake Moan* (1926), *Matchbox Blues* (1927), *Booger Booger* (1927), that transposed the left-hand piano boogie figures to the guitar, *See That My Grave's Kept Clean* (1927), and *Penitentiary Blues* (1928) but died in 1929 (the year that country blues became a brief fad); "Texas" Alger Alexander, a baritone who, unable to play the guitar, employed guitarist Lonnie Johnson and was the first to record the traditional *House Of The Rising Sun* (1928); "Blind" Willie Johnson, the greatest interpreter of religious music, who penned *Jesus Make Up My Dying Bed* (1927), *Dark Was The Night* (1927) for solo guitar and wordless humming (based on the hymn *Gethsemane*), and *Keep Your Lamp Trimmed and Burning* (1928); Huddie "Leadbelly" Ledbetter, discovered in 1933 in a prison by Alan Lomax, later a celebrity of New York's folk revival and thus the symbolic bridge between black and white folk music, who popularized Gussie Lord Davis' *Goodnight Irene* (1933), *Midnight Special* (1934), *Rock Island Line* (1936), *Pick A Bale Of Cotton* (1940) and *Cottonfields* (1941); and Mance Lipscomb (discovered only in 1959).

Atlanta's "Blind" Willie McTell developed a dazzling technique at the 12-string guitar that sounded almost polyphonic, and composed songs influenced by white folk music such as *Writin' Paper Blues* (1927), *Statesboro Blues* (1928), *Travellin Blues* (1929) and *Dying Crapshooter Blues* (1940).

Georgia's guitarist Arthur "Blind Blake" Phelps was fluent both in blues music, as in *West Coast Blues* (1926), that featured the line "we're gonna do that old country rock", and in ragtime music, as in *Southern Rag* (1927).

Alabama's pianist Charles "Cow Cow" Davenport recorded *Cow Cow Blues* (1928), another precursor of boogie woogie, and, generally speaking, helped coin a blues style for the piano.

Furry Lewis, John Hurt and Charley Patton were the guitarists who invented the "finger-picking" style of guitar playing (basically, imitating the structure of ragtime piano on the strings of the guitar, with the thumb strumming the strings to provide the rhythmic equivalent of ragtime's left hand, and the other fingers carrying the melody).

North Carolina's guitarist Elizabeth Cotton/Cotten developed a left-handed style (plucking the melody with her thumb on the high strings) and demonstrated it in her *Freight Train* (1958), composed at the age of 11 (in 1906) but recorded only at the age of 63.

Blues music was mainly vocal (it's whole reason to exist was in the lyrics), but the instrumental styles developed to accompany it would be no less influential on the future of popular music.

Between 1926 and 1929, several of the legends of the Delta had been recorded. During the Depression, black music continued to spread. But the social setting was changing dramatically, thanks to the ghettoes that had grown exponentially after the first world war: Harlem in New York and South Side in Chicago.

The most successful black singer of the 1930s was Tennessee's Leroy Carr, also a pianist who formed an influential duo with guitarist Scrapper Blackwell (the main guitar stylist of the era with Lonnie Johnson) for *How Long How Long* (1928), a song that broke the established rules of blues music (both vocal and instrumental), while his existential angst permeated the solo blues *Six Cold Feet In The Ground* (1935) and the tuneful *When The Sun Goes Down* (1935).

Another piano-guitar duo became a staple of the clubs of St Louis: demonic vocalist and pianist Peetie Wheatstraw (William Bunch) and guitarist Charley Jordan. Between his debut in 1930 and his death in 1941, Wheatstraw was one of the most popular and prolific bluesmen.

One of the great stylists of the blues was South Carolina's itinerant blind guitarist Gary Davis, who already in 1935 created a soulful fusion of blues and gospel, later perfected in *I Cannot Bear My Burden By Myself* (1949) and *Keep Your Lamp Trimmed and Burning* (1956), but didn't achieve recognition as an innovative guitarist until he turned sixty, with *Cocaine Blues* (1957), *Candy Man* (1957) and the instrumentals *Buck Dance* and *I Didn't Want To Join The Band* (1957), all off his seminal album **Pure Religion and Bad Company** (1957), *Death Don't Have No Mercy* (1960) and *Lovin' Spoonful* (1965). He played the guitar like he played the piano, and was not afraid of complex tunings, minor keys and dissonance, of mixing ragtime, country and marches with blues chords.

His fellow countryman Blind Boy Fuller (Fulton Allen) was influenced by Davis' guitar style, and his *Rattlesnake Daddy* (1935), *Big Leg Woman Gets My Pay* (1938) and *Step It Up And Go* (1940) harked back to the pre-blues era.

A watershed year is 1936, when Mississippi bluesman Robert Johnson cut his first record. A legend who lived only 27 years and recorded only 29 songs, but enough to establish a new (chilly and fatalistic) standard of delivery and accompaniment, Johnson perfected the styles of Charley Patton and Son House (and the guitar style of Lonnie Johnson) in the harrowing *Terraplane Blues*, *Cross Road Blues*, the bleak *Stones In My Passway*, *Come On In My Kitchen* (with his best bottleneck workout), *Love In Vain* (modeled after Leroy Carr's *When The Sun Goes Down*), *Dust My Broom*, and the lyrical *Hellhound On My Trail* (all recorded in 1936-37),

Booker "Bukka White" Washington was perhaps the last of the great Mississippi singer-guitarists, immortalized by *Shake 'Em Down* (1937) as well as *Fixin' to Die* (1940) and *Parchman Farm Blues* (1940), with Washboard Sam.

In 1939 Leo Mintz opened a record store in Cleveland, the "Record Rendezvous", that specialized in black music and was serving a white audience: black music found an audience beyond the ghetto.

Chicago: Urban Blues

The year 1916 was the year of the mass emigration of blacks from the South to the North. By the time the Depression stopped the flood, thousands of musicians had moved north, and transplanted their music (whether blues, spiritual or jazz) into the northern cities.

Urban blues was played in the "honky-tonks" (clubs that were serving alcohol illegally) and in the "gutbuckets" and other kinds of private parties. Urban blues was generally more aggressive, not so much because of the urban spirit but because of the noise that the bluesman had to compete with in those locales. The "Prohibition" probably helped replace classic blues with urban blues: classic blues relied on legal establishments, that had to close or change clientele, whereas urban blues was happy to serve the rough and wild clientele of the illegal establishments.

All of the Chicago protagonists were born in the South, mostly in Mississippi.

The star of Chicago, known also among white audiences as far as New York, was Big Bill Broonzy, who, arriving in 1928, chronicled the epics of city blacks in a long series of eclectic recordings, including: *Big Bill Blues* (1928), *Starvation Blues* (1928), *Keep Your Hands Off Her* (1934), *Too Many Drivers* (1939), *Key to the Highway* (1941).

The city performers introduced significant innovation in the instrumentation of blues music. For example, the piano became as commonplace as the guitar.

The most famous (and the first virtuoso) of the bottleneck/slide guitarists was Houston "Tampa Red" Woodbridge, who arrived in Chicago (from Florida) in 1925 and was one of the first black instrumentalists to make a recording. Unlike other southern bluesmen, whose playing was modal and in minor keys, Tampa Red's shimmering, clean style was influenced by ragtime and jug bands. His prolific career include *Through Train Blues* (1928), with Frankie Jaxon on vocals, *It's Tight Like That* (1928), a duet with vocalist Thomas "Georgia Tom" Dorsey and a massive hit, *Come On Mama Do That Dance* (1929), with the Hokum Jug Band (Jaxon on vocals), *Sugar Mama* (1935), *It Hurts Me Too* (1940).

Lonnie Johnson, Scrapper Blackwell and Tampa Red make up the triad of guitar stylists that determined the evolution of the instrument from little more than a rhythmic add-on to a full-fledged emotional tool. In fact, these three guitar wizards were responsible, more than anyone else, for making the guitar sound like a human voice. They cast a long shadow on all blues guitarists that came later.

Another virtuoso of the bottleneck guitar was Kokomo Arnold (in Chicago since 1930), who popularized *Milk Cow Blues* and *Sweet Home Chicago* (1930).

Big Joe Williams debuted with his *Highway 49 Blues* (1935) and the traditional *Baby Please Don't Go* (1935), arranged with fiddle and washboard, and then recorded *Crawlin' King Snake* (1941) with Sonny Boy Williamson on harmonica.

There was also a female guitarist, Lizzie "Memphis Minnie" Douglas, who arrived in Chicago in 1933, after recording *When The Levee Breaks* (1929) and *Bumble Bee* (1930) in Memphis, and converted to the urban style of Big Bill Broonzy with *Nothing In Rambling* (1940) and her signature song, *Me and My Chaffeur Blues* (1941).

The first great barrelhouse pianist was Roosevelt Sykes Bey, who moved to Chicago in 1929 and coined a rhythmic, pseudo-boogie style with *44 Blues* (1929), *The Night Time The Right Time* (1936) and *Driving Wheel* (1949). The other great barrelhouse pianist was Eurreal "Little Brother" Montgomery, arrived in 1928 from New Orleans, who debuted with *Vicksburg Blues* (1930). In those days, barrelhouse pianists were the equivalents of juke-boxes. Sykes and Montgomery were the first to introduce a personal style.

Sykes' disciple Memphis Slim (Peter Chatman), who reached Chicago in 1939 and had a hit with *Beer Drinking Woman* (1940), went on to form (1944) his Houserockers, who recorded *Rockin' The House* (1947) and *Nobody Loves Me* (1948, also known as *Everyday I Have The Blues*).

John Lee "Sonny Boy" Williamson (who moved to Chicago from Tennessee in 1937) integrated the blues harmonica into the blues singing, so that the two became one continuous voice. His *Skinny Woman* (1937), *Good Morning Little Schoolgirl* (1937) and *Hoodoo Hoodoo* (1946) became standards of a more rhythmic kind.

During the same period, Robert "Washboard Sam" Brown (who moved to Chicago in 1931) popularized one of the most humble of African-American instruments, the washboard.

Arriving in 1941 from Memphis, tenor Johnny Shines, who wandered with Robert Johnson, had to wait many years before his compositions, such as *Joliet Blues* (1946), were recorded.

Thundering vocalist and versatile pianist Albert "Sunnyland Slim" Luandrew, who moved from Mississippi to Memphis to Chicago (1942), was immortalized in *Sunnyland Train* (1929, but first recorded in 1951), *Johnson Machine Gun* (1947), with the young

Muddy Waters on guitar, *The Devil Is a Busy Man* (1948), *Brownskin Woman* (1948), *Shake It* (1951).

The main difference between the blues of the Delta and the blues of Chicago was that the former was mainly solo, while the latter was increasingly relying on a band format (guitar, harmonica, piano, drums, bass).

Ironically, blues music did not become popular among black people until the 1930s. The paying audience of a bluesman was usually a white audience, not a black audience. This was partly due to the fact that only whites were admitted to the clubs that sponsored the phenomenon, but also to the fact that blacks probably did not perceive the blues as entertainment. If a black had to pay a ticket, he would probably rather pay for a more lively kind of entertainment. Blues music was born and continued to thrive because white people liked it. And it spread across the country thanks to an indirect flow of money from the white middle class to the black ghettos via the music industry. During the 1910s blacks did not dream of becoming bluesmen: some of them "were" bluesmen, some were not. By the end of the 1930s playing the blues had become a honorable profession and many blacks aimed at starting a blues career.

Chicago: Gospel Music

While religious music was definitely a strong part of the lives of black slaves, there was actually a difference between what blacks sang in churches and what they sang outside. Most plantations had "praise houses" for the slaves to gather, pray and sing. Blacks also met in "camp meetings", that were largely outside the control of white people. In these places, the blacks sang lyrics that had references to their condition of slaves, and they danced as well (something that the churches did not quite tolerate), and they were free to indulge in their "savage" repertory of shouts, hand clapping, foot-stomping, etc. They also came to be centered on the call-and-response interaction between preacher and congregation.

It was relatively easy for blacks to identify with the Jews of the Bible: blacks too had been deported, and they too aspired to a homeland, a promised land (in fact the country north of the Ohio River, where blacks were free, was nicknamed "Jordan"). Several spirituals referred to the journey to freedom via the "Underground Railroad" (a secret network of abolitionists who helped blacks escape to the North) as the equivalent of the Jewish journey from Egypt to Palestine. A black woman named Harriet Tubman who worked for the "Underground Railroad" was referred to as "the Moses of the blacks". Songs such as *We Shall Overcome* were explicit about their real subject: freedom on this Earth, not only in Paradise.

Black religious hymns ("spirituals") such as *When The Saints Go Marching In* were among the oldest inventions of African-American music. In the years following the Civil War, they were popularized by the Fisk University Jubilee Singers, an "a cappella" group that in 1871 traveled throughout the USA and even abroad to collect funds for the university (one of the first black universities). Other universities followed suit (e.g., the Hampton Singers in 1873 at Virginia's Hampton Institute).

The process of black urbanization had also an impact on sacred singing. In the Baptist churches, the archaic form of spirituals that accompanied collective prayers evolved into the "gospel song". The main differences were the piano (spirituals were sung "a cappella") and the lead vocals, that were now taken on by the preacher himself. The effect was to reduce the freedom of the "performers". Originally the piano was meant to simply provide the rhythm but soon became a creative factor in itself, used to fill the pauses in the singing with all sorts of embellishments (arpeggios, glissandoes, etc). The demand for gospel hymns created a market for hymn writers, who specialized in adapting all sorts of melodies to the purpose of worshiping God.

Gospel music was popularized by Thomas Dorsey, the black Chicago pianist and songwriter, a former Atlanta vaudeville and barrelhouse pianist, as well as leader of the Wildcats Jazz Band that accompanied "Ma" Rainey in *Blame It On The Blues* (1924) and *Night Time Blues* (1924). Dorsey, who had already composed several "gospel" songs such as *If I Don't Get There* (1921) and *If You See My Savior* (1926), transported blues musicianship into the church. He also formed the first female gospel quartet and assembled the first large-scale gospel chorus (1931), struck gold when he composed *Precious Lord* (1932) and organized the first "National Convention of Gospel Choirs and Choruses" (1932). After this song became a hit (in 1937), Dorsey spent his life traveling from church to church, peddling his repertory of gospel songs, that also included *There'll Be Peace In The Valley* (1937) and *Search Me Lord*. In 1928, Mahalia Jackson was one of the singers who started their careers performing Dorsey's songs. And James Cleveland was among the first to hear Dorsey's choirs.

In the year 1930, the "Jubilee Meeting" of the National Baptist Convention included the first performance of gospel songs, and thus allowed the genre to come out of the ghettos.

However, gospel music was still strictly for churches. It was only later, in the 1930s, that some performers began to "export" gospel music to the night clubs. Notable among them was the thundering "Sister" Rosetta Tharpe, who appeared at the "Cotton Club" and who recorded Thomas Dorsey's *Rock Me* (1938), considered the first gospel record, *I Looked Down The Line* (1939), *This Train Is Bound For Glory* (1939), *Shout Sister Shout* (1941).

Throughout the 1930s, the preferred format remained the quartet, and the preferred style the "jubilee" (the standard set by the Fisk University Jubilee Singers): the Heavenly Gospel Singers (that recorded Thomas Dorsey's *Precious Lord*); the Dixie Hummingbirds, formed in 1928 in South Carolina (*Joshua Journeyed to Jericho*, 1939; *Jesus Walked the Water*, 1952); the Golden Gate Quartet, formed in 1934 in Virginia, a veritable orchestra simulated with vocals (*Jonah*, 1937; *Rock My Soul*, 1939); the Chuck Wagon Gang of Texas that debuted in 1936; the Five Blind Boys of Mississippi, formed by blind students in 1944 and led by the delirious tenor of Archie Brownlee (*Our Father*, 1951).

Male groups wore formal suits (such as tuxedoes) and beat the rhythm with finger snapping. Female groups wore church dresses and beat the rhythm with hand clapping. The latter were more likely to be accompanied by an organist.

The sound of the gospel quartet had an influence on the parallel development of the pop vocal groups.

Starting in 1925 in Ohio the Mills Brothers became a local sensation by recreating instruments with the voices, while usually limiting the accompaniment to a guitar. They were among the first performers to rely on a studio device (the microphone) for the sound of their music. They relocated to New York in 1930, where they continued to "impersonate" jazz music. Their interpretations of Nick LaRocca's *Tiger Rag* (1931), *Goodbye Blues* (1932), *Dinah* (1932), with Bing Crosby, Elmer Schoebel's *Bugle Call Rag* (1932), Hoagy

Carmichael's *Lazy Bones* (1934), *Paper Doll* (1943), that remained perhaps their signature song, Doris Fisher's *You Always Hurt the One You Love* (1944) and *The Glow Worm* (1952) were mellow sentimental ballads that redefined black music for the broader audience. They popularized the "barbershop harmonies", a sweet and romantic mutation of the jubilee quartets which would become the reference standard for all future vocal groups.

The Spirits Of Rhythm were a jazzier version of the Mills Brothers (they were a string band, not just a vocal group) and featured (since 1929) the acrobatic scat singing of Leo Watson derailing conventional pop material such as Harry Revel's *Underneath The Harlem Moon* (1932) and Gus Kahn's *Nobody's Sweetheart* (1932).

The Ink Spots, even more compromised with white pop music, crafted melodies such as *If I Didn't Care* (1939), *Address Unknown* (1939), *We Three* (1940), *Into Each Life Some Rain Must Fall* (1944) and *I'm Making Believe* (1944) with Ella Fitzgerald, *To Each His Own* (1946) and Billy Reid's *The Gypsy* (1946), that were characterized by very high falsettos and by a "talking chorus" (a bass voice set against contro a choir of tenors and falsettos), de facto the precursors of "doo-wop" music.

The Soul Stirrers, that relocated from Texas to Chicago in 1936, were one of the first gospel quartets to feature a solo vocalist, Rebert Harris, the author of *Walk Around* (1939) and the first gospel vocalist to sing in a falsetto register. After *By And By* (1950), Harris was replaced by the young Sam Cooke, who contributed *Be With Me Jesus* (1955) and *Touch the Hem Of His Garment* (1956). Cooke was then replaced by Johnnie Taylor.

Chicago: Boogie-woogie

The piano style that came to be called "boogie woogie" originated from the Piney Woods, in Louisiana, at the beginning of the 20th century. Here, black workers of the railway used to gather in a "barrelhouse" (basically, a tented saloon or a shack) to listen to their music. The entertainers of these rowdy crowds devised a dance version of rural blues music.

Just like in the saloons of the towns, the dominant instrument was the piano. Unlike the saloons, that usually did not admit black pianists for their white audience, the barrelhouses needed black performers to entertain a mainly black crowd. The itinerant pianists of the barrelhouses were blacks, and were free to emphasize the polyrhythmic figures of their African roots. They also had to play loud (i.e., be rather indelicate on the keys) in order to be heard over the noise of the barrelhouse. Furthermore, barrelhouse pianos were constantly out of tune: the musician had to compensate for the piano's imperfections with his speed and dexterity on the keyboard. Given that the barrelhouse could not hire more than one musician, the piano players developed a style that imitated the interplay of three guitars: one playing the chords, one the melody, and one the bass. Last but not least, the most natural rhythm to imitate in a barrelhouse was the rhythm of the steam train.

The barrelhouse style of piano playing spread with the railway, from the South to the North (1920s). The southern metropolis of Kansas City (that was replacing St Louis as the main center of the region, thanks to the railway junction and the highway interchange), the new magnet for black artists, was the natural place for the new style to become "permanent". Further north, Chicago was the second one.

It was in Chicago that a new craze appeared: the "boogie woogie". the ostinato bass of the left hand played the typical blues chords, while the right hand improvised the melodic elements in the treble. The genre had already existed for at least ten years (e.g., Cow Cow Davenport) before it became a sensation (1938), and it has at least three "inventors". Meade Lux Lewis, who was a cab driver for a Chicago taxi company (so was his friend Albert Ammons) recorded *Honky Tonk Train Blues* in 1927, but the song was released only two years later (it imitates the sounds of a train in motion). Jimmy Yancey started recording only in 1939 but was recognized as an influence by the early boogie pianists: his style in *Yancey Stomp* (1939), *The Fives* (1939) and *State Street Special* (1939) was almost purely percussive, while *Slow and Easy Blues* (1939) was actually in sixteen bars, *Yancey's Bugle Call* (1940) was full of suspense, and *Death Letter Blues* (1940) was a heart-wrenching blues melody. Clarence "Pinetop" Smith lived only 25 years, but, the year before dying, moved to the same apartment with Ammons and Lewis and recorded the archetype: *Pinetop's Boogie Woogie* (1928), the first recorded song that referred to the "boogie woogie". Note that boogie woogie emerged during the years of the Prohibition (1920-1933). If the title of inventor is disputed, there is no doubt when boogie woogie became a craze. It was announced by Albert Ammons' *Boogie Woogie Stomp* (1936), a cover of *Pinetop's Boogie Woogie* recorded with his Rhythm Kings, and by Pete Johnson, who teamed up with Kansas City's vocalist "Big" Joe Turner, the ultimate "shouter", for *Roll 'Em Pete* (1938), and then exploded after John Hammond assembled the piano trio of Albert Hammons, Meade Lux Lewis and Pete Johnson at New York's Carnegie Hall in 1938. Lewis penned some of the most sophisticated compositions of the boogie era: *Yancey Special* (1936), *Whistlin' Blues* (1937), *Cafe Society Rag* (1939), *Solitude* (1939), *Bear Cat Crawl* (1940), *Six Wheel Chaser* (1940). Pete Johnson, possibly the least gifted of the group, specialized in catchy numbers, such as *Blues On The Downbeat* (1939), *Death Ray Boogie* (1939), *Piney Brown Blues* (1940), the satori of his interaction with Turner, *Cuttin' the Boogie* (1941), one of many duets with Ammons of 1941. Albert Ammons was the most passionate of the trio, for example in the manic *Boogie Woogie Stomp* (february 1936) with his Rhythm Kings, *Mecca Flat Blues* (1939), *Shout for Joy* (1939) and *Bass Going Crazy* (1939). Ammons was also one of the first boogie woogie pianists to successful combine this piano style with a band. Clarence Lofton was a Chicago pianist who contributed to expand the horizons of boogie woogie with the haunting *South End Boogie* (1943), the intricate *Streamline Train* (1939) and the deviant blues of *I Don't Know* (1939). Swing bands appropriated the "new" style with Will Bradley's *Beat Me Daddy Eight To The Bar* and bandleader Tommy Dorsey's *Boogie Woogie*. In Kansas City, the band of pianist Jay McShann, with bluesman Walter Brown on vocals (and the young Charlie Parker on sax), had a huge hit, *Confessin' The Blues* (1941), by blending boogie woogie, blues and jazz.

Despite the fast pace (that became even faster, louder and more percussive in the 1950s), boogie woogie remained faithful to the blues chord progression.

Atlanta's pianist Piano Red (William Perryman) took boogie-woogie into the rock'n'roll era via *Rockin' With Red* (1950), *The Wrong Yo Yo* (1951) and *Dr Feelgood* (1962).

Virginia's white pianist James "Roy" Hall acted as the transmission chain between this generation of black boogie pianists and the generation of white rockers. His *Dirty Boogie* (1949),

Diggin' the Boogie (1956) and *Whole Lotta Shakin' Goin' On* (1956) boasted some of the most manic rhythms of the genre.

COUNTRY MUSIC

Southern States: Hillbilly Music

In 1910 ethnomusicologist John Lomax published "Cowboy Songs and Other Frontier Ballads" (that followed by two years the first known collection of cowboy songs), and in 1916 Cecil Sharp began publishing hundreds of folk songs from the Appalachian mountains (or, better, the Cumberland Mountains, at the border between Kentucky and Tennessee), two events that sparked interest for the white musical heritage, although the world had to wait until 1922 before someone, Texan fiddler Eck Robertson, cut the first record of "old-time music". These collections created the myth of the Appalachians as remote sanctuaries of simple, noble life, whose inhabitants, the "mountaneers", isolated from the evils of the world embodied the true spirit of the USA. Many of those regions were not settled until 1835, and then they were settled by very poor immigrants, thus creating a landscape of rather backward communities, still attached to their traditions but also preoccupied with the daily struggle for survival.

In 1922, a radio station based in Georgia (WSM) was the first to broadcast folk songs to its audience. A little later, a radio station from Fort Worth, in Texas (WBAP), launched the first "barn dance" show. In june 1923, 55-year old Georgia fiddler John Carson recorded (in Atlanta) two "hillbilly" (i.e., southern rural) songs, an event that is often considered the official founding of "country" music (although Texas fiddler Eck Roberton had already recorded the year before). The recording industry started dividing popular music into two categories: race music (that was only black) and hillbilly music (that was only white). The term "hillbilly" was actually introduced by "Uncle" Dave Macon's *Hill Billie Blues* (1924). In 1924, Chicago's radio station WLS (originally "World's Largest Store") began broadcasting a barn dance that could be heard throughout the Midwest.

With *When The Work's All Done This Fall* (1925), Texas-bred Carl Sprague became the first major musician to record cowboy songs (the first "singing cowboy" of country music). And, finally, in 1925, Nashville's first radio station (WSM) began broadcasting a barn dance that would eventually change its name to "Grand Ole

Opry". Country music was steaming ahead. Labels flocked to the South to record singing cowboys, and singing cowboys were exhibited in the big cities of the North.

Among the most literate songwriters were Texas-born Goebel Reeves, who penned *The Drifter* (1929), *Blue Undertaker's Blues* (1930), *Hobo's Lullaby* (1934) and *The Cowboy's Prayer* (1934), i.e. a mixture of hobo and cowboy songs, and Tennessee-born Harry McClintock, the author of the hobo ballads *Big Rock Candy Mountain* (1928) and *Hallelujah Bum Again* (1926).

Country music was a federation of styles, rather than a monolithic style. Its origins were lost in the early decades of colonization, when the folk dances (Scottish reels, Irish jigs, and square dances, the poor man's version of the French "cotillion" and "quadrille") and the British ballad got transplanted into the new world and got contaminated by the religious hymns of church and camp meetings. The musical styles were reminiscent of their British ancestors. The lyrics, on the other hand, were completely different. The USA disliked the subject of love, to which they preferred practical issues such as real-world experiences (ranching, logging, mining, railroads) and real-world tragedies (bank robberies, natural disasters, murders, train accidents).

The instrumentation included the banjo, introduced by the African slaves via the minstrel shows, the Scottish "fiddle" (the poor man's violin, simplified so that the fiddler could also sing) and the Spanish guitar (an instrument that became popular in the South only around 1910). Ironically, as more and more blacks abandoned the banjo and adopted the guitar, the banjo ended up being identified with white music, while the guitar ended up being identified with black music. For example, Hobart Smith learned to play from black bluesman Blind Lemon Jefferson, but went on to play the banjo while Jefferson played the guitar.

The role of these instruments was more rhythmic than melodic, because most performances were solo, without percussion. Some regions added their own specialties (such as the accordion in Louisiana), but mostly white music was based on stringed instruments. When not performed solo, it was performed by string bands, particularly after the 1920s, when the first recordings allowed musicians to actually make a living out of their "old-time music". The string bands of the 1920s included Charlie Poole's North

Carolina Ramblers, that augmented the repertory of old-time music with songs from minstrel and vaudeville shows, Ernest Stoneman's Dixie Mountaineers, and finally (but the real trend-setters for string bands) the hillbilly supergroup Skillet Lickers, formed in 1926 and featuring Riley Puckett on guitar, Gideon Tanner and Clayton McMichen on fiddles (and all of them on vocals), the first ones to record *Red River Valley* (1927).

The "hillbilly" format (led by the guitar and a bit more "cosmopolitan") was more popular in the plains, while the "mountain" format of the Appalachians (dominated by fiddle and banjo) remained relatively sheltered from urban and African-American influences.

Solo artists, or "ramblers", became popular after World War I, but often had to move to New York to make recordings. Some of them specialized in "event" songs, songs that chronicled contemporary events, such as Henry Whitter's *The Wreck Of The Old 97* (1923), that may have been the first "railroad song" (but actually used the melody of the traditional *The Ship That Never Returned*), later recorded by New York's singer Vernon Dalhart (1924) for the national audience (perhaps the first hit of country music), Andrew Jenkins' *Death Of Floyd Collins*, also first recorded by Dalhart (1926), about a mining accident, and Bob Miller's *Eleven Cent Cotton and Forty Cent Meat* (1928), *Dry Votin'* (1929), and especially *Twentyone Years* (1930), perhaps the first "prison song". Miller was, by far, the most prolific, writing thousands of hillbilly songs.

Hillbilly musicians also dealt with the opposite genre, the novelty song: Wendell Hall's ukulele novelty *It Ain't Gonna Rain No Mo* (1923), Carson Robison's whistling novelty *Nola* (1926), Frank Luther's comic sketch *Barnacle Bill The Sailor* (1928).

Very few of these singers were of country origins: Vernon Dalhart, Carson Robison and Bob Miller were New York singers who became famous singing hillbilly songs (and sometimes composing them, as in the case of Robison and Miller).

The real country musicians had been known mainly for their instrumental bravura. A national fiddle contest had been organized in Georgia already in 1917 (by the Old Time Fiddlers Organization). Two musicians important in the transition from the quiet and linear "mountain" style and the fast and syncopated "bluegrass" style were banjoists Charlie Poole of the North Carolina Ramblers (*Don't Let Your Deal Go Down*, 1925; *White House Blues*, 1926, better known as *Cannonball Blues)* and "Uncle" Dave Macon, the main "collector" of old-time music and one of the best-sold artists during the Roaring Twenties *(Keep My Skillet Good And Greasy*, 1924; *Chewing Gum*, 1924; *Sail Away Ladies*, 1927). If these two already used the banjo as much more than a mere rhythmic device, Dock Boggs was perhaps the first white banjoist to play the instrument like a blues guitar (in 1927 he recorded six plantation blues numbers and *Sugar Baby*, that was rockabilly ante-litteram). Sam McGee was one of the first to play the guitar like a bluesman, starting with *Railroad Blues* (1928). Georgia's blind guitarist Riley Puckett, the author of *My Carolina Home* (1927), played a key role in transforming the guitar from percussion instrument to accompanying instrument.

Un until the late 1920s, hillbilly artists were considered comedians as much as musicians. Many of them had a repertory of both songs and skits. The Skillet Lickers were probably instrumental in creating the charisma of the country musician, as opposed to the image of the hillbilly clown.

The Hawaian steel guitar, invented by Joseph Kekuku around 1885 in Honolulu, was a late addition to the line-up of string bands. The incidental music to Richard Walton Tully's play **Bird of Paradise** (1912) popularized the ukulele and the steel guitar in the USA, as did the Hawaiian pavillion at the "Panama Pacific Exhibition" of San Francisco in 1915. *On The Beach At Waikiki* (1915), composed by Henry Kailimai and Sonny Cunha, started a nation-wide craze. In 1916 all the record labels started selling records of Hawaiian music, including Sonny Cunha's *Everybody Hula* (1916), Richard Whiting's *Along the Way to Waikiki* (1917), *Hawaiian Butterfly* (1917), composed by Billy Baskette and Joseph Santly, and Walter Blaufuss' *My Isle of Golden Dreams* (1919). Hawaiian steel-guitar virtuoso Frank Ferera toured internationally. He had debuted on record with Stephen Foster's *My Old Kentucky Home* (1915). The craze subsided in the 1920s, but the steel guitar (first recorded by a hillbilly musician in 1927) would become more and more popular in the repertory of country music.

The first stars of the hillbilly genre were the members of the Virginia-based Carter Family, basically a vocal trio (Sara on lead vocals and autohapr, Alvin on bass vocals, and Maybelle on alto vocals and on guitar) that started out in 1926 and first recorded in 1927. Unlike their peers, who emphasized the instrumental sound, the Carter Family focused on songs. Collectively, they wrote over 300 songs, including classics such as *Will You Miss Me When I'm Gone* (1928), *Keep On The Sunny Side* (1928), a cover of Theodore Morse's 1906 song, *Foggy Mountain Top* (1929), *My Clinch Mountain Home* (1929), *Worried Man Blues* (1930), *Can The Circle Be Unbroken* (1935), *No Depression* (1936), and especially *Wildwood Flower* (1928), a traditional first published in 1860 that Maybelle turned into a guitar masterwork. Their vocal style was the quintessence of the "close-harmony" style of country music. Later, Maybelle (who plucked the melody on the bass strings) formed her own quartet with her three daughters (among whom June wrote *Ring Of Fire* and Helen wrote *Poor Old Heartsick Me*).

In 1924 with his first recording, *Rock All Our Babies To Sleep*, blind Georgia's guitarist Riley Puckett (already a radio star) introduced the "yodeling" style of singing (originally from the Swiss and Austrian Alps) into country music, the style adopted in 1927 by the first star of country music, Mississippi's Jimmie Rodgers, who wed it to the Hawaian slide guitar and, de facto, invented the white equivalent of the blues with *T For Texas* (1927), *Waiting For A Train* (1928), *In The Jailhouse Now* (1928), *Mule Skinner Blues* (1930). Ironically (but also tellingly), Jimmie Rodgers became the first star of this very white phenomenon by being the most influenced by the very black music of the blues. The year he died (1933) was a watershed year for country music.

Rodgers was influential in creating the myth of the Far West, which had already been fueled by the cowboy songs of Carl Sprague and Goebel Reeves. Thus "country" music became "country & western" music. Originally, country music was mainly from the Southeastern states (Virginia, Tennesse, Kentucky and neighboring states). But now the audience was becoming fascinated with the Southwestern states (Texas and neihboring states). The romantic allure of the mountain dweller was slowly being replaced by the romantic allure of the roaming cowboy.

Another country musician who, like Rodgers, harked back to the blues, was Louisiana's singer-songwriter Jimmie Davis whose songbook was no less impressive: *Pistol Packin' Papa* (1929),

Organ Grinder's Blues (1929), *Pussy Blues* (1929), *Nobody's Darling But Mine* (1935), *It Makes No Difference Now* (1938), *You Are My Sunshine* (1939).

In the meantime, two new styles were emerging: honky-tonk and western-swing. And two instruments debuted in those years that would become the staple of rock bands: Adolph Rickenbacker invented (1931) the electric guitar and Laurens Hammond invented (1933) the Hammond organ. The steel guitar was electrified shortly afterwards, and enthusiastically embraced by country musicians (another sign that the trend was away from the mountain purists).

It was Texas singer-songwriter Gene Autry's *Silver Haired Daddy Of Mine* (1931) a big hit that launched the "honky-tonk" style of country music. Debuting in the film **Tumbling Tumbleweeds** (1935), Autry (who in real life was not a cowboy at all) was also the first of the "singing cowboys" of Hollywood (before Roy Rogers, Tex Ritter, Johnny Bond, Jimmy Wakely) who contributed to move country music (originally an eastern phenomenon) to the "far west", at least in the popular imagination. He also recorded *Mother Jones* (1931), a labor song, besides a long list of western-flavored songs, such as *Mexicali Rose* (1936). Roy Rogers and songwriters Bob Nolan and Tim Spencer formed the genre's supergroup, the Sons Of Pioneers, who composed some of the genre's classics, starting with Bob Nolan's *Tumblin' Tumbleweeds* (1927).

Clyde "Red" Foley was the star of Chicago, popularizing country music in the big city with *Old Shep* (1935) and *Chattanooga Shoeshine Boy* (1950).

By now "hillbilly" was no longer a positive attribute, but rather a derogatory one, and thus "country & western" came to connote all white southern music. The performers wore country attires and mimicked the slang of cowboys. The fascination with the West spread to the big cities of the North thanks to fake hillbilly songs written by professional Tin Pan Alley songwriters, such as Bill Hill's *The Last Roundup* (1933), actually a catchy tune in the Broadway style, but nonetheless influential in creating the vogue of the Far West. This enabled Tex Ritter, who had never been cowboy but simply a rodeo attraction, to become a star in New York, thanks to his Texan accent, and then (1936) in Hollywood (*Rock'n'Rye Rag*, 1948).

Both honky-tonk and western-swing were, de facto, by-products of the shift of country music towards the western states (i.e. Texas).

In 1932 vocalist Milton Brown and fiddler Bob Wills cut the first records of a kind of country music influenced by jazz that was later dubbed "western swing" (by Foreman Phillips in 1944). Basically, the country & western music of rural towns merged with the swing of the big bands of urban jazz. The two pioneers then split. Brown's combo, the Musical Brownies, featuring fiddler Cecil Brower (who introduced Joe Venuti's style to country music), jazz pianist Fred Calhoun, Bob Dunn on one of the first amplified steel guitars and a rhythm section influenced by ragtime, ruled in Texas, while Wills' Texas Playboys, based in Oklahoma and featuring a country string section and a jazz horn section, and now fronted by Tommy Duncan, debuted on record in 1935 (with *Osage Stomp*, reminiscent of Will Shade's Memphis Jug Band) and went on to produce *Steel Guitar Rag* (1936), *New San Antonio Rose* (1940), their greatest hit, recorded with an 18-piece band, perhaps the first nation-wide hits of country music. *Time Changes Everything* (1940), *Smoke on the Water* (1944), *New Spanish Two Step* (1946).

From 1936 Chicago's fiddler and accordionist Frank "Pee Wee" King, who wrote *Bonaparte's Retreat*, *Tennessee Waltz* and *Slow Poke* (1950), led the most popular of the western swing bands, the Golden West Cowboys.

After the war, Spade Cooley (in Los Angeles) introduced a variant of western swing that de-emphasized the brass and reeds while returning to the more traditional sound of pop orchestras.

Western Swing marked the transition from the archaic string-bands to the dancehall orchestras. These bands were responsible for the introduction into country music of instruments such as drums, horns and electric guitar.

Texas singer Al Dexter had hits in both the honky-tonk style, such as *Honky Tonk Blues* (1934), and the western-swing style, such as *Pistol Packin' Mama* (1942), boasting a revolutionary arrangement of accordion, trumpet and steel guitar. San Diego's pianist Merrill Moore did the same after World War II, achieving a synthesis in songs such as *House Of Blue Lights* (1953) that heralded rock'n'roll.

The other major genre to surface during the 1930s was bluegrass music, but this one originated in the traditional southeastern areas ("bluegrass country" being the nickname of Kentucky). Several vocalist-instrumentalist couples (especially brothers) had appeared who played a more spirited music devoted to domestic themes.

Alabama's guitar-based Delmore Brothers (Alton was the main composer and lead vocalist) were instrumental in popularizing the "brothers style" thanks to their tenure with the "Grand Ole Opry" between 1932 and 1938. They were also important for bridging the world of white music and the world of black music. Their songs were bluesy, and they often interpreted gospel songs. Their greatest hits were in fact blues numbers, from *Brown's Ferry Blues* (1933) to *Blues Stay Away from Me* (1949). In 1944 they added the bluesy harmonica of Wayne Raney, and in 1946 they added electric guitar and drums. That is when they recorded their series of breathless boogies, one step away from rock'n'roll: *Hillbilly Boogie* (1945), *Freight Train Boogie* (1946), *Mobile Boogie* (1948), *Pan American Boogie* (1950). Other famous numbers were *Gonna Lay Down My Old Guitar*, *Midnight Special*, *Beautiful Brown Eyes* (1951).

Another "brother act" was that of the Blue Sky Boys, formed by Bill and Earl Bolick (respectively, mandolin and guitar), perhaps the most faithful to the "mountain" tradition in their versions of *Sunny Side Of Life* (1935), *Down On The Banks of the Ohio* (1936), *Story of the Knoxville Girl* (1937), *Are You From Dixie* (1939), *Turn Your Radio On* (1940).

The bluegrass style, that originated in the 1920s from both Kentucky and Bristol, on the Virginia-Tennessee border, was a by-product of the "brother style", except that it was fast, virtuoso and sometimes instrumental-only "mountain music" (the country equivalent of the dixieland in jazz). It derived from the string bands of the 1920s, with a banjo, fiddle, and mandolin leading the melody, backed by guitar and string bass. The notable addition to the arsenal of the string bands was the Italian mandolin, that became popular in the South with bluegrass music. The vocals were not as important as in the "brothers style", although often featured a high-pitched tenor voice. Bluegrass music relied on a mixture of techniques: mountain music's three-finger banjo picking, country & western's fiddle, the rhythmic guitar of the ramblers, the tenor-driven choir of religious hymns with bass-register counterpoint.

Kentucky-based mandolinist Bill Monroe, who had started a duo in 1934 with his guitarist brother Charlie, popularized the "bluegrass" style with *Kentucky Waltz* (1945), *Blue Moon Of*

Kentucky (1945) and *Footprints in the Snow* (1945), performed by his new band, the Blue Grass Boys, that eventually came to include virtuoso musicians such as Earl Scruggs on banjo, Chubby Wise on fiddle, Howard Watts on bass, and Lester Flatt on guitar, which were in turn replaced in the Sixties by a new generation of virtuosi (fiddler Richard Greene, guitarist Peter Rowan, banjoist Bill Keith). Monroe's spectacular mandolin style was documented on instrumental pieces such as *Rawhide* (1951) and *Roanoke* (1954). At the peak, Monroe's band was so focused on improvisation and technical skills that it sounded like a jazz group performing country music.

Flatt and Scruggs formed their own act in 1948, that, thanks to pieces such as *Foggy Mountain Breakdown* (1949), *Roll In My Sweet Baby's Arms* (1950), *Pike County Breakdown* (1952), *Flint Hill Special* (1952), and eventually the hit *The Ballad of Jed Clampett* (1962), competed with Bill Monroe. Flatt and Scruggs were also instrumental in introducing the dobro guitar (since 1955, played by Buck Graves), a variant of the Hawaian steel guitar, into country music.

Bluegrass acts of the 1950s included the Osborne Brothers (Sonny on banjo and Bobbie on mandolin), perhaps the most innovative of the new generation, as displayed in *Ruby* (1956); and the Stanley Brothers (Carter being the lead vocalist), much more focused on the vocal harmonies than on the instrumental counterpoint and solos, from the "high lonesome" style of *A Vision of Mother* to love songs such as *How Mountain Girls Can Love* (1959) to religious themes such as *Gathering Flowers for the Master's Bouquet* and Albert Brumley's *Rank Strangers* (1960).

Bluegrass would remain the branch of country music most obsessed with dazzling technical proficiency, whether vocal or instrumental.

Tennessee native Roy Acuff became the first star of Nashville thanks to two tunes already recorded by the Carter Family: *The Great Speckled Bird* (1936), based on the melody of *I'm Thinking Tonight Of My Blue Eyes*, and *Wabash Cannonball* (1936), one of the most celebrated "railroad songs". *The Precious Jewel* (1940), based on *The Hills of Roane County*, *Wreck On The Highway* (1942), one of the earliest car songs, Frank "Pee Wee" King's *Tennessee Waltz* (1947), were sung in an old-fashioned, mournful mountain style, and accompanied mainly with the dobro (James Clell Summey until 1938 and Beecher "Pete" Kirby after 1938). Country broadcasting had been dominated by string bands: Acuff's emotional solo performances changed the very perception of what country music ought to be. He was instrumental in turning country music into a business, and a huge nationwide business. The music publishing company he founded in 1942 with songwriter Fred Rose (credited with many songs that he actually only revised and published, including Hank Williams' *Kaw-liga* and *Take These Chains From My Heart*) became a gold mine.

Johnny Bond wrote *Cimarron* (1938), *I Wonder Where You Are Tonight*, *Hot Rod Lincoln*, *Your Old Love Letters* and *Tomorrow Never Comes*.

In 1939 the "Grand Ole Opry" moved to Nashville's "Ryman Auditorium" and was broadcasted by the national networks.

Nonetheless, the nation was still largely unaware of country music. It wasn't until 1942 that "Billboard" introduced a column on country music, and only in 1944 it introduced the charts for hillbilly songs.

New York: Dissent

If country music represented the quintessential values of the white population of the USA, and a positive attitude towards the "American way of life", others (harking back to the epics of the itinerant "hobos") were seeing through the "American Dream" and confronting the issues of poverty, fascism and racism.

In a somber guitar-based folk style, Oklahoma's Woody Guthrie wrote the **Dust Bowl Ballads** (1935, first recorded in 1940), the soundtrack of the Great Depression, to become the first major singer-songwriter of the USA. After moving to New York in 1940, he also graduated to being the voice of the political "opposition" with *Pretty Boy Floyd* (1939), the anthemic *This Land Is Your Land* (1940, first recorded in 1944), *Ludlow Massacre* (1944), *1913 Massacre* (1944), *Deportee* (1948), and the **Ballads Of Sacco & Vanzetti** (1947); but also composed popular songs such as *Oklahoma Hills* (1937), *Pastures Of Plenty* (1941), *Reuben James* (1941), *So Long It's Been Good To Know You* (1942), *Philadelphia Lawyer* (1946). His songs were mostly based on ancient hillbilly melodies.

The Left gained strength throughout the 1930s, finding shelter in the artists' lofts of New York's Greenwich Village. The "Village Vanguard", opened by Max Gordon in 1939 in that area (7th Avenue and 11th Street), was a jazz club but soon began to serve a white audience of political dissidents.

The viability of popular music as sociopolitical protest had been proven by *Brother Can You Spare A Dime* (1932), a song written by Yip Harburg (music by Jay Gorner), a veteran of the Broadway musical and the Hollywood soundtrack, and sung by Bing Crosby. In fact, the whole soundtrack of Victor Fleming's **Wizard of Oz** (1939), also written by Harburg (music by Harold Arlen), was meant as a commentary to the Great Depression.

Besides Guthrie, other folk musicians composed protest songs. For example, Earl Robinson wrote *Joe Hill* (1936) to commemorate a murdered union leader.

Another important strain of popular music had to do with folk music, which Guthrie and Robinson had already associated with social awareness. In 1940 Pete Seeger went further: he formed the Almanac Singers to sing protest songs (*We Shall Overcome*, *Guantanamera*), sometimes with communist overtones. In 1948 Seeger formed the vocal quartet Weavers loosely modeled after the Carter Family. Their arranger Gordon Jenkins added a string orchestra to their cover of Leadbelly's *Good Night Irene* (1949), thus creating the first folk-pop crossover. The collaboration with Gordon Jenkins continued with *The Roving Kind* (1950) and *Wimoweh* (1952). Their *If I Had A Hammer* (1949), *Where Have All The Flowers Gone* (1956), *Bells Of Rhymney* (1959) and *Turn Turn Turn* (1962) established the vogue of folk music, while *Wimoweh* (1961) even resurrected African folk music. His **Goofing Off Suite** (1955) was, de facto, the first record of "American primitivism".

Another pioneer of the folk revival, Burl Ives, popularized *Foggy Foggy Dew* (1945), a traditional English tune, *Blue-tailed Fly* (1948), a Civil War tune, Harry McClintock's *Big Rock Candy Mountain* (1948) and Stan Jones' *Ghost Riders In The Sky* (1949), based on the traditional *When Johnny Comes Marching Home*.

"Ramblin' Jack" Elliott Adnopoz became Guthrie's ambassador in Europe. Several black musicians (notably, Leadbelly and Josh White) benefited from the folk revival.

In fact, the folk revival was instrumental in rediscovering forgotten genres and musicians that could not possibly aim for the charts. For example, the tradition of "one-man bands" was kept alive in San Francisco by a black musician, Jesse Fuller, an old man (he debuted at 58) who played at the same time guitar, pedal bass, harmonica, hi-hats and castanets, immortalized by his *San Francisco Bay Blues* (1954). In 1948 Moe Asch founded Folkways, a record label devoted to folk music, but also to Latin-American music, to Native American music and to blues music.

New York became the stage for a movement of "folk revival" that spawned hits such as the Tarrier's *Banana Boat Song* (1956), that also launched the calypso craze, the Kingston Trio's traditional *Tom Dooley* (1958), Jimmy Driftwood's *Battle Of New Orleans* (1958), and *Soldier's Joy* (1958), all of them reconstructed from traditional melodies. Ethno-musicologists such as the New Lost City Ramblers assembled "lost" songs on albums such as **The New Lost City Ramblers** (1958), **Vol II** (1959) and **Songs from the Depression** (1960). The Limeliters assembled a multinational repertory on soothing collections such as **The Slightly Fabulous** (1961). The "Newport Folk Festival" (1959) created a vast audience for this music, an audience that increasingly came to be identified with the political Left and the young beatniks of the Greenwich Village.

These folksingers had little in common (stylistically or ideologically) with the hillbillies of country music, but they ended up creating the urban audience for country music. Country music, even in states that were rapidly urbanizing such as Texas, had been catering mainly to the countryside. The post-war generation of folksingers catered almost exclusively to the audience of the big cities. It wasn't long before country music learned that lesson.

Also part of the Leftist movement of ideas were the iconoclast satirists who attacked the "American way of life", contemporary politics and assorted taboos in the night clubs of New York: Richard "Lord" Buckley, Lenny Bruce and Tom Lehrer (chronologically). Their caustic humour actually anticipated the existential spleen and the political skepticism of the Greenwich Movement.

Texas and Tennessee: Country Music

The 1940s were mainly the years of "honky-tonk" music, a much more driving style than traditional Appalachian music, and the first urban form of country music. Originally named after the saloons where alcohol was being served illegally (which, in turn, took their name from the factories that made gin), honky tonk became even more popular at the end of Prohibition era. Its stars were from Texas: Ernest Tubb (*Walking The Floor Over You*, 1942), who was also the first country artist to employ an electric guitar, and William "Lefty" Frizzell, Rodgers' natural heir, one of the most innovative vocalists and a poignant songwriter (*If You've Got The Money I've Got The Time*, 1950; *Always Late*, 1951; *I Want to Be With You Always*, 1951; Danny Dill's folk ballad *The Long Black Veil*, 1959; *Saginaw Michigan*, 1964; *That's the Way Love Goes*, 1973). Floyd Tillman wrote *It Makes No Difference Now* (1938) and the "cheating song" *Slipping Around* (1949). Houston-based pianist Aubrey "Moon" Mullican predated Jerry Lee Lewis in fusing honky-tonk and boogie-woogie, two styles that had much in common, with Harry Choates' *New Jole Blon'* (1947) and *I'll Sail My Ship Alone* (1950). South Carolina's guitarist Arthur Smith did something similar with the instrumental *Guitar Boogie* (1945). Ted Daffan composed the classics *Worried Mind* (1940), *Born To Lose* (1943), *Headin' Down The Highway* (1945). Honky-tonk songs dealt with more prosaic themes such as alcohol (of course) and cheating.

Purists looked down on honky-tonk, that preserved little of the original spirit of country music, but Hank Williams shut them down with *Lovesick Blues* (december 1948) and *You're Gonna Change* (march 1949), followed by a repertory of both ballads and pseudo-blues. Among the former: *Cold Cold Heart* (december 1950), *Why Don't You Love Me* (january 1950), *Your Cheating Heart* (september 1952), *I Saw The Light* (april 1947). Among the latter: *Moaning The Blues* (august 1950), *Long Gone Lonesome Blues* (january 1950), *So Lonesome I Could Cry* (august 1949), *I'll Never Get Out Of This World Alive* (june 1952). Plus rhythmic songs that predated rock'n'roll, such as *Move It On Over* (april 1947), *Honkytonking* (august 1947), *Howlin' At The Moon* (march 1951). He died young (at 29), and his last songs, such as *Jambalaya* (june 1952) and Fred Rose's *Kaw-liga* (september 1952), already announced the age of exotica.

The star of honky-tonk who succeeded Williams, Webb Pierce, from Louisiana, adopted the electric guitar and steel guitar and moved towards pop and rock'n'roll in Merle Kilgore's *More And*

More (1954) and *Teenage Boogie* (1956). Ray Price, from Texas, bordered both honky-tonk and western swing in songs such as *Don't Let The Stars Get Into Your Eyes* (1952), *Crazy Arms* (1956), *City Lights* (1958). Hank Thompson's band, also from Texas, did the opposite (from western swing to honky-tonk), starting with *Wild Side of Life* (1952), basically a cover of Roy Acuff's *The Great Speckled Bird* (1936). Another Texan, Johnny Horton, adapted the style to the dancehalls and to rock'n'roll with songs such as *Honky Tonk Man* (1956).

Jimmie Rodgers' style was instead revived by Canadian-born Hank Snow, particularly in his own *I'm Moving On* (1950), one of the greatest hits of the post-war era, *The Golden Rocket* (1950) and *The Rhumba Boogie* (1951).

Among instrumental virtuosi, Merle Travis' finger-picking style (that was basically an adapation of a banjo technique to the guitar) turned the guitar into both a melodic and rhythmic instrument. To his contemporaries, he sounded like two guitarists, not one. He also recorded **Folk Songs of the Hills** (1947), including his own celebrated protest song *Sixteen Tons*, in a vein similar to Woody Guthrie's. *Smoke Smoke Smoke* (1947) which was his biggest hit.

His disciple Chet Atkins simplified Travis' style by using three fingers instead of only two. More importantly, Atkins pioneered the classic "Nashville sound" through compositions such as *Bluesy Guitar* (1946), a duet between electric guitar and clarinet, *Canned Heat* (1947), *Galloping on the Guitar* (1949), *Chinatown My Chinatown* (1952), *Country Gentleman* (1953), *Downhill Drag* (1953), that progressively downplayed the rustic role of the fiddle and the steel guitar while emphasizing a sweeter, poppier sound based on guitar and piano.

Jean Ritchie pioneered the revival of the dulcimer with records such as **Singing Traditional Songs of Her Mountain Family** (1952).

Les Paul, a white guitarist who played more often with jazz musicians than country ones, invented the solid-body guitar (1941), pioneered new recording techniques ("close miking", "echo delay", "multi-tracking") and engaged in archetypical experiments of tape manipulation and overdubbing in his 1948 songs *Brazil* and *Lover* (on which he played all instruments by himself), besides sprinkling his recordings with all sorts of sound effects.

Los Angeles-based pyrotechnic guitarist Joe Maphis was one of the first to use the instrument not only for the rhythmic accompaniment but also for the lead lines. He also composed *Dim Lights Thick Smoke* (1952) and *Fire On The Strings* (1954).

Other virtuosi included fiddler Vassar Clements and blind flat-picking guitarist Arthel "Doc" Watson, who recorded his first album, **Doc Watson Family** (1963), at the age of forty.

"Tennessee" Ernie Ford was the sex symbol of country music in the 1950s, and launched standards such as *Smokey Mountain Boogie* (1948), Johnny Lange's and Fred Glickman's *Mule Train* (1949) and *Shotgun Boogie* (1950), a progenitor of rock'n'roll.

Leon Payne, a member of Bob Wills' Texas Playboys, wrote *Lost Highway* (1949) and *I Love You Because* (1950)

Felice and Boudleaux Bryant were among the most successful Nashville songwriters, from *Hey Joe* (1953) to *Love Hurts* (1961) to *Rocky Top* (1967), and particularly for the Everly Brothers.

At the end of World War II, several studios had opened in Nashville, reflecting the growing popularity of the "Grand Ole Opry". Then musicians started relocating to Nashville. By 1954, when the "Country Music Disc Jockeys' Association" (CMA) was created, Nashville had as many songwriters as New York. Chet Atkins was one of the producers who, in the 1950s, crafted the "Nashville sound", basically country music played with a pop sensibility (the guitar and sometimes the piano replacing the fiddle, background vocals, string orchestra). Atkins was the man who buried the "high lonesome" Appalachian sound. In 1961 there were 81 radio stations devoted to country music, in 1966 there were 328. By 1963 one out of every two records of the USA was produced in a Nashville studio.

The Importance of Country Music

Country music had a profound impact on the subconscious of the USA: it provided the nation with an identity. Pop music (as performed in theaters, as published by Tin Pan Alley) was largely a European invention, so much so that European stars touring the USA were invariably given a royal welcome and billed as the "real thing". But country music was exclusively a US phenomenon: its performers were "American" (born and raise in the USA), its audience was "American", its stories were "American", its "sound" was "American". The white people of the USA could enjoy pop music on Broadway, but they could not identify with it in the same way that they could identify with the hillbillies and the cowboys. The sound of country music embodied the history of the USA, it represented its genome. As it developed from the 1920s to the 1960s, it simply continued to emphasize that "American" element, progressively removing the European elements: it sounded less and less like the English ballads and the Irish dances that originated it, and more and more like something completely new. From a musical viewpoint, country music emphasized first of all the story, then the voice, and last the arrangement. It was a secular music, devoted to personal, domestic or collective issues, but largely set in a secular universe. It was rational to the extent that its characters were trying to make sense of their life and their surroundings.

This contrasted with rhythm'n'blues, that emphasized first of all the voice, and then (ever more) the arrangement, and finally the story; that had a stronger mystical element (the legacy of the spirituals and of gospel music); that was fundamentally irrational, in that it accepted the human condition as inevitable.

RHYTHM'N'BLUES

New York: Jump blues

The blues was mutating according to the changing social and artistic landscape. The 32 beats of white pop music, the dramatic emphasis of gospel singers, the heavy rhythm of jump blues, the tight brassy riffs of swing orchestras, the witty attitude of minstrel shows, all had a role in making blues music more malleable and entertaining. Transplanted in the dancehalls, the juke joints and the vaudeville theaters, blues music became energetic and exuberant. Form (arrangement, rhythm and vocal style) began to prevail over content (message and emotion). While the lyrics were still repeating the traditional themes of segregation, the music was largely abandoning its original traits.

A new style was born in New York thanks to saxophonist, vocalist and bandleader Louis Jordan, who became one of the best-selling artists of his time. Jordan (who had inherited a band in 1938) shrank down the size of swing's orchestras, emphasized the dance rhythm (the "shuffle"), sharpened the sax and trumpet counterpoint, and sang the hardship of black life in a detached (almost ironic) tone. His Tympany Five, that ranged from five to nine members, penned *At The Swing Cats Ball* (1939), *Fore Day Blues* (1939) and *Somebody Done Hoodooed the Hoodoo Man* (1940) before becoming hit makers with *Outskirts Of Town* (1941), *Five Guys Named Joe* (1942), *Is You Is* (1944), *Caldonia* (1945), *Stone Cold Dead In The Market* (1945), a duet with jazz vocalist Ella Fitzgerald, *Choo Choo Ch'Boogie* (1946), the multi-million seller that changed the history of black music, *Beans and Cornbread* (1947). These songs defined "jump Blues", the uptempo, jazz-tinged style of blues that ruled the race charts after the war. Jordan was the link between blues, jazz and rock music. Few people noticed it, but Carl Hogan played a powerful guitar riff on Jordan's *Ain't That Just Like a Woman* (1945) that, ten years later, would make Chuck Berry's fortune.

Another intermediary between the swing orchestra and the jump-blues combo was Erskine Hawkins, who straddled the border between jazz and blues in *Tuxedo Junction* (1939), *After Hours* (1941), *Tippin' In* (1945).

New Orleans' barrelhouse piano blues survived in the early cuts of pianist Jack Dupree, *Dupree Shake Dance* (1941) and the drug song *Junker Blues* (1941).

Surprisingly, World War II fostered a boom of "race" music that enabled a more effective distribution of black music. It was during the war, in 1941, that a radio station in Arkansas (KFFA) hired Sonny Boy Williamson to advertise groceries, the first case of mass exposure by blues singers. It was during and right after the war that the growing business of "race" music spawned several labels (all of them founded and run by white people) devoted only to black music, such as Savoy, founded in 1942 in Newark (New Jersey) by Herman Lubinsky, King, founded in 1944 in Cincinnati (Ohio) by Syd Nathan, Atlantic, founded in 1947 in New York by songwriter Ahmet Ertegun, and Aristocrat, founded in 1947 in Chicago by by two Polish Jews, Phil and Leonard Chess.

Los Angeles: Sophisticated Blues

Los Angeles bluesman Aaron "T-Bone" Walker who, as a boy in his native Texas, had accompanied Blind Lemon Jefferson and had emerged as a guitarist in the medicine shows of Ida Cox and Ma Rainey, imported mellow jazz phrasing into the blues guitar (as Lonnie Johnson had already done), and decisevely adopted the electric amplification of the instrument, which, in turn, redefined the guitar as a dominant solo voice. *T-Bone Blues* (june 1940) and *Mean Old World* (july 1942) were recorded by swing orchestras. His fusion of deep-toned moaning rural blues and jubilant urban jump-blues, which is the raison d'etre of *Call It Stormy Monday* (september 1947) and *T-Bone Shuffle* (november 1947), take or leave the jazzy horns, but caused him a stylistic imbalance that culminated with the proto-psychedelic *Strollin' With Bone* (april 1950).

Another fusion of blues and jazz was conceived in Los Angeles by a white bandleader, Johnny "Otis" Veliotes, whose combo, that emerged with their noir instrumental version of Earle Hagen's *Harlem Nocturne* (1945) and stormed the charts with *Double Crossing Blues* (1950) and *Mistrustrin' Blues* (1950), was basically a shrunk-down version of the big-bands of swing, the epitome of all future rhythm'n'blues combos (guitar, piano, two saxes, drums, bass, vocalist). The musicians of his orchestra set the standard for the "solo" personality, indulging in spectacular interjections and elegant phrasing. Besides writing *Every Beat Of My Heart* (1951) and *Roll With Me Henry* (1955), Otis rode the wave of rock'n'roll with *Willie and the Hand Jive* (1958).

Another pioneer of the electric guitar, Lowell Fulson was also a guttural and soulful shouter who left a mark on the West Coast sound with *Three O'Clock Blues* (1946), *Trouble Blues* (1947), *Blue Shadows* (1950), *Reconsider Baby* (1954).

Jump-blues vocalist Amos Milburn delivered the explosive *Chicken Shack Boogie* (1948), besides *Roomin' House Boogie* (1949), *Let's Rock Awhile* (1950), three premonitions of rock'n'roll, and *One Bourbon One Scotch One Beer* (1953), one of the most anthemic drinking songs of all times.

Roy Milton crooned like a white pop singer in *RM Blues* (1945), the first "gold" record of rhythm'n'blues and another important step in the mutation of the boogie rhythm into rock'n'roll.

Charles Brown, the pianist who most closely resembled Nat King Cole, was a member of a similar trio, the Three Blazers, when he intoned *Drifting Blues* (1945), the first anthem of existential frustration, and *Merry Christmas Baby* (1949), while on his own he magnified Jessie Mae Robinson's *Black Night* (1951) and Leiber & Stoller's *Hard Times* (1951). In the age of boogie-woogie, he was, instead, the ultimate specialist of the crying blues, a master of the suicidal mood.

Another Californian master of the sentimental ballad, Percy Mayfield indulged in the bitter pathos of his solemn compositions *Two Years of Torture* (1949), *Please Send Me Someone To Love* (1950) and *Strange Things Happening* (1950), besides writing *Hit The Road Jack* (1961) for Ray Charles. Ivory Joe Hunter pushed the crossover towards country music itself with *I Almost Lost My Mind* (1950) and *Since I Met You Baby* (1955).

T-Bone Walker and Johnny Otis put California on the map of blues music. The 1940s witnessed a massive wave of immigration into the "golden state". Los Angeles' ghetto, Watts, thus became one of the largest in the country. Right afer the war, in 1946, three small independent labels ("indies") were founded in Los Angeles that specialized in black music: Specialty, founded by Art Rupe, Imperial, founded by Lew Chudd, and Modern, founded by Jules Bihari.

Interlude: Rocking Around the Clock

Black music was "rocking" harder and harder, as New Orleans' vocalist Roy Brown stated in his hits *Good Rockin' Tonight in Texas* (1947) and *Rockin' at Midnight* (1951), and Detroit's rhythm'n'blues saxophonist Wild Bill Moore claimed in *We're Gonna Rock We're Gonna Roll* (1948) and in the follow-up, *I Want To Rock And Roll* (1949), Cecil Gant proclaimed in *We're Gonna Rock* (1950), and saxophonist Jimmy Preston declared in **Rock The Joint** (1949), *Rock With It Baby* (1950) and *Roll Roll Roll* (1950).

Chicago: Rhythm'n'blues

During the industrial boom of the post-war era, Chicago became the main destination of black emigration. In 1946 the black ghetto, the South Side, became the second black city in the USA (after New York's ghetto, Harlem). The South Side was the place where the musical styles of the South met the musical instruments of the North. Chicago's blues style was not only faster and more turbulent than the Southern styles: it also adopted the horns and the electric guitar.

Eventually, a new term was coined for this aggressive kind of blues music: "rhythm'n'blues". Its birth date is disputed. In 1946 Muddy Waters cut the first records of Chicago's electric blues. In 1947 Billboard's writer Jerry Wexler coined the term "rhythm and blues" for Chicago's electric blues. In 1949 the Billboard chart for "race" records was renamed "rhythm and blues". The first major rhythm'n'blues festival was held in Los Angeles in 1950 (the "Blues & Rhythm Jubilee"), as important as the Carnegie Hall concert of 1938 that launched boogie woogie nationwide.

"Muddy Waters" (McKinley Morganfield), a Mississippi guitarist who reached Chicago in 1945, not only coined an influential style at the electric guitar, that upgraded the archaic forms to the amplified sound (yet another mutation of Son House's style), not only crafted classics such as *I Can't Be Satisfied* (1948), *I Feel Like Going Home* (1948), *Rollin' And Tumblin'* (1950), *Rolling Stone* (1950), *Honey Bee* (1951), *Mannish Boy* (1955), *You Shook Me* (1962), with Earl Hooker on slide guitar, *You Need Love* (1962), but also nurtured a group of talents (almost all of them originally from the Delta region) that included: guitarists Jimmy Rogers, also an impressive songwriter who wrote *That's Alright* (1953) and *Walking By Myself*

(1959), and Theodore "Hound Dog" Taylor; pianists Otis Spann (perhaps the greatest blues pianist of his generation) and Eddie Boyd (*Five Long Years*, 1952); bassist Willie Dixon; vocalist Iverson "Lousiana Red" Minter (*Red's Dream*, 1962); and harmonica players "Little Walter" Jacobs, the man who adapted the harmonica to the saxophone of bebop, immortalized by the instrumental *Juke* (1952) and *Mean Old World* (1952), Amos "Junior Wells" Blackmore, who recorded the classic **Hoodoo Man Blues** (1965) with his frequent collaborator Buddy Guy on guitar and *Southside Blues Jam* (1970) with Otis Spann on piano, Walter Horton and James Cotton.

Another Mississippi native, Elmore James, developed a percussive, torrential technique at the electric bottleneck guitar and pioneered distorted sounds, with a celebrated version of Robert Johnson's *Dust My Broom* (1952), that gave the name to James' band, the the Broomdusters (the only rivals of Muddy Waters' and Howlin' Wolf's bands), and with a series of breathtaking interpretations such as Robert Johnson's *Standing At The Crossroads* (1954, but issued as a single only in 1960), Tampa Red's *It Hurts Me Too* (1957), *The Sky Is Crying* (1959), *Shake Your Moneymaker* (1961) and *One Way Out* (1961), with Sonny Boy Williamson.

Another Mississippi refugee, vocalist J.B. Lenoir, was the first to aim blues music at contemporary political events, for example in the scathing *Korea Blues* (1951) and *Eisenhower Blues* (1955), and to indulge in histrionic behavior on stage (basically the progenitor of both Bob Dylan and Mick Jagger). He also assembled a band (two saxes, drums, bass, piano, and his own rhythm guitar) that changed the balance of instruments, as in the vibrant boogie *Mama Talk to Your Daughter* (1954).

Bassist, songwriter and vocalist Willie Dixon, yet another Mississippi emigrant who arrived in Chicago in 1937, was a sessionman since 1948, and established a new style with his "walking" bass lines, but, most importantly, composed some of the most influential songs of the blues repertory: *My Babe* (1955) for Little Walter Jacobs, *You Can't Judge A Book By Its Cover* (1962) for Bo Diddley, *Hoochie Coochie Man* (1954) and *I'm Ready* (1954) for Muddy Waters, *I Can't Quit You Baby* (1956) for Otis Rush, *21 Days in Jail* (1958) for Magic Sam, *Wang Dang Doodee* (1966) for Koko Taylor (Cora Walton), and especially the string of vibrant songs for Howlin' Wolf: *Evil* (1960), *Spoonful* (1960), *Back Door Man* (1961), *Little Red Rooster* (1961), *Shake For Me* (1961), etc.

Jimmy Reed, who moved from Mississippi to Chicago in 1948 and created standards such as *You Don't Have To Go* (1955), *Honest I Do* (1957) and *Baby What You Want Me To Do* (1959) transposed the boogie rhythm to the harmonica and to the guitar, using his bass player Eddie Taylor to simulate the left hand of the pianists. The result could sound anthemic, as in Luther Dixon's rebellious *Big Boss Man* (1961). His slow, hypnotic boogies were the epitome of the style that Louisiana bluesmen called "swamp blues".

John Lee Hooker, who relocated from Mississippi to Detroit in 1942, created an exuberant and anarchic synthesis of boogie woogie and talking blues, such as in the hypnotic *Boogie Chillen* (1948), *Crawling King Snake Blues* (1948), *I'm In The Mood* (1951), *Trouble Blues* (1955), *Dimples* (1956), *Boom Boom* (1962). Technically, he was one of the least sophisticated performers, so casual as to sound shabby and uncertain when he was, in fact, all mood and feeling.

This generation created the archetypical styles at their instruments, the styles that became the reference points for the following generations of blues and rock musicians. Their generation was also the last generation to be born in Mississippi (or nearby states). The following one would be fully urbanized, and something of the original mood would be lost forever.

Unlike rural blues music, that was meant to be personal and documentary, rhythm'n'blues was becoming only "good-time music", ever more emancipated from the original social meaning of black music.

Appreciation of the original blues was limited to the intellectuals of the Greenwich Village (New York), the same crowd that had rediscovered folk music and that loved political songs. After the 1938 concert at the Carnegie Hall, the duo of harmonica player Saunders "Sonny" Terry, raised on the East Coast, and guitarist Brownie McGhee, became a fixture of the Village. So did Leadbelly himself. So did Josh White from 1941, also a celebrated cabaret artist.

In Texas, the tradition of country-blues was continued by Sam "Lightnin'" Hopkins, one of the most eloquent and lyrical bluesmen of all times, despite using one of the most humble singing (or, better, half-singing) styles: *Katie Mae Blues* (1947) and *Short Haired Woman* (1947), both with Thunder Smith on barrelhouse piano, *Big Mama Jump* (1947), *Baby Please Don't Go* (1948), *Death Bells* (1949), *T-Model Blues* (1949), *Airplane Blues* (1949), *Shotgun Blues* (1950). He transformed the blues of the Delta into an electric, distorted form of boogie, while, at the same time, emphasizing the narrative aspect.

In the South, Sonny Boy Williamson II (real name Aleck Ford, also known as Rice Miller) established the harmonica as a fashionable instrument through his virtuoso accompaniments to *Nine Below Zero* (1951), *Don't Start Me To Talking* (1955), *Keep It To Yourself* (1956), *One Way Out* (1961), and *Help Me* (1963) that he recorded with Elmore James.

In Arkansas, Robert "Nighthawk" McCollum crafted a relaxed, intimate style, first rehearsed in *Sweet Black Angel* (1949).

The northern Mississippi school, christened "deep blues" in 1991 by critic Robert Palmer, was long lost, and rediscovered only decades later. Fred McDowell, first recorded in 1959, was perhaps the initiator, and the first bluesman to adopt the modal, tracey, droning, one-chord technique that would become typical of the region. His main disciple was R.L. Burnside, first recorded in 1967, who probably cut his best album at the age of 68, **Too Bad Jim** (1994). David "Junior" Kimbrough, who first recorded at the age of 61 for **All Night Long** (1992), was even more removed from the mainstream, playing raw hypnotic music reminiscent of ancient work songs and jungle polyrhythms Shunning the 12-bar dogma, they harked straight back to their African roots.

Post-war Gospel Music

Gospel music became a major business (no longer related to churches) after the war.

Mahalia Jackson, the virtuosa contralto of melismatic singing (improvising a rapid-fire sequence of notes on a single syllable of text), became the ambassador of gospel music to the world with international hits such as Kenneth Morris' *Dig A Little Deeper* (1947), Herbert Brewster's *Move On Up A Little Higher* (1948), the first nationwide hit single of gospel music, the traditional *Go Tell It On The Mountain* (1950), Kenneth Morris' *I Can Put My Trust In*

Jesus (1951), Lucie Williams' *In The Upper Room* (1952). She legitimized gospel music for a very large and international audience.

Mahalia Jackson was the exception to the rule that gospel music was still mainly a music for vocal quartets: the Swan Silvertones, featuring the falsetto of Claude Jeter, formed by four West Virginia miners in 1938 and converted to a melodic format with *Mary Don't You Weep* (1955), and the Sensational Nightingales, from South Carolina, featuring the baritone of Julius Cheeks, were among the most popular, still in the "jubilee" style.

Among female groups, the Ward Singers ruled Philadelphia, one of the greatest gospel vocalists of all times thanks to the voices of Clara Ward (Reverend Herbert Brewster's waltzing *Just Over the Hill*, 1949) and Marion Williams (Brewster's *Surely God is Able*, 1950). The Ward Singers were instrumental in freeing the female gospel quartet from the ecclesiastic dogma: they wore regular (actually, colorful) dresses instead of Church robes. Thus they looked and sounded like a pop group.

The Staple Singers, formed in 1951 in Chicago by Mississippi blues guitarist Roebuck "Pop" Staples and his four children, bridged two generations and two styles (blues and gospel) with *Uncloudy Day* (1956), *Will the Circle be Unbroken* (1957), *This May Be The Last Time* (1958), *Oh Lord Stand By Me* (1961). Roebuck Staples had introduced the blues guitar in gospel music in 1937, and went on to craft a gentle style based on tremolo and reverb.

Veteran choir leader James Cleveland penned one of gospel's greatest hits, *Peace Be Still* (1963). Edwin Hawkins recorded the hit version of the traditional *Oh Happy Day* (1969).

Kansas City: the Shouters

A visceral style of singing (or, better, "shouting") the blues developed in the dancehalls of Kansas City. The shouters fronted combos of the kind that had evolved in Chicago and Los Angeles, a poor man's version of swing orchestras. These combos were loud and unsophisticated. Their goal was to entertain an audience that was paying to dance. The vocalists had to shout in order to be heard. The boogie piano rhythm and the shrill sax solo were frequently the only elements that stood out, besides the vocals. But the "shouter" was not so much shouting as using the voice as an instrument: the function of the voice was no longer to narrate but to contribute to the overall sound. The three major Kansas City shouters were also deeply influenced by jazz's concept of time.

The foremost shouter was "Big" Joe Turner, the former partner of boogie pianist Pete Johnson, now a proto-rocker who constantly challenged the conventions of rhythm'n'blues, from *Cherry Red* (1939) to *My Gal's a Jockey* (1947) to Charles Calhoun (Jesse Stone)'s demonic *Shake Rattle An Roll* (1954), while balancing between melodic and jazzy ballads, such as Henry Van Walls' *Chains Of Love* (1951) and *Sweet Sixteen* (1952), and exuberant novelties, such as *Honey Hush* (1953), with Lee Allen on sax, and *T.V. Mama* (1954), with Elmore James on guitar. His stormy, booming vocals lifted blues music into a higher orbit.

His main rival was Jimmy Rushing, who typically performed as the booming tenor in big bands (mostly Count Basie's), as plastic as a saxophone, and sculpted the dramas of *I May Be Wrong* (1936), also known as *Boogie Woogie*, *Good Morning Blues* (1937), *Sent For You Yesterday* (1938), *Evil Blues* (1939), *I Want A Little Girl* (1940), *Goin To Chicago Blues* (1941).

Far less intimidating was Jimmy Witherspoon, a theatrical baritone who indulged in a more relaxed phrasing, *Confessing The Blues* (1945), *Ain't Nobody's Business* (1948), his own *No Rollin' Blues* (1950) and *The Wind Is Blowing* (1952).

In Chicago, the dominant shouter was Chester "Howlin Wolf" Burnett. A disciple of Charlie Patton in his native Mississippi, Wolf had already recorded *How Many More Years* (august 1951), *Moaning At Midnight* (august 1951) and *Saddle My Pony* (1952), and developed the symbiosis between his funereal vocals and Willie Johnson's heavy (and sometimes distorted) guitar riffs, the archetype of the guitar-voice dialogue in the electric age. Even more influential were the recordings with Hubert Sumlin on guitar, such as *Evil Is Going On* (may 1954), *Smokestack Lightning* (january 1956), based on Charley Patton's *Moon Going Down*, and his *Killing Floor* (august 1964), plus countless Willie Dixon songs. His savage, seismic and vitriolic blues implied not only a different message but a different way of communicating altogether. He was perhaps the first artist to figure out how to make thoroughly modern experimental music by emphasizing the authentic, most primitive elements of ancestral music; how to reconnect with the original creativity of the human soul.

In Los Angeles, jump blues was still the dominant paradigm. Majestic shouter Wynonie Harris delivered *Who Threw the Whiskey in the Well* (1944), *Wynonie's Blues* (1946), Roy Brown's epoch-defining *Good Rockin' Tonite* (1947), probably the first record to feature the backbeat rhythm, the titillating *All She Wants to Do is Rock* (1949) and *Good Morning Judge* (1950), and Hank Penny's *Bloodshot Eyes* (1951).

Roy Brown's fusion of the emotional melisma of gospel music and the pathetic wail of pop crooning in *Good Rockin' Tonite* (1947) *Boogie At Midnight* (1949), *Miss Fanny Brown* (1949), *Cadillac Baby* (1950), marked the appropriation of religious ecstasy by pagan performers. His melodramatic peak was the terrifying *Hard Luck Blues* (1950).

Roaring Divas

The "shouter" was a male role, but the female equivalent of a shouter was to be found both in sacred (gospel) and profane (rhythm'n'blues) music.

Johnny Otis' orchestra, in particular, was instrumental in launching the careers of top-notch female vocalists: Esther Phillips, the voice of Otis' own *Cupid's Boogie* (1950), Mae "Big Mama" Thornton, the roaring contralto of Leiber & Stoller's *Hound Dog* (1953) and the author of *Ball And Chain* (1967), and Etta James (Jamesetta Hawkins), the spirited and defiant heroine of Otis' *Roll With Me Henry* (1955), also known as *Dance With me Henry*, a duet with Richard Berry based on Hank Ballard's *Work With Me Annie*.

Chicago's Dinah Washington (real name Ruth Lee Jones), the profane counterpart to Mahalia Jackson, worked out a charismatic and thundering synthesis of gospel, blues, jazz and pop singing, a dramatic monologue venting her existential neurosis that forged the archetype for the "soul ballad". After moving from Alabama to Chicago in 1927, she became a gospel singer in a female choir and a jazz singer in Lionel Hampton's big band. Capable of turning any melody into a show of acrobatic melisma, she dominated the charts with an eclectic repertory that included Leonard Feather's *Evil Gal Blues* (1944) and *Baby Get Lost* (1949), Richard Jones' *Trouble In Mind* (1952), Gene DePaul's *Teach Me Tonight* (1954), Maria Grever's Latin-tinged *What a Difference a Day Makes* (1959), *This Bitter Earth* (1960).

New York-based Ruth Brown was the first diva to rival Dinah Washington. Among her stirring blues ballads were: *So Long* (1949), Rudy Toombs' *Teardrops From My Eyes* (1950), *5-10-15 Hours* (1952), Herb Lance's jazzy *He Treats Your Daughter Mean* (1953), Chuck Willis' *Oh What A Dream* (1954), *Mambo Baby* (1954), Leiber & Stoller's *Lucky Lips* (1953).

Faye Adams followed suit, also in New York, with *Shake A Hand* (1953), *I'll Be True* (1953) and *Hurts Me To My Heart* (1954). Mabel "Big Maybelle" Smith mastered an even more powerful voice for *Grabbin' Blues* (1953) and *Candy* (1956).

Lavern Baker, a Chicago native, moved from the sprightly and youthful *Tweedlee Dee* (1955) to Lincoln Chase's erotic *Jim Dandy* (1956) to the melancholy ballads *I Cried A Tear* (1958) and *Shake A Hand* (1959).

Koko Taylor (Cora Walton), who arrived in Chicago via Memphis in 1953, the first vocalist to claim the title of "queen of the blues" since World War II, growled *Honky Tonky* (1963), *I Got What It Takes* (1964) and Willie Dixon's *Wang Dang Doodee* (1966), before establishing her persona with a series of luxuriant albums starting with **I Got What It Takes** (1975).

This generation of female singers mixed sacred and secular aspects of black music in such an effective manner that they truly inverted the relationship between the text and the interpreter: the interpreter (the "recitation" of the vocalist) provided the meaning, whereas the lyrics and the melody merely helped deliver it. Their voices became the essence of the story to a degree that, until then, had been achieved only by theatrical actors. They lacked the technical refinement of opera singers, but introduced a psychological refinement that was unknown in western music.

Chicago: Post-war Blues Guitar

When blues music was accepted by the white masses (basically, with the advent of rock'n'roll), the influence was reciprocal: white popular music would never be the same again, but black music too would never be the same again. Rhythm'n'blues lost its rural character and began to resemble (both in format and in sound) white pop music with more vocal freedom and a simpler, rawer arrangement (the electric combo instead of the string orchestra).

The real winner of the transformation from blues to rhythm'n'blues had been the electric guitar, that was to dominate blues music for the next few decades.

Chicago's school of electric guitarists prospered with: Otis Rush, launched by Dixon's *I Can't Quit You Baby* (1956) and matured with *Double Trouble* (1958), with Ike Turner on guitar, and *So Many Roads So Many Trains* (1960); "Magic" Sam Maghett, one of the most lyrical and innovative guitarists, who moved from Mississippi to Chicago in 1950 and who died prematurely at 32 after penning *All Your Love* (1957), *Easy Baby* (1958), *All Night Long* (1958), with his most famous guitar break, the boogie instrumental *Riding High* (1966), the funky *She Belongs To Me* (1966) and the lively instrumental *Lookin' Good* (1967); Texas's Freddie King, mainly famous for his catchy instrumentals, such as *Hide Away* (1961), derived from a Hound Dog Taylor instrumental, *The Stumble* (1961), *Lonesome Whistle Blues* (1961), *San-Ho-Zay* (1961), *I'm Tore Down* (1961), and *Driving Sideways* (1962), but also successful with the romantic ballad *Have You Ever Loved A Woman* (1961); George "Buddy" Guy, capable of blending passages and savage arpeggio-laden guitar workouts as in *First Time I Met The Blues* (1960), *Broken Hearted Blues* (1960), *Let Me Love You Baby* (1961), and *Mary Had a Little Lamb* (1967); Earl Hooker, perhaps the last virtuoso of the slide guitar, a living vocabulary of extreme techniques, as certified by his own instrumental tracks *Blue Guitar* (1953), *Blues in D Natural* (1960), *Universal Rock* (1960) and *Tanya* (1962), as well as by his playing for others such as Robert Nighthawk's *The Moon is Rising* (1952) and Lillian Offitt's *Will My Man be Home Tonight* (1960).

Blues Guitar Elsewhere

Memphis' guitar stylist Albert King (born Albert Nelson) coined a strident propulsive phrasing language that emphasized tonal dynamics rather than melody, while, at the same time, fusing soul and blues in *Don't Throw Your Love on Me So Strong* (1961) and the stellar performances backed by Booker T. & the MG's: *Laundromat Blues* (1966), *Crosscut Saw* (1967), *Born Under a Bad Sign* (1967), *Cold Feet* (1967).

In Texas, Clarence "Gatemouth" Brown absorbed elements of country, cajun and jazz, while pitching his soft and fluid guitar phrasing against the backdrop of a big band: *Boogie Rambler* (1949), *Dirty Work At The Crossroads* (1953), *Okie Dokie Stomp* (1954), *Just Before Dawn* (1959).

Albert Collins' instrumental pieces, from *The Freeze* (1958) to *Don't Lose Your Cool* (1963), via his tour de force *Frosty* (1962), defined a "cool sound" based on loud sustained one-chord trebles.

In Los Angeles, Johnny "Guitar" Watson, perhaps the first guitarist to use the reverb and the feedback as musical elements, redefined blues music with the avantgarde *Space Guitar* (1954), *I'm Getting Drunk* (1954), *Hot Little Mama* (1955), and *Gangster Of Love* (1956). His canon was one of the most impressive of his era, or, for that matter, of any era, embodied in singles that few people heard but many guitarists would imitate for decades.

In New Orleans, Eddie "Guitar Slim" Jones (who died at 33) embellished his own *Story of My Life* (1953) and *The Things That i Used To Do* (1954) with guitar sounds never heard before and shouting influenced by gospel music.

Chicago's guitarist Luther Allison offered high-powered blues-rock on **Love Me Mama** (1969), while Frank "Son" Seals emerged with the full-throttle barrage of **The Son Seals Blues Band** (1973), on which he departed from the 12-bar dogma while retaining traces of Albert King's soul-blues fusion.

Memphis: Post-war Blues Crooning

Memphis was still a magnet for southern musicians, particularly the clubs of the Beale Street area.

Mississippi's blues pianist Ike Turner wrote and arranged (with his Kings Of Rhythm) Jackie Brenston's *Rocket 88* (1951), one of the contenders for the title of first rock'n'roll record, a boogie song that hailed the automobile and featured electric guitar and a wild sax solo, before turning to the vocal skills and sexy looks of his wife Tina in *A Fool In Love* (1960) and *It's Gonna Work Out Fine* (1961).

Memphis was, mainly, the epicenter of a mellow and elegant style of rhythm'n'blues. Riley "B.B." King's main merit was to make the blues palatable to white audiences. His hits were covers of other bluesmen, transformed into colloquial melodies sung in a gravelly gospel falsetto. His guitar stew of bent notes and singing notes was more a compromise than a synthesis between jazz great Charlie Christian and T-Bone Walker's lighter touches. The combination, from Lowell Fulson's *Three O' Clock* (1951) to his own *Rock Me Baby* (1964), which was the archetype for blues-rock, to Roy Hawkins' *The Thrill Is Gone* (1970), made him the most popular (if not the most original) bluesman of the rock era.

Rosco Gordon debuted, still a teenager, with *Booted* (1952) and *No More Dogging* (1952), that virtually invented the tempo of ska music, and became a popular entertainer with *Just A Little Bit* (1960).

Johnny "Ace" Alexander, who died at 25, continued the slide into the pop ballad with *My Song* (1952), *The Clock* (1953) and the posthumous *Pledging My Love* (1954).

Herman "Junior" Parker, a sensual crooner who was also an elegant harmonica player, specialized in simple atmospheric ballads such as *Feelin' Good* (1953, de facto a cover of John Lee Hooker's *Boogie Chillen*), *Next Time You See Me* (1957) and *In The DarK* (1961), but more interesting are the lugubrious love song *Mystery Train* (1953) and *Mother In Law Blues* (1956), penned by guitarist Pat Hare, one of the first virtuosi of the distortion.

The delicate baritone phrasing of Bobby Bland had more in common with Frank Sinatra and Bing Crosby than with the Delta bluesmen, as proven by massive hits such as Joe Medwick Veasey's *Further Up The Road* (1957) and *I Pity The Fool* (1961) and *Lead Me On* (1960), both written by Deadric Malone. The sound of these hits, and of the seminal **Two Steps From The Blues** (1961), was due in large part to the elaborate arrangements of Joe Scott, who also penned Bland's most authentic "blues" performance, *Ain't Nothin' You Can Do* (1964).

Less compromised with the pop ballad was Mississippi's "Little" Milton Campbell, a natural bridge between the Delta, Chicago (urban blues) and Memphis (soul), whose *We're Gonna Make It* (1965) and *Grits Ain't Groceries* (1969), which is a rewrite of Titus Turner's *All Around The World* (1958), fused Howlin' Wolf's shout and Bobby Bland's croon, while *That's What Love Will Make You Do* (1971) and *Walking The Back Streets and Crying* (1972) adopted the ornate arrangements of soul music and displayed an innovative guitar technique.

B.B. King, Bobby Bland and Little Milton made up the triad of soul-blues singers who tried to explain the blues via the elegant sound of soul music.

Among their followers, Los Angeles' Little Johnny Taylor (born Johnny Merrett) delivered powerful interpretations of Clay Hammond's anguished *Part Time Love* (1963), one of the all-time best-sellers of blues music, *Since I Found A New Love* (1964), *Zig Zag Lightning* (1966), Miles Grayson's *Everybody Knows About My Good Thing* (1971), Bobby Paterson's *Open House At My House* (1972).

New Orleans: Piano Blues and Swamp Blues

New Orleans, the historical capital of black music, developed its own style, that relied on booming riffs, on "jump" rhythms, and on a loud and heavy interplay of piano, sax and contrabass.

There were a number of bands in New Orleans that defined the local rhythm'n'blues sound. One bandleader stood out from the crowd. Dave Bartholomew, a trumpeter who started his own band in 1946 and raised talents such as drummer Earl Palmer, saxophonist Lee Allen and pianist Professor Longhair, was influential as an arranger and producer who crafted a sound that bridged jump blues, dixieland jazz and the carnival marches. His band specialized in warm relaxed piaces such as *Country Boy* (1949), *My Ding A Ling* (1951) and the proto-ska instrumental *The Monkey* (1957). But Bartholomew would always overload the "bass" range of the sound by piling up piano, bass, sax and drums to produce the "rumble" that became his trademark. He also wrote Smiley Lewis' *Blue Monday* (1953) and *I Hear You Knockin'* (1955), that features Huey Smith on piano, as well as most of Fats Domino's hits.

The other great bandleader, pianist Paul Gayten, wrote *Since I Fell For You* (1947) for Laurie Annie, *For You My Love* (1949) for Larry Darnell, *The Music Goes Round And Round* (1956), and *The Hunch* (1958), with Allen on sax and typical New Orleans piano.

For the bands of New Orleans, the piano was more than a mere addition to the vocals: often, it was the very foundation of the song.

The school was started by a Isadore "Tuts" Washington (who did not record until well into his seventies). His disciple Professor Longhair, also known as Fess (real name Henry Byrd), a husky vocalist, and wild performer in the barrelhouse tradition, who started out in Dave Bartholomew's band, invented a rolling bass riff that remained popular for decades. His signature tune *Mardi Gras in New Orleans* (1949), *Bald Hair* (1950), the Caribbean-tinged

Tipitina (1953), *Gone So Long* (1954), *She Walks Right In*, *Who's Been Fooling You*, *Big Chief* (1963) were his demonstrations of the New Orleans sound.

The New Orleans style entered a new era with Antoine "Fats" Domino, who, backed by Dave Bartholomew's band, broke all sales records for black artists with his warm casual falsetto and mellow boogie piano. His hits, such as *The Fat Man* (1949), a cover of Jack Dupree's *Junker Blues* (1941) that is a contender for the title of the first rock'n'roll song, *Goin' Home* (1952), *Going To The River* (1953), *Ain't That A Shame* (1955), and *I'm In Love Again* (1956), i.e. the traditional *Blueberry Hill*, *Blue Monday* (1957), the soul ballad *Walking To New Orleans* (1960), were mostly co-written with the bandleader and propelled by his band (mostly Earl Palmer on drums, Lee Allen on exuberant tenor sax).

Lloyd Price's career was established by a similar hit, *Lawdy Miss Clawdy* (1952), also with Dave Bartholomew's band and Fats Domino himself on piano, but then Price targeted the white audience with the folk traditional *Stagger Lee* (1959) and the smooth *Personality* (1959).

Boogie pianist Huey "Piano" Smith penned the novelty *Rocking Pneumonia And The Boogie Woogie Flu* (1957) *High Blood Pressure* (1958) and *Don't You Just Know It* (1958) with his group, the Clowns, before writing Frankie Ford's massive boogie *Sea Cruise* (1958).

Light and syncopated pianist Allen Toussaint, whose sound was defined by the instrumental *Java* (1958), became the most influential arranger and producer (besides songwriter) of the city through hits such as Jesse Hill's *Ooh Pooh Pah Do* (1960), Ernie K-Doe's super-catchy *Mother In-law* (1961), Chris Kenner's *I Like It Like That* (1961) and *Land of a Thousand Dances* (1963), Barbara George's *I Know* (1961), The Showmen's *It Will Stand* (1961), Lee Dorsey's *Ya Ya* (1961) and *Ride Your Pony* (1965), Benny Spellman's *Fortune Teller* (1962), Herb Alpert's *Whipped Cream* (1963), Aaron Neville's *Tell It Like It Is* (1966).

More or less in line with this New Orleans sound were a number of hits that benefited from the whole scene in the mid 1950s: Earl King's *Those Lonely Lonely Nights* (1955), Shirley (Goodman) and (Leonard) Lee's *Let The Good Times Roll* (1956), Clarence Henry's *Ain't Got No Home* (1956).

The other style that was popular in Louisiana was the "swamp blues", a hypnotic, haunting style derived from Jimmy Reed. Slim Harpo (James Moore) made Reed's sound palatable to a broader audience with the lascivious *I'm A King Bee* (1957), *Got Love If You Want It* (1957), *Rainin' in My Heart* (1961), the pulsating *Shake Your Hips* (1966), *Baby Scratch My Back* (1966).

Lightnin' Slim (Otis Hicks), the most introverted and lyrical of the three, sang *Bad Luck Blues* (1954) and *Rooster Blues* (1959) in an ominous bass register.

The main hit of swamp blues was *Sea Of Love* (1959), performed by The Twilights.

Oddly enough, it was a white Mississippi pianist, Mose Allison, to stand as the link between rhythm'n'blues and big-band swing. He was also the sensitive singer-songwriter of **Back Country Suite** (1957) **Creek Bank** (1958) and **Autumn Leaves** (1959), and the author of standards such as *Young Man Blues* (1957), *Parchman Farm* (1957) and *Seventh Son* (1958) that embodied his noir atmosphere and his languid existentialism, the epitome of the beatnik era.

Another popularizer of swing for the rhythm'n'blues audience was St Louis' tenor saxophonist Jimmy Forrest, whose massive hit *Night Train* (1952) was derived from Duke Ellington's *Happy Go Lucky Local* (1946).

Post-war Vocal Groups

Gospel quartets and barbershop quartets evolved into doo-wop groups via the experiments of the post-war generation.

New York's Ravens, despite their focus on covers of showtunes, such as Jerome Kern's *Ol' Man River* (1946), and Irving Berlin's *White Christmas* (1948), and covers of pop hits such as Ray Anthony's *Count Every Star* (1950), introduced the bass register of Jimmy Ricks as the lead vocals, an influential innovation that was particularly effective on the gutsier songs, such as *I Don't Have To Ride No More* (1950) and *Rock Me All Night Long* (1952).

Baltimore's Orioles introduced a mellower style with Deborah Chesler's *It's Too Soon To Know* (1948), and pioneered a vocal dynamics that juxtaposed a tenor (Sonny Tilghman) singing in a cold detached tone and a wordless falsetto in *Tell Me So* (1949), and became one of the first "race" groups to cross over into the pop charts with white songwriter Artie Glenn's *Crying In The Chapel* (1953).

Washington's Clovers pioneered with Ahmet Ertegun's *Don't You Know I Love You* (1951) and *Fool Fool Fool* (1951) the fusion of blues and gospel that was to obscure the old pop-jazz styling of the 1940s. The blues element was even stronger in Rudolph Toombs' *One Mint Julep* (1952) and in *Ting-a-ling* (1952), and the style kept evolving towards gospel with *Good Lovin'* (1953) and *Lovey Dovey* (1954), basically soul music ante-litteram. Bernie Wayne's *Blue Velvet* (1955) and Blanche Carter's *Devil Or Angel* (1956) marked a retreat towards mellow pop formats, but maintained a rare level of sophistication, while the sparkling melodies and rhythms of *Love Love Love* (1956) and Leiber & Stoller's *Love Potion Number Nine* (1959) targeted the rock audience.

A number of vocal groups remained closer to gospel than to pop and jazz. The main "rhythm'n'gospel" groups were: Dominoes, Midnighters, Five Royales, Drifters.

Billy Ward's Dominoes, based in Harlem, broke with the orthodox style of Ravens and Orioles, and pioneered the style with *Sixty Minute Man* (1951), a song of sexual innuendos delivered by the bass voice, and one of the first songs to use the expression "rock'n'roll", *Have Mercy Baby* (1952), *These Foolish Things Remind Me of You* (1952), *Money Honey* (1953) and *The Bells* (1953), besides launching the careers of Clyde McPhatter and then Jackie Wilson.

The erotic and visceral Midnighters, from Detroit, propelled by a driving rhythm of guitar, bass and drums, shocked the world of religious music with the obscene lyrics sung by Hank Ballard in *Get It* (1953) and especially *Work With Me Annie* (1954), which began one of the first teenage sagas of popular music. *Teardrops On Your Letter* (1958) was, de facto, already soul music. It was backed with *The Twist* (1959), Ballard's most famous invention (a revision of his *Is Your Love For Real* which was in turn a variation on the Drifters' *Whatcha Gonna Do*). It was the beginning of a new career, highlighted by the dance novelties *Finger Poppin' Time* (1960) and *Let's Go* (1960).

The Five Royales, from North Carolina, delivered the jubilant melodies and complex arrangements of *Baby Don't Do It* (1952), *Help Me Somebody* (1953), *Laundromat Blues* (1956). They relied on Lowman Pauling's compositional skills (he penned both *Think* in 1957 and *Dedicated To The One I Love* in 1958, both highly influential) and on his inventive guitar style. He virtually invented guitar distortion and feedback on 1958's *The Slummer The Slum*, and was perhaps the first guitarist to employ the "fuzztone". They bridged the gap between the black vocal groups and the first rock bands.

Clyde McPhatter moved to the Drifters, based in New York, and continued his gospel-pop mission with Jesse Stone's *Money Honey* (1953), his own *Honey Love* (1954), and Ahmet Ertegun's boogie *Whatcha Gonna Do* (1954). The new Drifters of 1959 were a completely different group, led by baritone Ben King, whose sophisticated vocals highlighted *There Goes My Baby* (1959), Jerry Leiber and Mike Stoller's first experiment mixing Latin percussions and strings, as well as Doc Pomus & Mort Schuman's diptych *This Magic Moment* (1960) and *Save The Last Dance For Me* (1960). The third season of the Drifters, with King replaced by Rudy Lewis, yielded Gerry Goffin & Carole King's *Up On The Roof* (1962), Mann & Weil's *On Broadway* (1963), and finally, with Johnny Moore replacing the late Rudy Lewis, Artie Resnick & Kenny Young's *Under The Boardwalk* (1964), arranged by Bert Berns with Latin percussions and strings. These hits, all produced by Leiber & Stoller, and including Ben King's solo *Spanish Harlem* (1961), also a Leiber/Stoller composition, and *Stand By Me* (1961), his secular version of a traditional gospel tune, were innovative and influenced both soul, pop and rock music.

Like Ballard, Frankie Lymon, a New York boy soprano who became the archetype of the teenage pop star, bridged the world of rhythm'n'blues and rock'n'roll with *Why Do Fools Fall In Love* (1955), a novelty that basically turned a child's wail ("ooh-wah oo-ooh wah-ah") into a melody, and *I'm Not A Juvenile Delinquent* (1956).

Doo-wop

The fusion between sacred and profane music of the blacks was finally embodied in a new vocal style, "doo-wop" (so called from the phonetic nonsense often used for the vocal harmonies), that emerged in the 1950s as a natural consequence of the developments of the previous decades. Its peak was probably between 1955 and 1962.

The song that, released in december 1954 in Los Angeles, started the fashion was *Earth Angel*, sung by The Penguins of baritone Curtis Williams and falsetto Cleveland Duncan. The song itself was a synthesis of several musical elements of the time: it is one of the many ballads of the era based on the chord changes of Rodgers & Hart's *Blue Moon*, and very similar to the Swallows' *Will You Be Mine* (1951) and to the Hollywood Flames' *I Know* (1953), Curtis Williams' previous group. It was composed by Williams' high-school buddy, Jesse Belvin, who basically recycled his *Dream Girl* (1953), and it was in the style of Belvin's other hits, *Goodnight My Love* (1953) and *I'm Only a Fool* (1954). In fact, it is Belvin that can be credited with the key synthesis of the song: between the idealized love of the 1950s (a modern equivalent of the medieval "amor cortese") and the teen angst that was about to explode in rock'n'roll. In fact, the song struck a chord mainly with the young white audience, once it was broadcast by disc-jockey Alan Freed.

Both the falsetto (deemed too feminine), the lyrics (deemed ridiculous) and the piano playing (the only instrumental accompaniment was Williams' simple piano figure, that created a danceable beat by hammering three times the same chord) were criticized as a symbol of artistic decadence. This was also the first song released by an independent label to reach the top of the charts (the cover by a white group sold even more). And, finally, this song marked the first time that a major musical phenomenon originated on the West Coast.

Los Angeles became the first stage for the doo-wop revolution. The Platters, propelled by the acrobatic tenor of Tony Williams (famous for his sobbing style at very high notes) and featuring one of the first female doo-wop singers (Zola Taylor), were the most conventional, still in the mellow sound of the Ink Spots, with tidy phrasing and orchestral arrangements: two hits written by their (and the Penguins') mentor Sam "Buck" Ram, *Only You* (1955) and *The Great Pretender* (1955), *My Prayer* (1956), that was a cover of Georges Boulanger's *Avant de Mourir*, Jerome Kern's *Smoke Gets In Your Eyes* (1958) and Ram's *Twilight Time* (1958). They were one of the very first groups to be promoted by their label (Mercury) as if they were white in an age in which radio djs were routinely "altered" about the race of the musicians.

The Jewels were perhaps the most unconventional, as proven by their raucous *Hearts of Stone* (1954).

The Coasters, mostly a vehicle for Leiber & Stoller's compositions, were the clowns of doo-wop, their jovial musical vignettes the equivalent of television's sit-coms. Each of their songs was also a social mini-drama, told (usually by tenor Carl Gardner) in the vernacular language and capped by a moral: *Riot In Cell Block No 9* (1954), *Smokey Joe's Cafe* (1955), *Searchin'* (1957), whose greatly-simplified instrumental part bore little resemblance to rhythm'n'blues, the lascivious *Youngblood* (1957), *Yakety Yak* (1958), a childish novelty (albeit permeated by teen angst) that introduced King Curtis Ousley's "yakety sax", *Charlie Brown* (1959), whose "fool voice" was still reminiscent of minstrel shows, and *Poison Ivy* (1959).

The main doo-wop artists in Chicago were the Flamingos, boasting the falsetto of John Carter who penned the sophisticated slow ballad *Golden Teardrops* (1953), later matched by *I'll Be Home* (1956) and *A Kiss from Your Lips* (1956).

New York had not been left in the dark by the doo-wop explosion. In fact, the Harptones had pioneered the genre with Louis Prima's *Sunday Kind Of Love* (1953), and the Crows' *Gee* (1953) was in the vanguard of the more rhythmic style that bordered on rock'n'roll. The Chords' claim to fame is only one song, *Sh-Boom* (1954), but it was another epoch-making song thanks to its bouncy rhythm and its charming vocal games: A bland cover by a white group, the Crew Cuts, reached the top of the charts and started the habit of turning black songs into watered-down versions sung by white kids. The Cadillacs, whose hit was Esther Navarro's *Spedoo* (1956), were influential for their onstage theatrics, the prototype for many soul artists of the following decade.

In New York, James Sheppard invented the "concept" album, except that it was not an album but a series of 14 singles that told the story of a teenage romance. It started with *Crazy For You* (1955), the elegant *Your Way* (1956) and especially *A Thousand Miles Away* (1956), by Sheppard's first group, the Heartbeats, followed by *I Won't Be The Fool Anymore* (1957), *500 Miles To Go* (1957) and *Down On My Knees* (1958). Shep and The Limelites, Sheppard's subsequent trio with no bass vocals, resumed the saga with *Daddy Home* (1961), perhaps the most intricate, and the end, *I'm All Alone* (1962).

Maurice Williams wrote a demented ditty over a Latin rhythm, *Little Darlin* (1957), for his original band, the Gladiolas, only to see it become a hit in the interpretation of Canada's Diamonds (but perhaps this was the only case in which the white cover improved the vocal arrangements over the black original), and then penned an even weirder hit over a Caribbean beat, *Stay* (1960), with the Zodiacs, shocking the white masses with his almost self-parodying falsetto.

Once doo-wop became big business, very few groups were able to emulate the artistic innovations of the pioneers. Fred Parris' *In The Still Of The Night* (1956) by the Five Satins (New Haven), was notable for replacing the traditional vocal counterpoint with an ostensible refrain of "shoo-doo-shoo-be-doo". *Book Of Love* (1958) by the Monotones was one of the "hardest" doo-wop songs. *Get A Job* (1958) by the Silhouettes was quite unique in being a nonsense protest song. *Maybe* (1958) was the first hit by a female doo-wop group, the Chantels. *Come Softly To Me* (1959) by the Fleetwoods was one of the few that mixed female and male voices. The Del-Vikings of *Come Go With Me* (1957) were the first multi-racial group to achieve nation-wide success. *My True Story* (1961) by the Jive Five boasted the crying lead vocals of Eugene Pitt. Richard Rodgers' *Blue Moon* (1961) by another multi-racial group, the Marcels, was one of the most amusing.

Among white groups who did not simply cover black groups, the Italo-Americans dominated: *Little Star* (1958) by the Elegants; *There's A Moon Out Tonight* (1958) by the Capris; *16 Candles* (1959) by the multi-racial Crests; *Sorry* (1959) by the multi-racial Impalas; *Denise* (1963), by Randy and the Rainbows; and Frankie "Valli" Castelluccio's Four Seasons, with *Sherry* (1962), *Big Girls Don't Cry* (1962) and especially *Walk Like A Man* (1963).

But maybe the most impressive achievement of white doo-wop groups was *Since I Don't Have You* (1959) by the Skyliners, orchestrated like a symphony by producer Joe Rock.

The Importance of Rhythm'n'Blues Music

What rhythm'n'blues achieved (in all its transmutations) was, socially speaking, to dispel the notion that black music was for black people only. But perhaps even more important was the progressive emancipation from the cliches of blues and jazz music: the arrangements became less and less sophisticated, the sound harder and harder, the guitars more versatile and sharp-edged, the vocals shouted or cried, the beat more aggressive, the lyrics more oriented towards the lifestyle of young people. Less style and more bodily movement. Less intellectual and more emotional. A side effect was to bring back to the surface the original ritual sexual element of African music. Indirectly, these changes meant that popular music was indulging in collective sexual innuendo, a sort of secret code for young people to communicate about taboo subjects.

Rhythm'n'blues also changed the profile of the audience. Where jazz catered to the audience of the clubs for the middle-class and (ever more often) the "aristocracy" of the city, rhythm'n'blues reached out to the working class and even to the street gangs. This was a rapidly-expanding market of urban masses that were benefiting from the economic boom of the post-war era. In fact, rhythm'n'blues can be said to have altered the balance, by overtaking jazz as the most popular form of black music. The fact that the more "populist" form became also the more "popular" reflected a profound change in the social fabric of the nation.

In other words, the stage was set for rock'n'roll to emerge. What was missing (the great drawback of rhythm'n'blues) was true creativity. Rhythm'n'blues (whether vocal or instrumental) was anchored to well-defined structures, that performers challenged only marginally. There were no significant attempts to create free-form structures, to integrate idioms of other cultures, to enlarge the orchestration to new instruments, to radically alter any of the fundamental dogmas of black-music performance. That will be, indeed, the revolution of rock music, which will progressively introduce the traditional European values of innovation and progress into the archaic values of African personal expression.

Both jazz and rhythm'n'blues may not have happened if white pop music (Tin Pan Alley) had not been stuck in a creative crisis. In the 1930s jazz bands took advantage of the vacuum caused by the Depression: jazz (swing) became popular when the masses had little else to listen (and especially dance) to. Rhythm'n'blues achieved the same feat in a similar time of crisis: at the end of World War II, Tin Pan Alley was incapable of producing exciting new music, and particularly exciting dance/party music that could stimulate the younger audience. Thus the white audience was led to rhythm'n'blues combos the same way their parents had been led to swing orchestras. (The exact same phenomenon would take place in the mid 1970s, when, again, white kids would look at black music, such as hip-hop, in an era of creative crisis for white rock music).

LATIN AMERICA

Argentina: the Tango

During the "belle epoque" (1890s), the working class of the "Boca" of Buenos Aires (Argentina) invented a new rhythm, the tango. "Tan-go" was the name given to the drums of the African slaves, and the music was influenced by both the Cuban habanera and the local milonga. The choreography originally devised in the brothels to mimick the obscene and violent relationship between the prostitute, her pimp and a male rival eventually turned into a dance and a style of music of a pessimistic mood, permeated by a fatalistic sense of an unavoidable destiny, a music of sorrow enhanced by the melancholy sound of the bandoneon. When lyrics were added, they drew from "lunfardo", the lingo of the underworld (the term originally meant "thief"). Tango was embraced enthusiastically in Europe and landed in the USA in the 1910s. The Viennese waltz and the Polka had been the first dances to employ the close contact between a male and a female. The tango pushed the envelope in an even more erotic direction. One of the earliest hits of tango was pianist Enrique Saborido's *Yo Soy La Morocha* (1906). By that time, tango had already established itself as a major genre among young Argentinians. Roberto Firpo is credited as having set the standard in 1913 for all future tango orchestras: the rhythm set by syncopated piano figures, the melodies carried by bandoneon and violin. Firpo's *Alma de Bohemio* (1914) and Gerardo Hernan Matos Rodriguez's *La Cumparsita* (1916) were among the early international hits. Bandoneon player Osvaldo Fresedo and violin player Julio de Caro were among the instrumental stars and composers of the 1920s. From his debut in 1917 to his untimely death in 1935, Carlos Gardel was the most charismatic vocalist, the master of erotic abandon. The tango craze took New York by storm during World War I. Rudolph Valentino created an international sensation in a steamy scene of his film "The Four Horsemen of the Apocalypse" (1921). But tango became a more intellectual affair during the 1930s, when literate songwriters created more poetic lyrics. Representative musicians of the decade are pianist Osvaldo Pugliese (*Recuerdo*) and violinist Elvino Vardaro. Bandoneon player Anibal Troilo ruled the 1940s.

Tango then became a dogma that allowed very little freedom. It was only in the 1960s that someone dared question the dogma.

Brazil: the Samba

Brazil's colonial history is unique in that the dominant white class showed some tolerance for the black slave class and the native pagans. The latter's traditions range from the African-derived voodoo (or, better, Candomble religion) of Bahia to Rio's Macumba religion. Unlike Mexico and Peru, where the original cultures were erased by the Spanish colonizers, Brazil retained them and simply recycled them into the general "saudade" (melancholy existentialism) of the Portuguese conquerors. The fundamental dichotomy of Brazilian music lies between Bahia and Rio. Bahia is the Brazilian equivalent of New Orleans: a melting pot where African traditions mixed with local and European concepts. Rio is both the capital of the aristocracy, where European culture was imported, and the underworld of the slums, where poor (black and white) immigrants from the rest of Brazil (including Bahia) lived in miserable conditions.

In the last decades of the 19th century, the orchestras of Rio de Janeiro (basically, woodwinds and horns, with the clarinet as the soloist) that performed European dance music (such as waltzes and polkas) were called "choro". Joaquim Antonio da Silva Calado, the band-leader of Choro Carioca, revolutionized the style by emphasizing virtuoso playing and improvisation, and by introducing the cavaquinho and the violao (a seven-string guitar). After him, the choro orchestras preferred the flute as the soloist, the violao as the bass, and cavaquinho as the rhythm. The great composers of choro were Chiquinha Gonzaga (a female and a pianist) and Ernesto Nazareth. But the choro ensembles abhorred the African percussion instruments.

The first appearance of the word "samba" dates from 1838. The "samba" was originally a dance of African origin, the mesemba, which came from Bahia and was probably related to the Candomble rituals. It wed a Brazilian dance, the "maxixe", which was an evolution of the habanera (a European dance craze created by Maurice Mouvet in 1912 on the basis of the Cuban habanera) and of the polka, and soon became a musical genre in its own. The samba was probably invented by African-Brazilians in the working-class slums of Rio de Janeiro. The rhythm of the samba was designed to fulfill three roles: to sing, to dance and to parade (at the carnival). The first record to be advertised as "samba" was a song by a black musician, Ernesto "Donga" dos Santos: *Pelo Telefone* (1916). Manuel "Duque" Diniz, a white Brazilian who had opened a maxixe academy in Paris, spread the samba dance craze to Europe in 1921, when he invited Os Oito Batutas, a black choro ensemble led by flutist and composer Pixinguinha ("the Bach of choro") which included Donga on guitar, on a tour to Paris. The combo brought the samba to Paris, but also brought something back to Brazil: trumpet, trombone, saxophone and banjo were added to the line-up, and the sound became more "Americanized", adapting to the sound of big-band jazz. Pixinguinha's *Carinhoso* (1928) was emblematic of the new style. A young white musician from the Rio middle class, Noel Rosa, became famous with the samba song *Com que Roupa?* (1930) and started a less "African" and more song-oriented form of samba. Vincent Youmans' film **Flying Down to Rio** (1933) popularized the samba dance in the USA. The first samba school was founded in 1928 in Rio, and samba schools proliferated in the 1930s. Samba was the generic name of the music employing a kind of rhythm, but there were different kinds of samba. Perhaps the most adventurous and extreme was the batucada. "Batucada" is both the name for a large samba percussion group, for a samba jam session, and for an intensely polyrhythmic style of drumming. A batucada can be played by ensembles with hundreds of percussionists. In Bahia, bloco afro and afoxe (two mainly percussive styles) combined to form samba-reggae. The choro was not dead: in fact, composers of the 1940s such as Benedito "Canhoto" Lacerda created most of the choro repertory.

Cuba: the Son

In the 20th century, Latin America produced a variety of genres born at the crossroads of European folk music, African music and native traditions. While not as popular as the popular music of the USA (also born out of the integration of European music and African music), Latin American genres share the same characters that made it a universal koine.

Cuba was the starting point for many of the Latin dances. At the beginning of the 20th century, Cuba's main music was the "son", a fusion of Spanish popular music and the African rhythm rumba (first mentioned in 1928 and probably related to the Santeria religion). Traditionally played with tres (guitar), contrabass, bongos and claves (wooden sticks that set the circular rhythm) the son of Cuba was popularized by the likes of Ignacio Pineiro, who had a hit with *Echale Salsita* (1929), and Miguel Matamores. The danzon, first documented by Miguel Failde Perez's *Las Alturas de Simpson* (1879), was a descendant of the French "contredanse" or contradanza, and in Cuba's 1920s the danzon became a version of the son for the upper classes, performed by "charangas" (flute and violin orchestras, in which the violin provided the main riff while the flute improvised). Charangas of the golden age include: Orquesta Neno Gonzalez (1926), Orquesta Belisario Lopez (1928), Orquesta de Cheo Belen Puig (1934), Orquesta Aragon (1939), Orquesta America (1942). In the 1930s, Spanish-Cuban bandleader Xavier Cugat (who formed the Waldorf-Astoria Orchestra in 1935) was for Latin music what the Beatles were for rock music: his orchestra created the commercial version of Latin music (largely devoid of artistic value but hugely popular) for the western masses. Also during the 1930s, the dance academia of Pierre and Doris Lavelle popularized Latin dancing in Britain (it was Pierre Lavelle who codified the moves of the rumba in 1955 and the moves of the samba in 1956). In the 1940s, Arsenio Rodriguez, a virtuoso of the tres (Cuban guitar), set the standard for the Cuban conjunto (adding congas, piano and trumpets to the traditional guitar-based sexteto) and thus spearheaded a kind of son based on the piano and the congas. For example, René Alvarez, Arsenio's former singer, formed Conjunto Los Astros in 1948, with multiple trumpets and piano.

Cuba's mambo, "invented" (or, better, imported from Congo) by bassist Israel "Cachao" Lopez and by his brother pianist Orestes of the Antonio Arcano's Orquesta Radiofonica with *El Danzon Mambo* (1937), fused rumba rhythms with big-band jazz (thus introducing syncopation into Cuban music), and was epitomized by Damazo Perez Prado's *Mambo Jumbo* (1948). Basically, the mambo was a danzon for the working class. The chachacha was a midtempo mambo figure that, after the 1953 recording of Enrique Jorrin's *La Enganadora* (1948) and especially Perez Prado's *Cherry Pink And Apple Blossom White* (1955), became a genre of its own, still performed by charangas (unlike the mambo, that was performed by smaller combos). The mambo became a USA craze in 1954.

"Salseros" were the conjunto groups (brass-driven dance bands) of the 1940s that played a bit of everything. The most celebrated Cuban vocalist of the era was Beny More, from *Yiri Yiri Bom* (1946) to *Maracaibo Oriental* (1954).

A fusion of Cuban music and jazz music (or "cubop") became popular after World War II, influencing some of the most important jazz musicians (e.g., Dizzy Gillespie). Puerto Rico pianist Noro Morales was the main practitioner of the quintet for piano and percussion (*Bim Bam Bum*, 1942; *Oye Negra*). Frank "Machito" Grillo's **Afro-Cuban Jazz Suite** (1950) was typical of the genre.

The foundations of post-war Latin music were laid by this generation. Cuban pianist Jose Curbelo played with Cugat and raised Ernesto "Tito" Puente, Ray Barretto and Pablo "Tito" Rodriguez, who raised Eddie Palmieri. The US singer Frank "Machito" Grillo played with Cugat and Norales, and then raised Puente.

Trinidad: the Calypso

Trinidad's calypso, first documented by an instrumental recorded in 1912 by George "Lovey" Bailey's orchestra, was another Latin dance to reach beyond Latin America. Calypso was originally sung in French, but the first recorded calypso song, Julian Whiterose's *Iron Duke in the Land* (1914), was already in English. Starting with the "Railway Douglas Tent" of Port-of-Spain in 1921, calypso was originally performed in "tents" (temporary dancehalls) during the period before carnival: the term stuck, and came to denote any club playing calypso. Most calypso records are still released just before or during carnival season. Hubert "Roaring Lion" Charles (who also called himself Rafael de Leon) was perhaps the first star, producing the standards *Send Your Children to The Orphan's Home* (1927), *Marry An Ugly Woman* (1934), *Three Cheers For The Red, White and Blue* (1936), *Netty Netty* (1937) *Mary Ann* (1945). Other classics of the early era were Raymond "Attila The Hun" Quevedo's *West Indian Federation* (1933), *Women Will Rule the World* (1935) and *Calypso Behind The Wall*, later covered by Belafonte as *Jump In The Line*, Frederick "Wilmoth Houdini" Hendricks' *War Declaration* (1934) and *He Had It Coming* (1939), covered by Louis

Jordan as *Stone Cold Dead in the Market* (1946), Neville "Growling Tiger" Marcano's *Money is King* (1935), Norman "King Radio" Span's *Matilda* (1938), Rupert "Lord Invader" Grant's *Don't Stop the Carnival* (1939) and *Rum and Coca Cola* (1944), Aldwyn "Lord Kitchener" Roberts' *Tie Tongue Mopsy* (1946), Irvin Burgie's *Day O* and *Island in the Sun*, both covered by Belafonte. They all had to travel to New York in order to record their songs. During the 1940s, Trinidad's musicians developed the concept of the steel band, which dramatically changed the sound of calypso. A 1946 concert in New York, "Calypso at Midnight", organized by Alan Lomax, and Sam Manning's revue **Caribbean Carnival** (1947), the first calypso show on Broadway, helped establish the genre. But it was in the 1950s that calypso became a "craze" in the USA, thanks mainly to Harry Belafonte's **Calypso** (1956), one of the first albums to sell over one million copies, that contained the *Banana Boat Song* (1956), originally composed by the New York folk group the Tarriers by fusing two Jamaican traditionals. Back in Trinidad, Francisco "Mighty Sparrow" Slinger released the first calypso album, **Calypso Carnival** (1958). Other Trinidad hits of the 1950s included Carlton "Lord Blakie" Joseph's *Steelband Clash* (1954), Slinger "Mighty Sparrow" Francisco's *Jean and Dinah* (1956), Fitzroy "Lord Melody" Alexander's *Mama Look A Boo Boo* (1956). Mighty Sparrow (*Ten To One Is Murder*, 1960; *Dan Is The Man*, 1963; *Melda*, 1966) and, to some extent, Lord Kitchener (*The Road*, 1963; *Rainorama*, 1973) continued to dominate during the 1960s. Songs by new artists included Mervyn "Mighty Sniper" Hodge's *Portrait of Trinidad* (1965) and McCartha "Calypso Rose" Lewis' *Fire In Your Wire* (1967), the first major hit by a female calypso artist.

POST-WAR POP MUSIC IN THE USA

USA: *After Tin Pan Alley*

From the moment that it became big business, pop music came largely from Tin Pan Alley's publishing houses. Tin Pan Alley thrived on the opera, ragtime, cakewalk, foxtrot and show tunes. As the latter came to represent more and more of the songwriter's business, in the 1930s Tin Pan Alley moved north, near the Broadway theaters, between 42nd and 49th street. Unfortunately for them, before World War II the market came to be dominated by the "Big Bands", that accounted for almost 85% of the best-sellers between 1937 and 1941. Big bands tended to perform the music written by the bandleader, thus the publishing houses were the real losers.

Surprisingly, World War II fostered an economic boom and, indirectly, helped the music industry develop in different directions. It was during the war that Bing Crosby's *White Christmas* (1942) became the best-selling song of all times (and would remain so for 50 years) It was during the war that the first "disc jockeys" followed the US troops abroad. It was during the war that Capitol was founded in Hollywood, the first major music company not to be based in New York (1942), and Mercury was founded in Chicago (1945). It was during the war that the "barber-shop quartets" evolved from the slow, melancholy style of the Ink Spots to the casual, innovative style of Ravens, Orioles, Clovers. At the end of the war, the nation was electrified. War was over, the USA had won, peace reigned, and wealth was spreading. The new mood helped popular music too.

By the end of World War II, the landscape had been dramatically altered by the radio, the jukeboxes, a broader availability of records and turntables, and a proliferation of dance halls. The singer, not the bandleader, returned to be the charismatic focus of attention. This launched a second golden age for the publishing houses.

The biggest star of the war years, though, was still Bing Crosby, thanks to his multi-million seller: Irving Berlin's *White Christmas* (1942).

During World War II, the three Andrews Sisters were the second main sensation after Bing Crosby: *Bei Mir Bist Du Schoen* (1938), originally composed by Sholom Secunda for a 1932 Yiddish musical, Don Raye's *Boogie Woogie Bugle Boy* (1941), Sam Stept's *Don't Sit Under the Apple Tree* (1942), *Pistol Packin' Mama* (1943), Jeri Sullavan's and Paul Baron's *Rum and Coca-Cola* (1944).

Among white female singers, only Peggy Lee (Norma Egstrom), the former vocalist of Benny Goodman's orchestra, could compete with the great black vocalists of blues and jazz music. She not only sang, but almost acted, the songs she sang, particularly her own compositions, such as *Why Don't You Do Right* (1942) and *Manana* (1948).

Frances "Dinah" Shore was the most successful female singer of the war years, first with the Xavier Cugat orchestra (*Quiereme Mucho*, 1939) and then on her own with *Yes My Darling Daughter* (1940), *Blues In The Night* (1942), *I'll Walk Alone* (1944), *The Gypsy* (1946), *Anniversary Song* (1947). Her success was crucial in emancipating the female voice from the band after a decade in which female singers had become, de facto, instruments in the hands of the bandleader.

The epitome of the transition from the bandleader to the singer was singer Frank Sinatra, one of the creative forces of jazz phrasing ("the voice") and the quintessential Italian baritone. He took Bing Crosby's romantic crooning to new evocative (and swooning) heights. He sang with the big bands of Harry James (1939), Tommy Dorsey (1940-42), of whom Sinatra basically emulated vocally the expansive trombone style, Count Basie and Duke Ellington. His hits were mere vehicles for his phrasing: Johnny Mercer's *Dream* (1945), Victor Young's *Stella by Starlight* (1947), Ken Lane's *Everybody Loves Somebody* (1948), Frank Loesser's *Luck Be A Lady Tonight* (1950), Johnny Richards' *Young At Heart* (1954), Vernon Duke's *April In Paris* (1959), Bert Kaempfert's *Strangers In The Night* (1966), etc. His albums, starting with the chamber-jazz arrangements of **Swing Easy** (1954), were among the most refined of the 1950s. **In The Wee Small Hours** (1955), arranged by Nelson Riddle, is a contender for the title of first concept album. **Songs For Swinging Lovers** (1956), again arranged by Riddle, fused swing's big band and string orchestra.

Perry Como was the quintessential entertainer to make the transition from the radio to the television. In 1942 he had started his own radio show, that he transferred successfully to the new medium in 1948. Perry Como established his romantic aura with Ted Mossman's *Till the End of Time* (1945), a pop adaptation of Chopin's *Polonaise in A-flat Major*, Bennie Benjamin's *Surrender* (1946), Leo Robin's *Prisoner of Love* (1947), Al Hoffman's *Chi-Baba Chi-Baba* (1947), Slim Willet's *Don't Let The Stars Get In Your Eyes* (1952), Al Hofman's *Hot Diggity* (1956), Lou Stallman's *Round And Round* (1957), Burt Bacharach's *Magic Moments* (1958), and Lee Pockriss' *Catch A Falling Star* (1958), but he began to sound terribly antiquated in the age of rock'n'roll.

New Orleans' jazz trumpter Louis Prima became a Las Vegas entertainer famous for his *Bell-Bottom Trousers* (1945) and *I've Got You Under My Skin* (1959).

The hits of operatic balladeer Frankie Lane (LoVecchio), mostly arranged by Mitch Miller and arranged by Carl Fischer, not only marked the decline of the old crooning style but also inaugurated the studio as a place where a "sound" was created (not just a performance recorded): Helmy Kresa's *That's My Desire* (1947), the country hit *Mule Train* (1949), Beasley Smith's *That Lucky Old Sun* (1949), Terry Gilkyson's *The Cry Of the Wild Geese* (1950). Lane sold over 100 million records.

Mario Lanza (real name Alfredo Cocozza) was an operatic tenor who continued the process of displacing of the crooning style with Nicholas Brodsky's *Be My Love* (1950), *The Loveliest Night of the Year* (1951), a cover of Juventino Rosa's *Over The Waves* (1888), and assorted arias from operas.

Tony "Bennett" Benedetto sang similar material to Sinatra's but in a register that was more operatic. He also sang generic melodies from all sorts of sources: Arthur Hammerstein's *Because of You* (1950), Richard Adler's *Rags to Riches* (1953), *Stranger in Paradise* (1953), based on a Borodin aria, George Cory's *I Left My Heart in San Francisco* (1962).

Laine and Bennett were merely the vanguard of the "Italian" connection, that peaked with Dean Martin (Dino Crocetti), the crooner of Harry Warren's *That's Amore* (1953), *Sway* (1954), i.e. the English version of *Quien Sera*, Terry Gilkyson's *Memories Are Made of This* (1956).

Billy Eckstine, who had been running one of the last big bands of the swing era (featuring Miles Davis, Charlie Parker, Dizzy Gillespie and many others), was the first black vocalist able to compete with the heavy-weights of the white pop ballad, thanks to Willard Robison's *Cottage For Sale* (1945), Leo Robin's *Prisoner Of Love* (1946), Burton Lane's *Everything I Have Is Us* (1947), Rodger's *Blue Moon* (1948), that he interpreted à la Sinatra, Victor Young's *My Foolish Heart* (1949), Al Hoffman's *I Apologize* (1951).

Jazz pianist Nat "King" Cole (Nathaniel Coles), who reached Los Angeles in 1937, was the second. Cole led an influential piano-guitar-contrabass trio for his mellow tunes *Straighten Up And Fly Right* (november 1943), *For Sentimental Reasons* (august 1946), *Harmony* (august 1947), *Nature Boy* (august 1947), the first hit with the backing of a traditional pop orchestra instead of the trio, *Mona Lisa* (march 1950), backed by Les Baxter's orchestra, *When I Fall In Love* (december 1956), his zenith of pathos (lushly arranged by Gordon Jenkins). The arrangements of these hits pioneered chamber jazz. More importantly, Cole bridged pop and jazz, as well as white and black psyche: he introduced black sex appeal into white popular culture and romanticism into black popular culture.

Another black singer, Sammy Davis Jr, also a comedian and a dancer, combined Bob Hope, Fred Astaire and Frank Sinatra in one persona.

Eddie Fisher bridged the generation of these pop singers and the generation of rock'n'roll with lively interpretations of Guy Mitchell's *Thinking Of You* (1950), Tolchard Evans's *Lady of Spain* (1952) and *Oh Mein Papa/ I'm Walking Behind You* (1953), the English version of a German song.

Few female singers managed to stand up to the male stars. Doris Day, America's eternal virgin, the vocalist in the most popular white dance band of the 1940s, Les Brown And His Band of Renowns, popularized *Sentimental Journey* (1945), which would remain her signature song (composed by Les Brown's arranger, Ben Homer), Jule Styne's *It's Magic* (1948), Oscar Brand's *A Guy Is A Guy* (1952), Sammy Fain's *Secret Love* (1953), Jay Livingston's *Que Sera Sera* (1956). Teresa Brewer, one of the first teenage idols, had two world-wide hits: Bernie Baum's *Music Music Music* (1950) and Sidney Prosen's *Till I Waltz Again With You* (1952). Jo Stafford, former singer in Tommy Dorsey's band, had the most acrobatic phrasing, running the gamut from the tender *Candy* (1945) to the mocking *Timtayshun* (1947) to Pee Wee King's *You Belong To Me* (1951).

The most successful white harmony quartets before the age of doo-wop were the Four Aces, from Pennsylvania, with *Sin* (1951), *Tell Me Why* (1952), Jule Styne's *Three Coins In A Fountain* (1953) and Sammy Fain's *Love Is A Many-Splendored Thing* (1955), followed by the Four Lads, from Toronto (Canada), with the exotic *The Mocking Bird* (1952) and Robert Allen's sentimental *Moments To Remember* (1955).

The Four Freshmen, from Indianapolis, pioneered an intricate style of close-harmony vocals (already practiced by Herb Ellis' trio Soft Winds in 1947), debuted it in George Forrest's *It's a Blue World* (1952), refined it on **Voices In Modern** (1954) and adapted it to jazz on **Four Freshmen and Five Trombones** (1956). It revolutionized the polyphony of the harmony quartet, leading to Gene Puerling's Hi-Lo's in Los Angeles, so named because of their broad vocal range, first documented on **Listen to the Hi-Lo's** (1954), which in turn led to the Beach Boys.

Influenced by gospel rather than by opera, Johnny Ray's shamelessly emotional style and spare arrangements, first demonstrated in Churchill Kohlman's *Cry* (1951), marked the end of the big-band era.

More than any other arranger, Miller was responsible for shaping the concept of "soundscape", the sonic landscape in which the singer's melody floats and soars. He augmented the conventional orchestra with instruments by the intriguing register (cello, French horn, harpsichord) and even with sound effects. Mitch Miller continued to pursue the strategy of ethereal orchestrations, originally developed for Frankie Lane, with another romantic idol, Johnny Mathis, whose hits included *Wonderful Wonderful* (1956), *Chances Are* (1957) and *Twelfth Of Never* (1957). Miller was, in many ways, the predecessor of the Brian Wilsons and the George Martins who would use the studio as an instrument.

After the Metro-Goldwyn-Mayer (MGM) film company opened a recording business to sell their movie soundtracks (1946), the mainstream popular music was controlled by six "majors: Columbia, RCA Victor, Decca, Capitol, MGM, Mercury. A gap was being created between these six majors, that sold white music for white people, and the small independent labels that were sprouting up around the country. The first confrontation had taken place in 1941, when radio stations refused to accept the higher royalties requested by the ASCAP, that controlled most of the New York artists, and started BMI (Broadcast Music Inc), which mainly represented independent country and blues artists from the rest of the nation. Tin Pan Alley and the ASCAP were marketing to adult white families, not black families and not young people. But the independent radio stations had more success among young white people, a market that was virtually unexplored.

In 1948, Moe Asch founded Folkways, a label devoted to resurrecting folk music, and Pete Seeger formed the Weavers, the first major group of folk revival.

Jazz and folk musicians shared the same clubs and lofts, and inevitably came to influence each other. The intellectuals of the Greenwich Village were listening to both. In 1948 Billboard introduced charts for "folk" and "race" records, the latter being a euphemism for "black people's records" (and renamed in 1949 "rhythm'n'blues"). In 1950 Elektra was founded in New York to promote both scenes, and Dutch electronics giant Philips entered the recording business.

Another strain in popular music, "exotica", was created piecemeal starting from the late 1940s. First (1947) Korla Pandit (John Red), pretending to be an Indian guru and playing a Hammond organ, started a Hollywood-based tv program that, indirectly, publicized exotic sounds. Then (1948) Rodgers & Hammerstein's **Tale Of The South Pacific** became a Broadway hit. Finally (1950) Les Baxter's **Music Out of the Moon** incorporated exotic themes in instrumental easy-listening music.

New York pianist Raymond Scott (real name Harry Warnow) never actually composed anything for cartoons, although he became famous for cartoon music. Scott composed quirky tunes with odd time signatures set to a frantic pace, all recorded with his jazz quintet, from *The Toy Trumpet* (1936) to *Bumpy Weather* (1939). Starting in 1941, Carl Stalling used snippets of Scott's tunes for countless episodes of "Bugs Bunny", "Daffy Duck" and "Porky Pig". Raymond Scott moved on, founding (1946) "Manhattan Research", the world's first electronic music studio, for which he invented several electro-mechanical devices that predated synthesizers, sequencers and samplers. His most intriguing projects were perhaps the **Rock and Roll Symphony** (1958) and the three-LP electronic album **Soothing Sounds for Baby** (1962), a predecessor of both ambient and minimalist music.

New York: Easy Listening

Burt Bacharach was the master of the mellow jazz-infected orchestral melody. If Cole Porter's songs had been the quintessence of calculated aristocratic elegance, the songs of Bacharach were the quintessence of spontaneous middle-class elegance: casual, unassuming, almost involuntary. His golden years were the ones with lyricist Hal David, a collaboration that yielded an endless series of classics of easy listening: *Magic Moments* (1958), sung by Perry Como, *Only Love Can Break a Heart* (1962) for Gene Pitney, *Wishin' And Hopin'* (1964) for Dusty Springfield, *Always Something There to Remind me* (1964) for Lou Johnson, *Walk On By* (1964), *Valley of the Dolls* (1968) and *I'll Never Fall in Love Again* (1969) for Dionne Warwick, *Raindrops Keep Falling on My Head* (1969) for B.J. Thomas, *Arthur's Theme* (1981) for Christopher Cross, *That's What Friends are For* (1986) for Warwick, etc.

The most Bacharach-esque of the songs of the following decade was perhaps Charles Fox's *Killing Me Softly* (1971), that Roberta Flack turned into a smash hit two years later. Fox also penned *I Got A Name* (1973) for Jim Croce, theme songs for tv series such as **Happy Days** and **The Love Boat**, and songs for Roger Vadim's **Barbarella** (1968).

Roberta Flack also recorded another Bacharach-esque hit: Ewan MacColl's *The First Time Ever I Saw Your Face* (1971).

Paul Williams' *Evergreen* (1976) for Barbra Streisand and *That What Friends Are For* (1985) for Dionne Warwick were also in the Bacharach style.

WORLD MUSIC ON THE RISE

Jamaica: the Mento

The first Jamaican recording studio opened in 1951 and recorded "mento" music, a fusion of European and African folk dance music. The island was awash in rhythm'n'blues records imported by the so called "sound systems", eccentric traveling dance-halls run by no less eccentric disc-jockeys such as Clement Dodd (the "Downbeat") and Duke Reid (the "Trojan"). The poor people of the Jamaican ghettos, who could not afford to hire a band for their parties, had to content themselves with these "sound systems". The "selectors", the Jamaican disc-jockeys who operated those sound systems, became the real entertainers. The selector would spin the records and would "toast" over them. The art of "toasting", that usually consisted in rhyming vocal patterns and soon evolved in social commentary, became as important as the music that was being played.

In 1954 Ken Khouri started Jamaica's first record label, "Federal Records". He inspired Reid and Dodd, who began to record local artists for their sound system. Towards the end of the 1950s, amateurs began to form bands that played Caribbean music and New Orleans' rhythm'n'blues, besides the local mento. This led to the "bluebeat" groups, which basically were Jamaica's version of the New Orleans sound. They usually featured saxophone, trumpet, trombone, piano, drums and bass.

Soon the bass became the dominant instrument, and the sound evolved into the "ska". The "ska" beat had actually been invented by Roscoe Gordon, a Memphis pianist, with *No More Doggin'* (1951). Ska songs boasted an upbeat tempo, a horn section, Afro-American vocal harmonies, jazzy riffs and staccato guitar notes.

A few years later a Jamaican singer named Theophilus Beckford cut the first "ska" record, *Easy Snapping* (1959), and the word "reggae" was coined (1960) to identify a "ragged" style of dance music, with its roots in New Orleans' rhythm'n'blues.

In 1930 Ethiopia was the only black African country to be still free from European white colonial occupation. That year prince Ras Tafari Makonnen ascended to the throne, assuming the title of Emperor Halie Selassie I. While his "empire" was short-lived (Benito Mussolini invaded Ethiopia just five years later), the widely-covered story of his coronation and of his claim to be the incarnation of the Judeo-Christian god Yahweh inspired blacks living outside Africa. The Jamaican activist Marcus Garvey had already started an Afro-nationalist movemement in Jamaica and in 1927 had prophesied the coming of the messiah of God (called "Jah" in Ethiopia). Leonard Howell's libel "The Promise Key" (1935), written just before Mussolini overthrew the "emperor", identified the messiah with the "Ras Tafari". Rastafari therefore became both a religious and a political movement in Jamaica, paralleling the purely secular "Black Power" movement of the USA. The new Jamaican music became its soundtrack.

Ghana: the Highlife

Ghana, the first African country to win independence from a European colonizer (in 1957) and the economic miracle of Africa at the end of the century, was the birthplace of highlife music. Originally the name given by the blacks to the music of the white social elite, it evolved from the fusion of rural "palm-wine" music for guitar, percussion and concertina, church music, Latin ballroom music, military music and African tribal music. The black bands that used to play at parties thrown by white people started playing also for black people, and their sound became more and more Africanized. The guitar-based fusion was mature in the 1930s, when it was interpreted for the masses by Jacob Sam (his *Yaa Amponsah* dates from 1928), heavily influenced by the Cuban orchestras. In the 1950s, especially after independence, highlife bandleaders Emmanuel Tettah Mensah (leader since 1948 of the twelve-piece orchestra Tempos, the charismatic archetype of the highlife dance band), King Bruce, Jerry Hansen, Stan Plange, E.K. Nyame, leader of the most popular guitar-band, drummer Guy Warren, Nigerian trumpeter Victor Olaiya, Nigerian guitarist Bobby Benson, were influenced by swing bands of the USA. The Tempos exported highlife to Nigeria in 1951, and Nigeria soon came to rival Ghana for highlife supremacy.

Congo: the Soukous

During the 1950s, when they experienced rapid urbanization and a relatively booming economy, the two French-speaking colonies of the Congo area (capitals in Brazzaville and Kinshasa) witnessed the birth of an African version of the Cuban rumba played by small US-style orchestras (called "kasongo", "kirikiri" or "soukous") with a touch of jazz and of local attitudes: Joseph "Grand Kalle" Kabasselleh's African Jazz (that counted on vocalist Tabu Ley, guitarist "Docteur" Nico Kasanda, saxophonist Manu Dibango), Jean Serge Essous' O.K.Jazz (featuring the young Franco), Orchestre Bella Bella, etc. Each orchestra became famous for one or more "dances" that they invented. So soukous (as Ley dubbed it in 1966) is actually a history of dances, rather than one monolithic genre (Ley's definition originally applied only to a frenzied version of rumba). A guitarist named Jimmy Elenga introduced "animation": instructions yelled to the crowd in order to direct their dances. Animation eventually became part of the dance, delivering both the identity of the dance, the (ethnic) identity of the band and a (more or less subtle) sociopolitical message. As dictators seized power in both Congos, musicians emigrated to other African countries, to Europe and to the USA, thus spreading soukous around the world, while in Zaire (Congo Kinshasa) soukous bands were used for Maoist-style propaganda purposes ("l'animation politique").

A key figure was "Franco" (Francois Luambo Makiadi), the guitarist who in 1958 evolved the O.K.Jazz into the 20-member T.P.O.K.Jazz (including saxophonist "Verkys" Kiamanguana Mateta) and was largely responsible for the relaxed, sensual, languid version of soukous that became predominant, before the 1967 arrival of guitarist Mose Fan Fan led to a more lively sound. His collaboration with Tabu Ley, **Omana Wapi** (1976), contained only four lengthy dances.

Tabu Pascal (aka Tabu Ley Rochereau) formed African Fiesta in 1963 (initially with Dr Nico, who co-wrote the classic *Afrika Mokili Mobimba*) and then renamed it Afrisa in 1970, with vocalist Sam Mangwana and guitarist Huit-Kilos Bimwela Nseka. From the beginning, Ley played the Latin rhythms on the drums of rock music, thus merging (at least ideally) rumba and rock. His Fiesta also turned the soukous concert into a happening that was reminiscent of the sexy shows of Parisian cabarets.

South Africa: the Mbaqanga

South Africa had a melting pot of its own. In the black urban centers where different tribes met, and met with foreign slaves, a dance style called "marabi" evolved. It was originally a humble form of music, but it became similar to the jazz music played by swing bands in the USA when it was adopted by the relatively wealthy and free blacks of Sophiatown, a suburb that had become a sort of Johannesburg's Harlem. In 1955 it was destroyed by the white racist government, an event that led to the radicalization of South African jazz music.

The most influential phenomenon in South-African music was the evolution of Zulu township music, or mbaqanga (originally the name of a soup of the 1950s), a lilting style that relies on driving rhythm. Early South-African songs include Solomon Linda's *Mbube* (1939), the base for *The Lion Sleeps Tonight*.

By the end of the 1950s South African music was on the rise. South-African composer Todd Matshikiza's musical **King-Kong** (1959) fused classical, jazz and African music, while Nigerian hand drumming virtuoso Babatunde Olatunji shocked the USA with **Drums of Passion** (1959) for percussion ensemble. (He would continue to pursue his aesthetic of drumming-induced trance with the **The Invocation** of 1988 and the 21-minute *Cosmic Rhythm Vibrations* of 1993).

Much of South-African music of the 1950s was born at the crossroads of jazz and folk music. In fact, an important moment for the emancipation of the local scene was Todd Matshikiza's musical **King-Kong** (1959), that exported to the USA a fusion of classical, jazz and African idioms, and that featured both trumpeter Hugh Masekela and vocalist Miriam Makeba.

Miriam Makeba, an activist in the civil-rights movement of the USA, recorded in a pop-jazz style, often accompanied by her husband Hugh Masekela.

Trumpet player Hugh Masekela, who had led the first jazz record of the African continent, **Verse I** (1960), with a sextet named the Jazz Epistles that featured pianist Dollar Brand, fused the South-African tradition of work and church songs (the South-African equivalent of the blues and gospel of the USA) and Zulu mbaqanga rhythms with the structure of jazz and pop-jazz music, on albums such as **The Lasting Impression** (1965).

Brazil: Bossanova

A major stylistic revolution took place in Brazil during the 1950s: when white young middle-class intellectuals merged a gentler, slower form of the samba with jazz music, and shifted the lead to the guitar: bossanova was born. Thus, it was a music of the bourgeoisie, not of the working class. Indeed, bossanova songs left behind the underworld of samba, where people struggled to make a living, and shifted to the world of beaches, romance and lazy bohemian life. And, in fact, bossanova soon became a favorite style of easy-listening and lounge music.

Antonio Carlos ("Tom") Jobim began a collaboration with Vincius de Moraes when he scored the soundtrack for the latter's play, **Orfeu da Conceicao** (1956), which included his first standard, *Se Todos Fossem Iguais a Voce*. After Jobim composed the classic *Desafinado* (1957), the two released **Cancao do Amor Demais** (1958), featuring Eliseth Cardoso on vocals and Joao Gilberto on guitar, which contained Jobim's *Chega de Saudade*, the song that established bossanova in Brazil. Jobim and Moraes also wrote *Garota de Ipanema* (1962), which turned bossanova into a world-wide phenomenon.

The jazz world of the USA welcomed the Brazilian style on **Jazz Samba** (1962), a collaboration between guitarist Charlie Byrd and saxophonist Stan Getz.

Other notable protagonists of bossanova were Luiz Bonfa` (*Manha de Carnaval*, 1958), Jorge Ben (*Mais Que Nada*, 1963), Sergio Mendes (the most shameless perpetrator of Brazilian easy-listening).

USA: Latin Pop

At the end of the 1950s exotic sounds were still percolating into the national psyche of the USA, with the emphasis shifting towards Latin America. Harry Belafonte's *Banana Boat Song* (1957) launched "calypso" in the USA, Ritchie Valens' *La Bamba* (1958) created a tex-mex version of rock'n'roll, the Drifters' *There Goes My Baby* (1959) introduced Latin rhythm to pop music, Herp Albert's instrumental *Lonely Bull* (1962) coined another hybrid, dubbed "ameriachi", and Jose Fernandez Diaz's *Guantanamera* (1963) became a folk standard.

In Cuba in 1955, Los Papines fused the violin-based music of charangas and the trumpet-based music of conjuntos, thus creating a new standard for Cuban-inspired pop music. But, as Fidel Castro seized power in Cuba (1959), the epicenter of Latin music moved to other islands and then south. Eduardo Davidson's *La Pachanga* (1959), recorded by Orquesta Sublime, introduced Cuba to a Colombian dance (which was confusingly called "charanga" in the USA). Charanga and pachanga became brief fads in the USA, while the "son" left Cuba and migrated to Puerto Rico.

Puerto Rico had its own tradition of "bomba" and "plena", to which percussionist Rafael Cortijo, leader of a conjunto since 1954, had added trumpets and saxophones (*El Bombon De Elena*). His conjunto and his husky vocalist Ismael Rivera (*El Nazareno*, *Quitate de la Via Perico*), notorious for the improvised call-and-response vocals of the "sonero" tradition, harked back to the African roots of Caribbean music without any distinction between styles. Both vocally and rhythmically they created a "sauce" of Caribbean music. El Gran Combo, formed by pianist Rafael Ithier, continued Cortijo's mission in a lighter vein, with *La Muerte* (1962) and *Ojos Chinos* (1964).

In the 1960s, the Puertorican-son hybrid reached the Puertorican colony in New York. Here, the son adopted the format of the big band, as in Jimmy Sabater's *Salsa y Bembe* (1962) and vibraphonist Cal Tjader's *Salsa del Alma* (1964).

The Cuban expatriates that relocated in New York contributed greatly to the assimilation of the genre in US culture: vocalist Celia Cruz (*Burundanaga*, 1956; *Yerbero Moderno*, 1956), flautist Jose-Antonio Fajardo (*La Charanga*), jazzy congueros Candido Camero and Ramon "Mongo" Santamaria (*Mazacote*, 1958; *Afro Blue*, 1959; Herbie Hancock's *Watermelon Man*, 1963), violinist Felix "Pupi" Legarreta, who fused charanga and jazz on **Salsa Nova** (1962). Santamaria, who arrived in New York in 1950, paid tribute to his Cuban roots on **Yambu** (1958) and **Mongo** (1959), that were performed with other Latin percussionists.

The evolution of son continued in New York via Dominican flautist Johnny Pacheco, leader of the quintessential charanga (featuring singer Pete "El Conde" Rodriguez) but also the leader of the "Africanization" of the charanga (arrangements limited to trumpets, piano and percussion), New York's pianist Charlie Palmieri, who formed in 1959 the influential charanga Duboney (four violins and Pacheco on flute), New York's percussionist

Ernesto "Tito" Puente (*Oye Como Va*, 1962), New York's drummer Ray Barretto, who experimented with rhythm'n'blues and jazz, Puertorican bongo player Roberto Roena (*Mi Desengano*, 1976). New York's pianist Eddie Palmieri, the leader of La Perfecta (a smaller conjunto more prone to improvisation), in 1962 pioneered "trombanga", a sound based on two trombones and a flute (in alternative to the charanga sound). His timbale player Jose-Manuel Oquendo transformed Cuba's carnival rhythm Mozambique into a hypnotic beat for the dancehalls. They all crossed over into jazz and rhythm'n'blues. Notable albums include Puente's **Dance Mania** (1958), Duboney's **Pachanga At The Caravana Club** (1959), Pablo "Tito" Rodriguez's **West Side Beat** (1961), Bobby Valentin's **Ritmo Pa Goza** (1966), Eddie Palmieri's **Lo Que Traigo Es Sabroso** (1964) and **Superimposition** (1969), Barretto's **Acid** (1967) and **The Message** (1972), Cortijo's **Maquina de Tiempo** (1974). Latin New York also secreted the boogaloo, a fusion of black soul music and the Cuban mambo, as in Eddie Palmieri's *Ay Qye Rico* (1968). New York-born Willie Colon, originally a trombonist, was the first major Puertorican star, his orchestra and his singer Hector Lavoe capable of albums such as **El Malo** (1967) and **El Bueno, El Malo y El Feo** (1975), besides the classics *Che Che Cole* (1969) and *Gitana* (1984).

A key event in 1967 was the meeting between Puertorican vocalist Ismael Miranda (then still a teenager) and the orchestra of New York's pianist Larry Harlow, best documented on **Abran Paso** (1970). They revitalized the sound of son for the audience of rock music.

Arabs: Maqam

While widely imitated around the world, the classic "maqam" Islamic style, that basically modulated a monophonic melodic figure, was rarely heard outside the Arab world. This musical system, one of the most intricated modal systems in the world, harks back to the heyday of the Arab empire and was organized during the Ottoman empire. The system (which is not an equally-tempered intonation system, and based on roughly 17 notes to the octave, with plenty of regional variations) prescribes a number of maqamat, that can be used either as finished compositions (typically for solo vocal performances) or as blueprints for composition. The maqam scale has, of course, an influence on the tuning of instruments. There are five makamat for the five daily calls to prayer, but there are also dozens of regional maqamat: Turkey's makam system lists more than 200 distinct modes. It is likely that the Ottomans simply unified a body of styles that they collected from Greece to Central Asia.

Maqam was best represented by Egyptian girl prodigy Umm Kalthum, who first recorded in 1925 and whose orchestra was organized by virtuoso oud player Mohammad el Qasabgi (author of most of her love songs), and by Lebanese Nuhad "Fayrouz" Haddad, who first aired in 1950. Mohammed Abdel Wahab and Riad El-Sombati were the most influential composers of the more traditional music for classical poems. The latter composed several of Umm Kalthum's most ambitious songs: *Salou Qalbi* (1946), a rendition of Omar Khayyam's *Rubayyiat el Khayyam* (1950) and *Al-Atlal* (1966). Among Wahab's collaborators was the Egyptian singer and multi-instrumentalist Abdel Halim Hafez, who rarely recorded. He employed the quasi-psychedelic Egyptian guitarist Omar Khorshid, who later also played for Umm Kalthum.

Indian Classical Music

Indian classical music is based on the ragas ("colors"), which are scales and melodies that provide the foundation for a performance ("raga" in southern India, "raag" in northern India and Pakistan). Unlike western classical music, that is deterministic, Indian classical music allows for a much greater degree of "personalization" of the performance, almost to the level of jazz-like improvisation. Thus, each performance of a raga is different. The goal of the raga is to create a trance-like state, to broadcast a mood of ecstasy. The main difference with western classical music is that the Indian ragas are not "composed" by a composer, but were created via a lengthy evolutionary process over the centuries. Thus they do not represent mind of the composer but a universal idea of the world. They transmit not personal but impersonal emotion. Another difference is that Indian music is monodic, not polyphonic. Hindustani (North Indian) ragas are assigned to specific times of the day (or night) and to specific seasons. Many ragas share the same scale, and many ragas share the same melodic theme. There are thousands of ragas, but six are considered fundamental: Bhairav, Malkauns, Hindol,

Dipak, Megh and Shree. A raga is not necessarily instrumental, and, if vocal, it is not necessarily accompanied. But when it is accompanied by percussion (such as tablas), the rhythm is often rather intricate because it is constructed from a combination of fundamental rhythmic patterns (or talas). The main instrument of the ragas is the sitar, although historically the vina zither was at least equally important. Carnatic (Southern Indian) ragas constitute one of the oldest systems of music in the world. They are based on seven rhythmic cycles and 72 fundamental ragas. The founder of the Karnataka school is considered to be Purandara Dasa (1480). Carnatic music is mostly vocal and devotional in nature, and played with different instruments than Hindustani music (such as the mridangam drum, the ghatam clay pot, the vina sitar as opposed to sitar, sarod, tanpura and tabla). The fundamental format of Carnatic songs is the "kriti", which are usually set in the style of a raga (the raga serves as the melodic foundation). The golden age of Carnatic music was the age of Syama Sastri, who died in 1827, of Tyagaraja, who died in 1847 and who composed the *Pancharatna Krithis* as well as two "operas", *Prahalada Bhakti Vijayam and Nauca Charitam*, and of Muthuswami Dikshitar, who died in 1835 after composing the *Kamalamba Navavarnams* and *the Navagraha krithis*.

Among influential Carnatic musicians, T. R. Mahalingam or "Mali" pioneered continuous flute playing in the 1950s and Palghat Mani Iyer introduced a highly emotional manner of playing mridangam in the 1940s.

However, Indian classical music is mainly a vocal (not only instrumental) art. "Khayal" emerged over the centuries as the vernacular (and romantic) version of "dhrupad" (the oldest extant vocal religious and aristocratic style). Both the sitar and the tabla were probably introduced (in the 18th century) to complement khayal singing. The greatest interpreters of "khayal" documented on record were probably the Pakistani brothers Nazakat Ali Khan and Salamat Ali Khan, who debuted in 1941.

Among women one of the most revered Carnatic singers in the 1950s was Madurai Shanmukhavadivu Subbulakshmi.

A number of musical schools ("gharanas") developed in North India (Hindustan). For example, Abdul Karim Khan created the

Kirana gharana, and Alladiya Khan created the Atrauli-Jaipur gharana.

The Bangash family is credited with the development of the sarod, the second most popular stringed instrument in Hindustani after the sitar. When he migrated to India from his native Afganisthan, Mohammed Hashmi Khan Bangash fused the two traditions on the Afghan instrument rabab, and in the early 19th century his son Ghulam Bandegi Khan Bangash simply modified the rabab to better express this hybrid. Amjad Ali Khan was the descendant of this gharana who fully embraced the recording medium, starting with the ragas of **Amjad Ali Khan** (1967).

The austere, pure Pakistani-born vocalist Pandit Pran Nath, a master of the Kirana style since 1937, moved to the USA in 1970, performing the first morning ragas ever in the USA. His emphasis on perfect intonation and emotional subtlety influenced minimalist composers LaMonte Young and Terry Riley. He only recorded three albums: **Earth Groove** (1968), containing two traditional ragas, *Raga Bhupali Maha Dev* and *Raga Asavari*, **Ragas Yaman Kalyan and Punjabi Berva** (1972), containing his *Raga Yaman Kalyan*, **Ragas of Morning and Night** (1986), containing two 1968 compositions (*Raga Darbari* and *Raga Todi*). He also composed *Raga Anant Bhairavi* (1974), *Raga 12-note Bhairavi* (1979), *Darbar Daoun* (1987), and *Aba Kee Tayk Hamaree* (1989) for voice and string quartet.

Interest in Indian music (until then largely unknown in the west) was triggered by Bangladesh-born sarod player Ali Akbar Khan's 1955 concert in New York. Eventually, western curiosity for Indian music wed the hippy ethos and (thanks mainly to the Byrds' *Eight Miles High*) "raga-rock" became a sonic emblem of the Sixties. Khan's album **Music of India - Morning and Evening Ragas** (1955), containing two side-long ragas (the traditional *Rag Sindhu Bhairavi* and his own *Rag Pilu Baroowa*), was the first Indian classical recording to appear in the West, and the first recording of ragas on an LP. Khan had become famous in India with *Raga Chandranandan*. The popularity of Khan's and Ravi Shankar's concerts led to a stream of recordings in the Sixties, mostly featuring 20-minute long ragas: several EPs from 1961 to 1964, later collected on **Sarod** (1969), **Traditional Music of India** (1962), **The Soul of Indian Music** (1963), **Ustad Ali Akbar Khan** (1964), **India's**

Master Musician by Shankar (recorded in 1963), **Classical Music of India** (1964), **Master Musicians of India** (1964) by Shankar and Khan, containing *Raga Palas Kafi* and *Raga Bilashkani Todi*, **The Soul of Indian Music** (1965), **Sarod** (1965), **Master Musician of India** (1966), containing a 22-minute version of Khan's own *Raga Chandranandan*, **Two Ragas for Sarod** (1967), etc. In 1967, Khan founded the Ali Akbar College of Music in the San Francisco Bay Area, to provide education in the classical music of North India. Among his later performances, there are still impressive ones such as *Raga Basant Mukhari*, off **Artistic Sound of Sarod** (1985). He remained faithful to his roots longer than other Indian performers, eventually experimenting with synthesizers on **Journey** (1991) and with instruments of the western symphonic orchestra on **Garden of Dreams** (1994), basically a raga symphony for a chamber orchestra.

Another disciple of Ali Akbar Khan's father Allaudin Khan, sitar player Ravi Shankar, would become the star of Indian music. He first toured the west in 1956, when he was already a veteran and made friends among pop stars (George Harrison of the Beatles became his student in 1966). Among his historical performances are his masterpiece *Raga Jog*, from **Three Ragas** (1961), the *Raga Rageshri*, on **Improvisations** (1962), and the **Ragas and Talas** (1964), containing the *Raga Jogiya* and the *Raga Madhu Kauns*. **Improvisations** (1962), a collaboration with flautists Paul Horn and Bud Shank, was the first meeting of jazz and raga. Shankar pioneered the "east-west" fusion with **West Meets East** (1967), a terrible collaboration with British violinist Yehudi Menuhin containing both a raga and a sonata. Shankar was also instrumental in turning the raga into a product of mass consumption (he performed at both the 1967 Monterey Festival, the 1969 Woodstock Festival and the 1971 Concert for Bangla Desh), but he soon repudiated his "pop" period and returned to classical music. Nonetheless, he continued to experiment with western music (he performed with western symphonic orchestras and soloists), and, later, starting with **Tana Mana** (1987), even with electronic keyboards. He is a composer, not only a performer, including two sitar concertos (the second, *Raga-Mala*, debuted in 1980).

The same ashram of Ali Akbar Khan's father raised flautist Pannalal Ghosh and sitarist Nikhil Banerjee.

The other major sitarists of Ravi Shankar's generation were Vilayat Khan (a pupil of Wahid Khan, another legendary sitarist) in Indore (central India) and Abdul Halim Jaffer Khan in Kolkata (eastern India).

After relocating to Britain in 1952, Indian violinist John Mayer, had already composed *Raga Music* (1952) for solo clarinet, a *Violin Sonata* (1955), the suite *Dances of India* (1958) for sitar, flute, tabla, tanpura and orchestra, and a *Shanta Quintet* (1966) for sitar and strings. He formed the mixed-race ensemble Indo-Jazz Fusions with jazz saxophonist John Harriott. Mayer thus predated Shankar with the **Indo-Jazz Suite** (october 1965) and **Indo-Jazz Fusions** (september 1966), two albums (mostly composed by Mayer) recorded by a double quintet: Harriott's jazz quintet and an Indian quintet led by Mayer plus Diwan Motihar on sitar, flute, tanpura and tabla. He pursued this idea on **Hum-Dono** (1969), featuring Indian guitarist Amancio D'Silva, trumpeter Ian Carr and vocalist Norma Winstone.

The same sitarist, Diwan Motihar, plus Keshav Sathe on tabla and Kasan Thakur on tanpoura, recorded **Jazz Meets India** (october 1967) with a European quintet led by Swiss pianist Irene Schweizer and featuring German trumpeter Manfred Schoof and drummer Mani Neumaier.

Another precursor of the "east meets west" movement was Shankar's favorite tabla player Allah Rakha, who recorded a duo with jazz drummer Buddy Rich, **Rich A La Rakha** (1968).

Shankar frequently performed with tabla player Alla Rakha. His son Zakir Hussain, also a virtuoso of the tablas, came to the USA in the late 1960s and went on to star in two of the most progressive projects of world-music, Mickey Hart's **Diga Rhythm Band: Diga** (1976) and jazz guitarist John McLaughlin's Shakti. Hussain's **Making Music** (1987), featuring Hariprasad Chaurasia on bansuri, Jan Garbarek on saxophone and John McLaughlin on guitar, was a milestone in jazz-Indian fusion. Another legendary student of Alla Rakha was Yogesh Samsiji.

However, by the time that jazz discovered Indian music, both Davy Graham and Sandy Bull had already toyed with ragas (both in 1963) and in 1965 Robbie Basho had started a whole career based on merging Indian and USA music. Lengthy hybrids such as Paul Butterfield's *East-West* (1966), the Doors' *The End* (1967) and Pink

Floyd's *Set The Controls For the Heart of the Sun* (1967) were already trend-setting.

France: the Chansonniers

During the first decades of the 20th century, Paris was the cultural capital of Europe. Impressionist painters, decadent poets, populist novelists, pioneering filmmakers and folk singers created a colorful milieu that came to be identified with the eccentric side of the "Belle Epoque", the so called "Boheme", centered around the district of Montmartre. Their favorite entertainment was much freer than what the prevailing moral dogmas prescribed. The performers of the "cafe`-concerto" began to sing both satirical and socially-aware tales, while the "cabarets" indulged in crazy dances and outrageous ballets. Entertainment became both a celebration of individual pleasure and a meditation on collective misery. la canzone satirica, che acquistera` via via toni ora grotteschi ora ironici. The tone of popular music turned grotesque, tragic and colloquial, frequently enhanced by "maudit" overtones. Its content shifted towards populist themes, so that popular music became a chronicle of real life. Musicians were also influenced by poets and playwrights, a factor which accounts for the continuous increase in intellectual depth of their songs. Furthermore, popular music came to coexist with avantgarde artists and subversive comedians. Politics, art and entertainment cross-fertilized each other in the cabarets of Paris.

Aristide Bruant, the hero of the "Chat Noir" (which opened in 1881), was the first "auteur" of popular music, followed by Maurice Chevalier and Josephine Baker in the new century.

At the end of World War II, a new spirit revitalized the tradition of the "chansonniers", and new musical ingredients (particularly from the USA) fostered greater complexity and variety. Those were the years of existentialism, and the chansonniers of Paris reflected that zeitgeist. They focused on the working class and the misfits, and they shunned the conformist bourgeoisie: Georges Brassens, whose anarchic epos permeates albums such as **Chante Les Chansons Poetiques** (1953), **Le Parapluie** (1954) and **Les Trompettes De La Renommee** (1962); Jacques Brel, whose melancholy romanticism overflows from *Quand On N'a Que L'Amour* (1957) and *Ne Me Quitte Pas* (1959); Leo Ferré, a militant chansonnier influenced by the surrealists (*Paris Canaille*, 1954; *L'Amour*, 1956) who struck a

philosophical balance between the poet and the politician on **Ferre'
64** (1964); the elegant tenderness of Charles Aznavour (Chahnour
Varenagh Aznaourian) and Gilbert Becaud (*Et Maintenant*, 1962).

The epoch was perhaps best defined by the melodramatic
romanticism of Edith Piaf (Edith Gassion). She was the
quintessential singer of lost love, but frequently set it against a
decadent backdrop of of sex, death and drugs: Michel Emer's
L'Accordeoniste (1940) her own *La Vie en Rose* (1947), Marguerite
Monnot's *Les Trois Cloches* (1946) and *Milord* (1959), Gilbert
Becaud's *Je T'Ai Dans la Peau* (1952) Norbert Glanzberg's *Mon
Manege a Moi* (1958), Charles Domont's *Non Je Ne Regrette Rien*
(1960).

In the 1950s she had to compete with the morbid eroticism of
Juliette Greco, whose early hits were written by famous poets and
set to music by Jozsef Kosma: Raymond Queneau's *Si Tu
T'Imagines* (1949), Jules Laforgue's *L'Eternel Feminin* (1951),
Jacques Prevert's *Je Suis Comme Je Suis* (1951) and *Les Feuilles
Mortes* (1951).

France: the Ye'ye Generation

With the arrival of rock'n'roll in France (Johnny Hallyday), the
chansonniers began to fall out of favor. Even if rockers were never
too popular in France, the "ye'ye" generation identified with younger
and less serious performers. Francoise Hardy was the first ye-ye girl
to write her own songs, the natural link between the chansonniers
and folk-rock. The dreamy, languid, melancholy, angelic, elegant
and seductive style of melodic gems such as *Tous Les Garcons Et
Les Filles* (1962) was thoroughly new. It embodied the hopes and
the angst of her generation.

Serge Gainsbourg (Lucien Ginzburg) destabilized the ye-ye scene
with his sensual and "confidential" songs that, instead, harked back
to the beatnik mood: *Le Poinconneur des Lilas* (1959), *Couleur Cafe*
(1964), *Je T'Aime Moi Non Plus* (1967), *Comment Te Dire Adieu*
(1968), *Soixante Neuf Annee Erotique* (1969). The peak of his
lascivious art was perhaps *Histoire de Melody Nelson* (1971), a
seven-song suite (arranged by Jean Claude Vannier) that chronicles
a pervert's escapade with a nymphet.

Algeria: the Rai

A music whose revolutionary message could compare with the protest songs of the USA and France was the Algerian rai.

At the turn of the century, the port of Oran, or, better, its decadent milieu of sailors, prostitutes and artists, experienced a boom in music that could rival New Orleans or Kansas City. The "cheikhs" and "cheikhas" (young male and young female performers) created a new style that fused Berber, Bedouin and Spanish elements. Conservative clerics disapproved, but Algeria was a colony of France. In the 1930s that music was called wahrani and had already acquired distinct political overtones. This time it was the colonial oppressors who disapproved. Cheikha Rimitti was the first star, the best known of the "shaabi musicians" who cut the soundtrack for Algeria's independence war.

In the 1960s, trumpet player Bellamou Messaoud coined a westernized form of rai, replete with elements of flamenco, blues, rock, jazz and funk, arranged with guitars, saxophone and accordion. He replaced wahrani's qasbah flute with the trumpet. He was appropriately nicknamed **Le Pere du Rai** (1989).

In 1967 the Algerian government banned rai (as well as alcohol). This sent the music underground, and producer Rachid Baba Ahmed became its reference point, helping the chebs and chebas, who took the place of the "cheikhs" and "cheikhas", record cassettes that would spread around the country and in Europe despite the official ban.

Russia: the Intelligentsia

At the same time that protest songwriters were emerging in Europe and the USA, a much more literate generation of songwriters emerged in the Soviet Union, the most brutal regime of the time. Because the censorship organs of the Soviet Union refused to publish any of their works, poets such as Bulat Okudjava since 1946, Alexander Galich (Aleksandr Ginzburg) since 1961, Novella Matveeva, Vladimir Vysotsky in the 1960s and Yuliy Kim since 1956 resorted to music in order to have their lyrics heard by the people. Usually, they set such lyrics to simple accompaniments of acoustic guitar.

Something similar would happen two decades later in Czechoslovakia with Slavek Janousek, Jaromir Nohavica and Jim Cert.

Latin America: the Nueva Cancion

Eduardo Falu virtually founded the modern folk movement of the Spanish-speaking countries of Latin America. His art peaked with the **Romance de la Muerte de Juan Lavalle** (1965), written by poet Ernesto Sabato.

The most famous folksinger to come out of that school was Mercedes Sosa, who debuted with the traditional songs of **La Voz de la Zafra** (1959) and whose most ambitious recording was the concept **Cantata Sudamericana** (1973), composed by Ariel Ramirez and written by Felix Luna.

A better singer-songwriter was Violeta Parra in Chile, who composed the touching *Gracias a la Vida* (1966), one year before committing suicide.

One of the most popular folk groups of the continent was Cuncumán, led in Chile by Victor Jara, who became a national hero when he was tortured and killed in 1973 after a fascist coup.

POST-WAR COUNTRY MUSIC

The Nashville Sound

Chet Atkins' invention (the "Nashville sound", designed as much for the rural southern states as for the big northern cities) spawned the country-pop crossover of Eddy Arnold (*I'll Hold You In My Heart*, 1947; *Bouquet of Roses*, 1948), George Morgan (*Candy Kisses*, 1949); Jim Reeves (*Mexican Joe*, 1953; *Four Walls*, 1957; Joe Allison's *He'll Have to Go*, 1959), Carl Smith (*Loose Talk*, 1954), Faron Young *Live Fast Love Hard Die Young*, 1955; Willie Nelson's *Hello Walls*, 1961), "Sonny" James Loden (*Young Love*, 1956), Ferlin Husky (*Gone*, 1957), Stonewall Jackson (*Waterloo*, 1959), Roger Miller (Ray Price's *Invitation to the Blues*, 1958; *Dang Me*, 1964; his hobo song *King of the Road*, 1965; *England Swings*, 1965), Marty Robbins (Melvin Endsley's *Singing the Blues*, 1955; *A White Sport Coat*, 1956; *El Paso*, 1959), George Jones (JP Richardson's *White Lightning*, 1959; Darrell Edwards' *Tender Years*, 1961; Dickey "Lee" Lipscomb's *She Thinks I Still Care*, 1962; *Walk Through This World With Me*, 1967; Bobby Braddock's *He Stopped Loving Her Today*, 1980), pianist Charlie Rich (*Lonely Weekends*, 1960; *Sittin' and Thinkin'*, 1962; Kenny O'Dell's *Behind Closed Doors*, 1973; *The Most Beautiful Girl*, 1973), Leroy Van Dyke (Kendall Hayes' *Walk On By*, 1961, the top selling country hit of all times), Porter Wagoner (*Misery Loves Company*, 1962; Bill Anderson's *The Cold Hard Facts Of Life*, 1967),, Jimmy Dean (*Big Bad John*, 1961), Dave Dudley (*Six Days On the Road*, 1963), who inaugurated the genre of "trucking songs", former rocker Harold Lloyd "Conway Twitty" Jenkins (*It's Only Make Believe*, 1958; *Next in Line*, 1968; *Hello Darlin'*, 1970), David Houston (*Almost Persuaded*, 1966), Jack Greene (*There Goes My Everything*, 1967), Mac Davis (*In The Ghetto*, 1969; *Baby Don't Get Hooked On Me*, 1972), and Charley Pride, the first black star of Nashville (*All I Have To Offer You Is Me*, 1969).

Ray Price's operatic and throbbing Texan honky-tonk paid off after he formed the Cherokee Cowboys thanks to Ralph Mooney's *Crazy Arms* (1956), his own *You Done Me Wrong* (1956), Billy Walker's *I've Got a New Heartache* (1956), Bob Wills' *My Shoes*

Keep Walking Back to You (1957), and Bill Anderson's *City Lights* (1958).

There had been female pop stars who had successfully recorded country material, such as yodeler Patsy Montana (Rubye Blevins) with *I Wanna Be A Cowboy's Sweetheart* (1935), the first million-seller by a female country singer, Molly O'Day with *The Tramp On The Street* (1949), Patti Page (Clara Fowler) with her version of Frank "Pee Wee" King's *Tennessee Waltz* (1950), one of country music's biggest hits, and Larry Coleman's *Changing Partners* (1953), but it was Kitty Wells (Muriel Deason) who legitimized female country singers with Jay Miller's *It Wasn't God Who Made Honky Tonk Angels*, 1952), and opened the doors of Nashville to: Patsy Cline (Virginia Hensley), whose hits included Don Hecht's *Walking After Midnight* (1957), Hank Cochran's *I Fall To Pieces* (1960), which marked her conversion to the pop ballad, Willie Nelson's *Crazy* (1961), Hank Cochran's *She's Got You* (1962), and Don Gibson's *Sweet Dreams* (1963), which became her signature song; Brenda "Lee" Tarpley (Ronnie Self's *I'm Sorry*, 1960); Skeeter Davis, one of the poppiest of Atkins' singers (*I'm Falling Too*, 1960; *My Last Date*, 1961; *The End Of The World*, 1963; *I Can't Stay Mad At You*, 1963); Loretta "Lynn" Webb (*Success*, 1962; *Don't Come Home A-Drinkin*, 1965; the autobiographical *Coal Miner's Daughter*, 1970); Tammy Wynette (Billy Sherrill's *I Don't Wanna Play House*, 1967; *Stand By Your Man*, 1968).

These were all song-oriented stars, with hardly anything to say other than their voice. The notable exception was Jean Shephard, whose album **Songs Of A Love Affair** (1956) was one of the first concept albums in the history of popular music.

Also an exception was Dolly Parton, equally adept at singing (*Dumb Blonde*, 1967; *Joshua*, 1970; *Jolene*, 1974; Mann & Weil's *Here You Come Again*, 1977; *9 To 5*, 1980; *Think About Love*, 1985) and songwriting (*My Tennessee Mountain Home*, 1969; *Coat Of Many Colors*, 1971; *I Will Always Love You*, 1974; *Wildflowers*, 1987).

Properly speaking, the "Nashville sound" started in the mid 1950s.

The quintessence of the "Nashville sound" was embodied in the instrumentals cut by Atkins' studio pianist Floyd Cramer, such as *Last Date* (1960) and *On The Rebound* (1961), a style derived from a style that Los Angeles' pianist Don Robertson had pioneered with

Hank Locklin's multi-million seller *Please Help Me I'm Falling* (1960).

Among session guitarists, Jerry Reed (*Guitar Man*, 1967) and Lenny Breau were perhaps the most influential.

Nashville Songwriters

Johnny Cash bridged the world of country music, rock'n'roll and the folk revival with the epic narratives of *Folsom Prison Blues* (1956), *I Walk The Line* (1956), which remained his signature song, *Ballad Of The Teenage Queen* (1958).

The Louvin Brothers were the main defenders of the old order, both musically (they harked back to the Appalachian sound) and morally (they sang of churches and domestic joys), but their songs, such as *You're Running Wild* (1956) and *My Baby's Gone* (1959), evolved the vocal harmonies of the Delmore Brothers towards the style of the Everly Brothers, and their album **Tragic Songs of Life** (1956) pioneered the intimate singer-songwriter style.

Don Gibson wrote three classics: *Sweet Dreams* (1955), *Oh Lonesome Me* (1958), and *I Can't Stop Lovin You* (1958).

John Loudermilk's million-sellers (for other artists), such as *A Rose And A Babe Ruth* (1956) for George Hamilton, *Waterloo* (1959), *Sad Movies* (1961), *The Language Of Love* (1961), *Norman* (1962), *Abilene* (1963) for George Hamilton, *Tobacco Road* (1964), and *Indian Reservation* (1971), ran the gamut from pop to folk, from rock to country.

Songwriter Bill Anderson rejuvenated country music with the realism of *City Lights* (1958), launched by Ray Price, and the romanticism of *Mama Sang A Sad Song* (1962), besides writing *The Cold Hard Facts Of Life* (1967) for Porter Wagoner, while Harlan Howard represented the conservative wing of Nashville with *Pick Me Up On Your Way Down* (1958) and *Heartaches by the Number* (1959), both written for Ray Price.

Shel Silverstein composed (with a self-parodying sense of humour) *The Unicorn Song* (1961), *A Boy Named Sue* (1969), *Queen Of The Silver Dollar* (1973), and recorded loony collections such as **Freaking At the Freakers Ball** (1979).

A genre within the genre was the "truck-driving song". Perhaps the most sophisticated were produced by Woodrow "Red" Sovine: *Giddy up Go* (1966), *Phantom 309* (1967), *Teddy Bear* (1976).

Mickey Newbury was a songwriter specializing in heartbreaking stories, such as *Just Dropped In* (1968) and *She Even Woke Me Up To Say Goodbye* (1969), who also crafted the historical saga of *An American Trilogy* (1971).

Even more sophisticated was Tom Hall, the dramatic poet of small-town America: *Harper Valley PTA* (1968) for Jeannie Riley, *Ballad Of Forty Dollars* (1968), *A Week In A County Jail* (1969), *Salute To A Switchblade* (1970), *Kentucky Feb 27 1971* (1971), *Trip To Hyden* (1971), *The Year That Clayton Delaney Died* (1971), *Old Dogs, Children and Watermelon Wine* (1973), *Pamela Brown* (1974). These detailed narrative songs emphasized the dignity of hillbillies.

Dallas Frazier, the author of the silly novelty *Alley Oop* (1960), credited to the Hollywood Argyles, was actually a serious storyteller whose ballads were bleak frescoes of ordinary hard lives: *There Goes My Everything* (1966), *The Son Of Hickory Holler's Tramp* (1968), *California Cottonfields* (1969).

Bob McDill was a specialist of gentle romantic country music, as proven by *Amanda* (1973), sung by Don Williams.

In Texas, country music coexisted shoulder to shoulder with "tex-mex", the music (accordion-driven, and based on polka and waltz) of the chicanos. Freddy Fender was the main chicano to cross over into country music, with *Wasted Days And Wasted Nights* (1959), and then pop music, with *Before The Next Teardrop Falls* (1975).

Bakersfield: Honky-tonk

However, the most exciting place to be (artistically, if not commercially, speaking) was Bakersfield, a California town northeast of Los Angeles, where two giants of country music founded a new school of (hard-edged) honky-tonk at a time when Nashville was selling out to orchestral pop.

The lively, cadenced sound of Buck Owens' songs straddled the border between country music and rock music because it was driven by two guitars, a country (slide) guitar and a rock (electric) guitar (Don Rich), the two pillars of his Buckaroos: *Under Your Spell Again* (1959), which sounded like soul music, Johnny Russell's *Act Naturally* (1963), which sounded like rock'n'roll, *Under the Influence of Love* (1961), *Love's Gonna Live Here* (1963), *Tiger By*

The Tail (1964), Rich's *Waiting in Your Welfare Line* (1966), *Tall Dark Stranger* (1969).

Merle Haggard, a fan of Lefty Frizzell who grew up both an old-fashioned rambler and a modern juvenile delinquent (thus destined to bridge country music and rock music), adopted a similar two-guitar sound. From Wynn Stewart's *Sing Me A Sad Song* (1965) to Liz Anderson's existential dirges *Strangers* (1965) and *I'm A Lonesome Fugitive* (1966), from his first album of (mostly) original compositions, **Swinging Doors** (1966), containing *The Bottle Let Me Down*, from the transitional hits *Sing Me Back Home* (1967), *I Threw Away the Rose* (1967) and *Today I Started Loving You Again* (1968) to the mature social fresco of *Hungry Eyes* (1969), from the anti-hippie anthem *Okie From Muskogee* (1969) to the workers' lament of *If We Make It Through December* (1974), via the concept album **Someday We'll Look Back** (1971), Haggard paid tribute to his own depressing autobiography and to the even more depressing condition of the white working class.

Nashville: Country-pop

On the other side of the barricade, Kenny Rogers, a former member of the New Christy Minstrels, applied his slow, flowing baritone in mellow and bland story-ballads such as Mickey Newbury's *Just Dropped In* (1968), Mel Tillis' *Ruby Don't Take Your Love To Town* (1969), *Lucille* (1977), Don Schlitz's *The Gambler* (1978), *Coward Of The County* (1979). The string orchestra accompanied most of his romantic hits: *She Believes In Me* (1979), Lionel Richie's *Lady* (1980), *Don't Fall In Love With A Dreamer* (1980), Bob Seger's *We've Got Tonight* (1983), the Bee Gees' *Islands In The Stream* (1983).

The simple, laid-back mood of Glen Campbell was revealed by John Hartford's *Gentle On My Mind* (1967), and became the main vehicle for Jimmy Webb's songs.

Bobby Goldsboro, Roy Orbison's former guitarist, was the ultimate romantic of country music, with Bobby Russell's *Honey* (1968), *Autumn of My Life* (1968), *Watching Scotty Grow* (1970), *With Pen In Hand* (1972).

Ray "Stevens" Ragsdale was the main composer of novelty ditties, a subgenre that became extremely popular in the 1960s, such as *Ahab The Arab* (1962), *Gitarzan* (1969) and *The Streak* (1974), although his biggest hit was the social meditation of *Everything Is Beautiful* (1970).

Soul Music
The Founding Fathers of Soul Music

The gospel revival and doo-wop merged into the great season of soul music. Soul music was enabled by the commercial boom of "race" music, that had led to the creation of channels and infrastructures run by black entrepreneurs for black artists. This class of black entrepreneurs hired and trained a generation of session musicians, producers and arrangers (not to mention songwriters) who were specifically meant to serve the needs of black music. Soul music was also enabled by an unstoppable trend towards black and white integration, as more and more white folks accepted the idea that black culture was not evil or degrading, simply different (African instead of European). The sociopolitical inroads made by jazz also helped legitimize black pop music with the white masses. Soul music was also, indirectly, helped by rock music, precisely because rock music made white pop music sound so obsolete. Rock music buried white pop music but did not quite offer an alternative. On the other hand, rock music legitimized black pop music (rock music was basically a white version of rhythm'n'blues), and black pop music did offer an anternative to the Italian crooners and the likes.

As the civil rights movement staged bigger and bigger demonstrations and increased African-American pride, soul music became more than party music for young blacks: it became a rallying flag for the black nationalist movement. While never truly political in nature, soul music's ascent in the pop charts came to represent one of the first (and most visible) successes of the civil-rights movement.

Soul music was born thanks to the innovations of a generation of post-war musicians who, essentially, turned gospel music into a secular form of art.

Los Angeles-based vocalist (inspired by Charles Brown and therefore Nat King Cole) and pianist Ray Charles Robinson, soon to become the most famous blind person in America, succeeded by setting mundane lyrics to gospel tunes, famously in *I Got A Woman* (1955), and coined a hybrid blues-jazz-gospel group sound with the lengthy *What'd I Say* (1959), before turning into one of the first crossover black artists with Hoagy Carmichael's *Georgia On My Mind* (1960), Percy Mayfield's *Hit The Road Jack* (1961), Don Gibson's *I Can't Stop Loving You* (1962), Fred Rose's *Take These Chains From My Heart* (1963), an ideological turn illustrated by the best-selling album **Modern Sounds In Country And Western Music** (1962).

Georgia's vocalist James Brown and his band (featuring Jimmy Nolen on guitar, the inventor of the 16-note strumming style that defined funk music once and for all, Alfred "Pee Wee" Ellis on alto sax, Maceo Parker on tenor sax, Fred Wesley on trombone, and, in the 1970s, William "Bootsy" Collins on bass), clarified the relation between sexual lust and religious fervor via *Please Please Please* (1956), *Try Me* (1958) and *I'll Go Crazy* (1960). It took several years for the rest of soul music to catch up with his intuition, but eventually his monotonous and anti-virtuoso style created a new kind of music. Brown coined a frenzied style of choppy rhythms and jazzy horns, coupled with stage histrionics and a grotesquely choreographed show, first documented on **Live At The Apollo** (1962). At the same time, his visceral falsetto shrieks amid guttural lascivious wails (and lyrics full of sexual innuendos) invented a new narrative form. With *Out Of Sight* (1964), *Papa's Got A Brand New Bag* (1965), *I Got You* (1965) and *Cold Sweat* (1967), Brown coined a purely-percussive style of soul, the predecessor of "funk". and associated himself with black nationalism starting with *Say It Aloud I'm Black and Proud* (1968). The novelties *Give It Up* (1969), *Mother Popcorn* (1969) and *Superbad* (1970) further streamlined the idea and led to the quintessential Brown-ian funk songs, *Sex Machine* (1970), with Bootsy Collins on bass (and a piano figure that virtually invented house-music), and *King Heroin* (1972). The deadly combination of psychotic falsetto, metallic guitar strumming, fractured bass lines, noisy horn section and pulsing polyrhythm was dance-music to the square.

Chicago-raised Sam Cooke, who had already contributed *Be With Me Jesus* (1955) and *Touch the Hem Of His Garment* (1956) to the Soul Stirrers, used his crisp melismatic tenor to deliver Bumps Blackwell's *You Send Me* (1957), one of the biggest hits of the era, and some of the most imitated ballads of the pop-soul genre: Lou Adler's *Only Sixteen* (1959), *Wonderful World* (1960), and then, after producers Hugo (Peretti) & Luigi (Creatore) adopted him,

Twistin' The Night Away (1961), *Cupid* (1961), *Bring It On Home To Me* (1962), *Another Saturday Night* (1963), the prophetic *A Change Is Gonna Come* (december 1963) that would become a signature song of the Civil Rights Movement.

Detroit-born Jackie Wilson, McPhatter's substitute in the Dominoes and perhaps the greatest vocal gymnast of the era, benefited from three Berry Gordy compositions, *Reet Petite* (1957), *To Be Loved* (1958) and especially *Lonely Teardrops* (1958), that formed the model for lavishly arranged melodramatic ballads exuding his sexual charisma such as *A Woman A Lover A Friend* (1960), *Doggin' Around* (1960), *Baby Workout* (1963) and the acrobatic, multi-octave *Danny Boy* (1965).

Brown and Charles (the two sound stylists) were raised in the South, whereas Cooke and Wilson (the two vocal virtuosi) were fully urban.

Another of the soul pioneers, Detroit-based vocalist "Little Willie John" Woods introduced the quavering gospel falsetto (that James Brown learned from him). The melancholy of *Need Your Love So Bad* (1956), perhaps his most intense performance, and *Sufferin' With The Blues* (1956) established the quintessential soul mood, while his versions of Otis Blackwell's *Fever* (1956) and of Titus Turner's *All Around The World* (1958) created an even more passionate style of singing.

New York gospel singer Roy Hamilton, who had achieved stardom status with his interpretation of Alex North's *Unchained Melody* (1955), created a gospel-tinged pop style, best epitomized by later material such as *Don't Let Go* (1958), that was influential on soul music.

Soul Singer-songwriters

Soul music was perceived to be a music for vocalists, but songwriters were, from the beginning, no less important to define the style.

Chuck Wills was a delicate and evocative singer from Atlanta, who penned his own *My Story* (1952), *You're Still My Baby* (1954), *I Feel So Bad* (1954) and *It's Too Late* (1956), before striking gold with *CC Rider* (1957), an adaptation of Ma Rainey's standard from the 1920s.

South Carolina-born baritone Brook Benton (Benjamin Peay), a former member of the Golden Gate Quartet, was the main songwriter of this generation, dishing out *A Lover's Question* (1958), a hit for Clyde McPhatter, *It's Just A Matter of Time* (1959), *Thank You Pretty Baby* (1959), *So Many Ways* (1959), *The Ties that Bind* (1960), *The Same One* (1960), *Kiddio* (1960), etc.

Another South Caroliner, Don Covay moved away from his dance novelties *Bip Bop Bip* (1959) and *Pony Time* (1961) to pen soul ballads such as *You Can Run* (1962) for Jerry Butler, *Letter Full Of Tears* (1962) for Gladys Knight, his two classics *Mercy Mercy* (1964) and *See Saw* (1965), and the mega-hit *Chain Of Fools* (1967) for Aretha Franklin.

Bobby Womack, Sam Cooke's guitarist, wrote *Lookin' For A Love* (1962) and *It's All Over Now* (1964) that crossed over into rock'n'roll, and later would reinvent his career as a romantic soul balladeer with *That's the Way I Feel About 'Cha* (1971) and *Woman's Gotta Have It* (1972).

Nina Simone (Eunice Waymon), the "high priestess of soul", an eclectic interpreter of both blues, jazz and pop classics, composed *My Baby Just Cares For Me* (1958), *Mississippi Goddam* (1963), *Four Women* (1966), and *Young Gifted And Black* (1969). *Please Don't Let Me Be Misunderstood* (1964) was written for her by songwriters Bennie Benjamin and Sol Marcus. As the controversial lyrics of these songs prove, the angry young woman of soul music also represented the link with the folksingers of the "Movement".

Chicago's soul music was dominated by the artistic persona of guitarist, songwriter, arranger and vocalist Curtis Mayfield, whose Impressions created a smooth, majestic, orchestral, jazzy style with carefully crafted vocal and horns arrangements to accompany his allegorical messages: *For Your Precious Love* (1958), one of the candidates to first soul record, *Gypsy Woman* (1961), the rumba-like *It's All Right* (1963) the anthemic *Keep On Pushin'* (1964) and *People Get Ready* (1965), the baroque *Choice of Colors* (1969). As a solo artist, Mayfield pioneered the format of the extended message-oriented psychedelic funk-pop shuffle on his concept albums **Curtis** (1971) and **Roots** (1972), and then applied the idea to the danceable soundtrack for the film **Superfly** (1972).

Soul and Rock

While they had little in common, soul and rock interacted from the beginning.

Cleveland's shouter "Screamin'" Jay Hawkins, the first great gothic perfomer, who had studied opera and whose stage antics were the horror counterpart to the sexual histrionics of most black singers, experimented bizarre vocal styles in his demented melodramas *I Put A Spell On You* (1956) and *Constipation Blues* (1967), with Plas Johnson on sax.

Virginia's demonic soul-rocker Gary "U.S. Bonds" Anderson coined the rough, exuberant rhythm'n'blues sound of *New Orleans* (1960), Gene Barge's *Quarter to Three* (1961), *School's Out* (1961).

Soul Styles

Soul music retained its vocals-driven image, typical of all pop music, but, like so much pop music, its hits became increasingly dependent on the skills of the arrangers and producers. In other words, soul music mutated transparently from a vocal style into a sound style.

This mutation took place mainly in four places: New York, Memphis, Detroit, Philadelphia. And it corresponded with four independent labels, respectively: Atlantic (founded in 1947 by white songwriter Ahmet Ertegun), Stax (founded in 1959 by white country fiddler Jim Stewart), Tamla Motown (founded in 1959 by black entrepreneur Berry Gordy), and, much later, International (founded in 1971 by Kenny Gamble and Leon Huff).

The sound of Atlantic was largely the invention of producer (and former critic) Jerry Wexler, hired in 1953. The peak of Atlantic's reign on soul music came in 1967 when Wexler started working with arranger Arif Mardin and engineer Tom Dowd.

Former Philadelphia preacher Solomon Burke transferred the fervor of his sermons into the stirring rhythms of black dance music. Needless to say, his live shows became legendary for their delirious intensity, second only to James Brown. His material ranged from Virgil Stewart's *Just Out Of Reach* (1961), possibly the first country crossover by a soul artist, to Bert Berns' *Cry To Me* (1961), Gene Pitney's *If You Need Me* (1963), Alain Toussaint's *Got To Get You Off My Mind* (1964), Bert Berns' *Everybody Needs Somebody To*

Love (1964), his own *The Price* (1964), perhaps his vocal masterpiece, and Don Covay's *Tonight's The Night* (1965).

Wexler's greatest discovery was Aretha Franklin, a Detroit gospel singer whom Wexler turned into the female counterpart of Ray Charles, pitting her exuberant and aggressive vocals (that mixed blues phrasing and melisma) and her romantic lyrics against sensual and agitated rhythms. But Franklin's strategy was, in a sense, the opposite of Charles': instead of secularizing sacred music, Franklin sanctified her own private life. Charles transferred religious love into bodily love, while Franklin exalted bodily love as a vehicle to salvation or redemption. She staged with church fervor the most intimate female emotions, such as the need to be loved, the frustration of not being loved, and the ecstasis of being loved. Compared with the attitude, the material was negligible, and it came from disparate sources (blues, pop, soul): Ronnie Shannon's *I Never Loved A Man* (1967), Otis Redding's *Respect* (1967), which she transformed into a piano-based anthem of female pride, Ronnie Shannon's *Baby I Love You* (1967), Don Covay's *Chain Of Fools* (1967), Carole King's and Gerry Goffin's *A Natural Woman* (1967), which acted as the complementary anthem to *Respect*, her own *Since You've Been Gone* (1968), her own *Think* (1968), Burt Bacharach's *I Say A Little Prayer* (1968).

Vocalists of other big cities shared the same spirit.

Fontella Bass was perhaps the most vibrant soul singer of the Chicago area, breathing life into Oliver Sain's *Don't Mess Up A Good Thing* (1965) and Raynard Miner's *Rescue Me* (1965), with the young Maurice White on drums, before joining the jazz avantgarde (the Art Ensemble Of Chicago). Predating Franklin, her touch was bluesier and less poppy.

Los Angeles-based vocalist Dobie Gray (Leonard Ainsworth) recorded in a sandpaper voice Billy Page's *The In Crowd* (1965), the quintessential mod anthem, *Out On The Floor* (1966), and Mentor Williams' *Drift Away* (1973).

Southern Soul

The sound Of Stax, an elegant hybrid of rhythm'n'blues and country'n'western with simple arrangements and sober rhythms, was largely the sound of its session musicians (and their first producer, Chips Moman). The Mar-Kays' instrumental hit version of Chips

Moman's *Last Night* (1961) pretty much set the standard for all subsequent Stax productions: punchy horns section (two trumpets and two saxophones) and powerful rhythm section (groovy organ, staccato guitar, bass and drums). The band's guitarist, Steve Cropper, one of the most original guitarists since Lowman Pauling, whose stinging riffs bridged country and blues, joined saxophonist and keyboardist Booker Jones and drummer Al Jackson to form Booker T. & The MGs, that released the similar instrumental shuffle *Green Onion* (1962), while trumpet player Wayne Jackson formed the Memphis Horns. These remained the house bands for all Stax musicians.

Among the classics crafted by this "team" were: Carla Thomas' *Gee Whiz* (1961), produced by Chips Moman, and *B-A-B-Y* (1966), written by Isaac Hayes, songwriter William Bell's *You Don't Miss Your Water* (1962), Rufus Thomas' dance novelties, such as *Walking The Dog* (1963) and *Do The Funky Chicken* (1970), Eddie Floyd's *Knock On Wood* (1966), a Cropper composition, Arthur Conley's *Sweet Soul Music* (1967), an Otis Redding rewrite of Sam Cooke's *Yeah Man* that sounded like the label's aesthetic manifesto, Albert "King" Nelson's *Born Under A Bad Sign* (1967), a William Bell song that crystallized the Stax ensemble sound, the hits for Johnnie Taylor (another ex-Soul Stirrers), such as Isaac Hayes' *I Had A Dream* (1967) and *Who's Making Love* (1968), and those for Sam (Moore) and Dave (Prater), *Hold On* (1966) and *Soul Man* (1967), both composed by Isaac Hayes, etc.

The Memphis sound was epitomized by Wexler's productions for Wilson Pickett, setting the singer's wicked and visceral delivery against Steve Cropper's lean/mean guitar and against the house band's majestic explosions of sound (frantic horns, gospel choir, fearsome drums). Steve Cropper composed his classics *In The Midnight Hour* (1964) and *634-5789* (1966). Then came equally invigorating performances for Chris Kenner's *Land Of 1000 Dances* (1966), and Bonnie "Mack" Rice's *Mustang Sally* (1967). *Funky Broadway* (1967) was the cover of a genre-defining song, already written and performed in James Brown's vein by Arlester "Dyke" Christian, the voice and the brain behind Dyke & The Blazers.

The moving voice of Georgia-born Otis Redding, who died at 26, created a new emotional standard for southern soul. Equally important were the tight arrangements of guitarist Steve Cropper, in which the instrumental backing de facto replaced the gospel choir, turning the traditional call-and-response structure into a dialogue between voice and horns, and between voice and guitar. His own *These Arms Of Mine* (october 1962) and *Pain In My Heart* (september 1963), which was a cover of Irma Thomas' *Ruler of My Heart* (1962), Steve Cropper's *Mr Pitiful* (december 1964), his own *Respect* (july 1965), a metaphorical declaration of black pride camouflaged as a sexual plea, opened an almost metaphysical dimension to soul music, backed by one of the greatest rhythm sections of the time (Cropper on guitar, Booker T. Jones on piano, Donald Dunn on bass, Al Jackson on drums, and occasionally Isaac Hayes on organ). His version of Jerry Butler's *I've Been Lovin' You Too Long* (april 1965) became the quintessential seduction song. The last two gems that he composed with Cropper, *Fa-fa-fa-fa-fa* (august 1966) and *Dock Of The Bay* (december 1967), were increasingly tender, ethereal and extraterrestrial.

Overton Wright cried and sobbed in *That's How Strong My Love Is* (1964), *You're Gonna Make Me Cry* (1965), and *Eight Men Four Women* (1967), three of the most melodramatic performances of southern soul, as well as wailing in the intense and haunting Willie Mitchell productions of *Ace Of Spades* (1970), *A Nickel and a Nail* (1971), and *I'd Rather Be Blind Crippled and Crazy* (1973).

Another influential Memphis singer, James Carr recorded Baker and McCormick's *Pouring Water On A Drowning Man* (1966) and especially Chips Moman's poignant *Dark End of the Street* (1967), as well as two Obie McClinton compositions, *You've Got My Mind Messed Up* (1966) and *A Man Needs A Woman* (1968).

If Memphis was the epicenter, it certainly wasn't the only source of southern soul.

The queen of New Orleans soul was Irma Thomas, who penned three self-written gems such as *Don't Mess With My Man* (1961), *Ruler Of My Heart* (1962) and *Wish Someone Would Care* (1964), as well as premiering Jerry Ragavoy's *Time Is On My Side* (1964).

Joe Tex (Joseph Arrington), from Texas, sang witty stories in a rather limited falsetto against Memphis-style arrangements, alternating his singing with sermon-style raps. *Hold What You've Got* (1964) was the first southern soul song to become a national hit, followed by *The Love You Save* (1965), the dance novelty *Skinny Legs And All* (1967) and *I Gotcha* (1972). His album **From the**

Roots Came the Rapper (1971) was one of the first instances that a street poet was called a "rapper", and included extended versions of Burt Bacharach's *I'll Never Fall In Love Again* and Jim Doris' *Oh Me Oh My*.

The purest phrasing was Percy Sledge's, the devoted Alabama tenor of *When A Man Loves A Woman* (1966), composed by Jimmy Hughes' organist Andrew Wright and bassist Calvin Lewis, and featuring "church" organ by Dewey Oldham, who composed Sledge's other two jewels, *It Tears Me Up* (1966) and *Out Of Left Field* (1967). Another impeccable demonstration of his country-soul style was *Take Time To Know Her* (1968).

The next big thing to happen to southern soul was Isaac Hayes' extended orchestral raps, that debuted on **Presenting** (1967) with a lengthy cover of Erroll Garner's *Misty*, and that matured on the four-song album **Hot Buttered Soul** (1969), including colossal covers of Jimmy Webb's *By The Time I Get To Phoenix* and Burt Bacharach's *Walk On By*. This style of subdued singing and lavish production was further revolutionized by the soundtrack to the film **Shaft** (1971), that added a strong funky undercurrent, setting the stage for disco-music.

Willie Mitchell organized another artistic colony in Memphis by hiring veterans of Booker T. And The MG's and producing the mellow hits of singer-songwriter Ann Peebles, notably *Slipped Stumbled and Fell In Love* (1971), *I'm Gonna Tear Your Playhouse Down* (1973) and *I Can't Stand The Rain* (1974).

Mitchell's southern-soul productions also propelled the erotic hymns of Al Green: Green's own *Tired Of Being Alone* (1971) and Mitchell's *Let's Stay Together* (1971), *Look What You Done To Me* (1972), *I'm Still In Love With You* (1972), as well as Green's own *Take Me To The River* (1974). These productions expressed the ultimate contradiction of soul music, the tension between sex and God.

Detroit Soul

The sound of Detroit's soul music was the sound of Berry Gordy's Tamla Motown, the greatest success story of a black entrepreneur in the music business.

Gordy borrowed the concept from the assembly lines of Detroit's car industry: Tamla's hits were manufactured on industrial scale by a team of skilled professionals. Composers and producers included the trio of Brian Holland, Lamont Dozier and Eddie Holland (alias H-D-H), the duo of Nick Ashford and Valerie Simpson, as well as Norman Whitfield and Smokey Robinson. Sessions musicians (the Funk Brothers) included bassist James Jamerson (one of the most influential bassists of all times), drummer Benny Benjamin, saxophonist Hank Crosby, trombonist Paul Riser, trumpet player Herbie Williams, guitarists Robert White, keyboardists Joe Hunter and Earl Van Dyke.

Gordy's "Motown sound" was the least "black" and most "white" of the various soul styles. His hits were catchy and elementary. Arrangements overflew with strings and other orchestral instruments. Rhythms were driving and infectious. The vocals and the instrumental backdrop had little of the psychological sophistication of southern soul: Tamla's hits were emphatic and epic. The "call-and-response" structure was largely abandoned, and the new center of the song became the melodic "hook". The lyrics targeted the lifestyle of teenagers.

The first hits were, actually, plain party music: Barrett Strong's *Money* (1960), written by Berry Gordy, the Miracles' *Shoparound* (1960), written by Smokey Robinson, the Contours' *Do You Love Me* (1962), written by Berry Gordy, Martha (Reeves) & The Vandellas' *Dancing In The Street* (1964), written by William Stevenson, pianist Frederick "Shorty" Long's *Devil With A Blue Dress On* (1964), and saxophonist Junior Walker's instrumental *Shotgun/ Hot Cha* (1965).

H-D-H, the greatest tunesmiths of the era, also wrote *Heat Wave* (1963) and *Nowhere To Run* (1965), whose booming arrangement was an exercise in excessive rapture, for Martha & The Vandellas, *Please Mr Postman* (1961) for the Marvelettes, *Can I Get A Witness* (1963) and *How Sweet It Is To Be Loved by You* (1964) for Marvin Gaye, and virtually all the hits for the Supremes, a female trio (the most commercially successful in history), and for the Four Tops, a male quartet.

The simple, infectious melodies of the Supremes embodied the romantic exuberance of the Sixties: *Where Did Our Love Go* (1964), *Baby Love* (1964), *Stop In The Name Of Love* (1965), *I Hear A Symphony* (1965), *My World Is Empty Without You* (1965), *You Can't Hurry Love* (1965). On her own, Diana Ross indulged in vocal tours de force for Ashford's and Simpson's *Ain't No Mountain High Enough* (1970), Gerry Goffin's pathetic *Do You Know Where Are You Going To* (1975), and Pam Sawyer's and Marilyn McLeod's erotic disco monolith *Love Hangover* (1976).

The Four Tops excelled both at melodrama, as in *Baby I Need Your Loving* (1964) and *Reach Out I'll Be There* (1966), both marked by Levi Stubbs' blues lament and highly emotional harmonies, besides H-D-H's cataclysmic arrangement (the latter a concerto for piano and strings), and at sprightly party dance music, such as *I Can't Help Myself* (1965) and *Same Old Song* (1965). With the mystical overtones and morbid introversion of *Standing In The Shadows Of Love* (1966) and *Bernadette* (1967) they transcended passion and ghetto.

The H-D-H trio rank among the greatest pop phenomenon of all times. Their songs were a simplified form of soul music, but these were the kind of black music that white radio stations had no problem broadcasting. They were meant to inspire dances at private parties, they complied with the conventions of the romantic ballad, they were sung by polite singers, and they implied no more than the usual stories of falling in love and heartbreak. There were none of the controversial elements of the Afro-American culture that had alarmed white parents when their children were listening to rhythm'n'blues.

Norman Whitfield penned some of the most dramatic and creative productions, from the epochal *I Heard It Through The Grapevine* (1967), a concentrate of anxiety (largely packed by the instrumental choreography of piano, guitar, drums, strings and horns), sung by Marvin Gaye and later Gladys Knight And The Pips, to most of the Temptations' classics, from Edwin Starr's *War* (1970) to Rare Earth's *I Just Want To Celebrate* (1971).

The Temptations, featuring baritone David Ruffin and tenor Eddie Kendricks, were more stylish than the Four Tops thanks first to the baroque productions of Smokey Robinson's *My Girl* (1965) and *Since I Lost My Baby* (1965), and then to the psychedelic visions of Norman Whitfield: *Cloud Nine* (1968), *Runaway Child* (1969), *I Can't Get Next To You* (1969), *Psychedelic Shack* (1970), *Ball Of Confusion* (1970), and the suite *Masterpiece* (1973), ever more bizarre despite lighter fare such as the ballad *Just My Imagination* (1971) and the funky *Papa Was A Rolling Stone* (1972).

William "Smokey" Robinson was both a gifted melodic composer, a fluent vocalist, a consummate poet and a creative arranger. He composed the Miracles' *Shoparound* (1960), Mary Wells' *My Guy* (1964), the Temptations' *My Girl* (1965) and *Since I Lost My Baby* (1965), Marvin Gaye's *Ain't That Peculiar* (1965), *One More Heartache* ((1966), and *I'll Be Doggone* (1965). The Miracles were his own group, and they delivered his best material: *You Really Got A Hold On Me* (1963), *The Tracks Of My Tears* (1965), *I Second That Emotion* (1967) and the baroque, breathtaking *The Tears Of A Clown* (1970). Robinson did not merely create catchy refrains, he created mini-dramas or mini-symphonies. He also became the epitome of the romantic soul vocalist of the post-Cooke era.

One of the most expressive male vocalists of the era, Marvin Gaye, capable of impersonating both the party dancer, the romantic lover, the hostile mod/punk and the political activist, breathed life into H-D-H's *Can I Get A Witness* (1963) and *How Sweet It Is To Be Loved By You* (1964), Smokey Robinson's *I'll Be Doggone* (1965), *One More Heartache* ((1966) and *Ain't That Peculiar* (1965), Norman Whitfield's *I Heard It Through The Grapevine* (1967), Ashford's and Simpson's *Ain't No Mountain High Enough* (1967). Gaye the songwriter exploded in 1971, with the socially aware and orchestrally-arranged concept album **What's Going On** (1971), one of the albums that shifted the emphasis from the "song" to the ambience. The less intense and dense **Let's Get It On** (1973) was more sound-oriented and returned to his erotic persona, a transition towards the abstract melodic fantasies of **I Want You** (1976), co-written with Leon Ware.

Stevie "Wonder" Judkins/Morris, the blind multi-instrumentalist *enfant prodige* of Henry Cosby's *Fingertips* (1963), Henry Cosby's and Sylvia Moy's *Uptight* (1966) and *My Cherie Amour* (1969), Ron Miller's and Bryan Wells' *A Place In The Sun* (1966) and *Yester-me Yester-day* (1969), grew up to become an adventurous composer and arranger. Wonder crafted concept albums that moved from the format of the extended song towards the format of the electronic-funk-jazz-pop jam via production tours de force: **Music Of My Mind** (1972), a collaboration with electronic musicians Robert Margouleff and Malcolm Cecil of the Tonto's Expanding Head Band, the first collection written, produced and played (mostly) by himself (already a veteran at the age of 22); **Talking Book** (1972), with the funky work-out *Superstition* and the romantic *You Are The Sunshine Of My Heart*; **Innervisions** (1973), a social fresco of symphonic proportions; the monumental and ambitious **Songs In The Key Of Life** (1976); and the mostly instrumental **Journey Through the Secret Life of Plants** (1979). Till the end, his artistic life was schizophrenic in its attempt to please both the masses, with catchy tunes such as *I Just Called To Say I Love You* (1984) and *Part-time Lover* (1985), and his spiritual alter-ego.

In 1973 Motown moved from Detroit to Los Angeles, a sign that an era had come to an end.

The importance of soul music

Soul music was, fundamentally, a consequence of rock music. The leadership went from the blacks (rhythm'n'blues) to the whites (rock'n'roll) back to the blacks (soul). Soul music was everything that rock music was: dance music, personal expression, teenage angst, political rebellion. Rock'n'roll had stolen the body (the sound) of rhythm'n'blues, and soul music stole the soul (the spirit) of rock'n'roll.

From a musical point of view, the aesthetic priorities of soul music were rather different from those of blues music. The singer was still the center of action, but the arrangement (the ambience, the soundscape) was way more important than in rhythm'n'blues. The great figures of soul music were, first and foremost, arrangers.

The mystical element of blues music was largely lost, replaced by sociopolitical awareness and a philosophical inquiry into the meaning of life; or simply by enjoyment of life. In many ways, one could claim that soul music was the result of black musicians adopting the European stance about artistic matters: intellectual, creative, melodic.

At the same time, soul music introduced a new form of dancing: elegant, sensual and nonetheless primal.

Philly Soul

During the 1970s, Tamla Motown was replaced at the helm of soul music by Philadelphia International. Kenny Gamble and Leon Huff added lavish orchestrations and disco rhythms to the new wave of Detroit's soft soul music. Their house band, the MFSB, was their equivalent of the MG's. Their sound was defined via the Intruders'

Cowboys to Girls (1968), Jerry Butler's *Only The Strong Survive* (1969), the O'Jays' *Back Stabbers* (1972), female trio Three Degrees' *When Will I See You Again* (1974), and, above all, *If You Don't Know Me By Now* (1972) and *Don't Leave Me This Way* (1976) by Harold Melvin and the Blue Notes, featuring the young Teddy Pendergrass. The other local producer-composer, Thom Bell, created an even softer sound via the Delfonics' *La-La Means I Love You* (1968), the Stylistics' *Betcha By Golly Now* (1972), the Spinners' *I'll Be Around* (1972), etc. In 1974, Philadelphia ruled the charts (Bell had eleven hits, Gamble & Huff had ten).

Art Soul

With the cerebral and elegant productions of Isaac Hayes' **Hot Buttered Soul** (1969), Marvin Gaye's **What's Going On** (1971), Curtis Mayfield's **Superfly** (1972), and Stevie Wonder's **Music Of My Mind** (1972), soul music had recognized its crisis, and entered a new era. Instead of the assembly-line approach and the song format of the early era, the new era valued an author-oriented approach and the suite format.

A typical product of the era was Los Angeles' multi-instrumentalist Shuggie Otis, the son of Johnny Otis, who embraced the aesthetics of Sly Stone and Marvin Gaye on his fourth album, **Inspiration Information** (1975), a work that he composed, played and produced on his own, a stylistic tour de force, heavy on drum-machine and keyboards as well as strings and horns, that concocted an orchestral and sometimes electronic blend of funk, soul and psychedelic-rock.

However, the 1970s were a decade of steady decline for soul music. First it was funk music that reduced the market for soul musicians (and, in fact, many of them simply adopted the funky beat). Then it was disco music that made soul music sound antiquated as party music. Finally, hip-hop music introduced a completely new paradigm (both vocal and rhythmic) for black music.

THE POST-WAR MUSICAL

New York: the Post-war Musical

After World War II, the most adventurous musicals followed in the footsteps of **Oklahoma** (1944), and showtunes dominated US popular music.

Jule Styne composed **High Button Shoes** (1947), with *I Still Get Jealous* and *Papa Won't You Dance With Me*, and especially **Gentlemen Prefer Blondes** (1949), based on Anita Loos' 1925 novel, with *Diamonds Are A Girl's Best Friend*. His other musicals included songs such as *It's Magic* (1948), *Three Coins In The Fountain* (1954), *The Party's Over* (1956), *Everything's Coming Up Roses* (1959), until **Funny Girl** (1964), the musical biography of Fanny Brice, that launched the career of Barbra Streisand.

Frank Loesser delivered the hit of the decade: **Guys and Dolls** (1950), that included *Sit Down You're Rockin' the Boat, I've Never Been In Love Before* and *Luck Be A Lady Tonight*. **The Most Happy Fella** (1956), with *Standing On The Corner*, was even more ambitious. He also composed *See What the Boys in the Backroom Will Have* (1939), *Praise the Lord and Pass the Ammunitions* (1942, his greatest hit), *I Don't Want To Walk Without You Baby* (1942), *Spring Will Be A Little Late This Year* (1944), *On A Show Boat to China* (1948), *Baby It's Cold Outside* (1949).

The new standard of quality was set by composer Frederick Loewe and lyricist Alan-Jay Lerner. Loewe's score for the fairy tale **Brigadoon** (1947), that included *Almost Like Being In Love* and *There But For You Go I*, was typical of his delicate romanticism and eclectic style. After **Paint Your Wagon** (1951), with *I Talk To The Trees, Wanderin' Star* and *They Call The Wind Mariah*, the duo reached their zenith with **My Fair Lady** (1956), an adaptation of George Bernard Shaw's **Pygmalion** (1914) that boasted countless catchy tunes (*With A Little Bit of Luck, I Could Have Danced All Night, On The Street Where You Live*, that was a major hit for years). They also penned Vincent Minnelli's film **Gigi** (1958), with *Thank God For Little Girls*, and the eccentric **Camelot** (1960), based on Terence-Hanbury White's **The Once And Future King** (1958).

Classical composer and conductor Leonard Bernstein brought to the musical his exuberant creativity: the jazz dance fantasia **On The Town** (1944), the eclectic **Wonderful Town** (1953), the comic operetta **Candide** (1956), based on Voltaire's novel, and finally **West Side Story** (1957), the decade's masterpiece, an adaptation of Shakespeare's **Romeo and Juliet** set in the world of street gangs, with lyrics by Stephen Sondheim and an endless parade of memorable melodies (*America, Dance at the Gym, Tonight, I Feel Pretty, Gee Officer Krupke, Maria* and *Somewhere*) set to rousing rhythms. This musical was, de facto, a most serious attempt at creating an "American" opera as a genre distinct from European opera. Leonard Bernstein also scored Elia Kazan's films **On The Waterfront** (1954) and **East of Eden** (1954).

In Europe, a notable musical was Marguerite Monnot's **Irma La Douce** (1956). In London, the first major sensation of the post-war musical was Lionel Bart's rock'n'roll score for Frank Norman's play **Fings Ain't What They Used To Be** (1959), set in the underworld, followed by Bart's most successful work, **Oliver** (1968). Leslie Bricusse composed **Stop The World I Want To Get Off** (1961).

Show tunes declined rapidly after the advent of rock music. Unlike jazz, that had coexisted peacefully with the Broadway musical, and the "fake" rock'n'roll of Elvis Presley and the Beatles (who were still, basically, singers in the old tradition), "progressive" rock music of the Sixties seemed antithetic to the whole notion of the show tune. The musical seemed to be dying a slow but unstoppable death, despite Jerry Herman's **Hello Dolly** (1964), a musical adaptation of Thornton Wilder's play **The Matchmaker**, Sheldon Harnick's **Fiddler on the Roof** (1964), an adaptation of Sholom Aleichem's stories, and John Kander's **Cabaret** (1966), the most original productions of the Sixties. The age of the hippies was better represented by small-budget off-Broadway productions such as Galt MacDermot's **Hair** (1968), with *Aquarius* and *Let the Sunshine In*, **Oh Calcutta** (1969), an erotic revue devised by British drama critic Kenneth Tynan.

The rock influence peaked in the 1970s with Charles Strouse's **Applause** (1970), a rock adaptation of Joseph Mankiewicz's film **All About Eve** (1950), Andrew Lloyd Webber's **Jesus Christ Superstar** (1971), Jim Jacobs' and Warren Casey's **Grease** (1972), a nostalgic collage of rock melodies from the Fifties plus their own

Greased Lightnin' and John Farrar's *You're The One That I Want*, Pete Townshend's **Tommy** (1975), adapted from the Who's 1969 rock opera, and Richard O'Brien's **The Rocky Horror Picture Show** (1975), a spoof of horror and sci-fi stereotypes with strong sexual overtones, one of the greatest (and wildest) musicals of all times.

A country where the musical comedy boomed in those years was Italy, whose variety show had been strongly influenced by the US invasion of 1943. Armando Trovajoli composed the two most popular musicals: **Rugantino** (1962), that included his hit song *Roma Nun Fa La Stupida Stasera*, and **Aggiungi un Posto a Tavola** (1974).

The decline of the Broadway musical had several concomitant causes. First and foremost, the competition of television soap operas, that catered to the same audience as the musical. Then the escalating production costs, that simply made it too risky a venture for entrepreneurs who could invest their money in more reliable ventures (a film can be shown in thousands of theaters at the same time). In terms of "taste", the musical never truly managed to assimilate the new taste that developed with the advent of rock'n'roll, disco music and hip-hop. Somehow, the musical had successfully assimilated new genres (ragtime, jazz) up until the Sixties. In the Sixties, rock music introduced not only a new musical paradigm but also new forms of consumption (from Woodstock to the video clip) that were simply not compatible with the theatrical format. Finally, there certainly was a change in the national psyche: as the Cold War forced the USA to abandon its childhood (made of easy victories against clearcut enemies such as the Indians and the Nazis) and entered its adulthood (a difficult time of subtle strategizing and risky undertakings on a global scale), the musical had a hard time abandoning its childhood, and eventually fell out of synch with the rest of society.

New York: the Concept Musical

Just when the musical seemed doomed to become only a footnote in the history of rock music, along came a new generation of literate, vibrant "authors", who actually redefined the very notion of the "author" as well as the very notion of "musical".

Bob Fosse's musicals were a first significant step in redefining the musical. Fosse showed little interest in storytelling, plots and characters. He was a musical artist for the sake of the art of the musical, in a sense a true post-modernist genius: his musicals were about the musical. Each musical was a manneristic exploration of themes prevalent in the history of the musical, whether sex or dancing. **Pippin** (1972), scored by Stephen Schwartz (*Corner of the Sky*), **Chicago** (1975), scored by John Kander (*All That Jazz*), **Dancin'** (1978), a loose collage of vintage dance-related numbers (famous as "the musical that got rid of the author").

The towering musical genius of the musical at end of the century was Stephen Sondheim, who revealed his complete persona of both creative composer and virtuoso lyricist with **A Funny Thing Happened on the Way to the Forum** (1962), a cunning musical adaptation of the farces of Roman playwright Plautus. However, he best channelled his aesthetic vision into his later "concept" musicals, that, typically complex and dark in nature, confronted contemporary and universal issues, straddling the line between William Shakespeare and Ingmar Bergman, and, in the process, neglected the melodic aspect in favor of analytic depth: **Company** (1970), the manifesto of his major theme (middle-class alienation), **Follies** (1971), a meditation on nostalgia, **A Little Night Music** (1973), a musical adaptation of Ingmar Bergman's film **Smiles of A Summer Night** (1955), that, despite the intellectual setting, produced Sondheim's only hit song ever, *Send In The Clowns*, the kabuki pastiche **Pacific Overtures** (1976), that includes scene conceived as stand-alone mini-musicals, the operatic drama, **Sweeney Todd** (1979), **Sunday in the Park with George** (1984), a bold musical biography of French painter Georges Seurat, **Into the Woods** (1987), almost a multi-textured literary exegesis of the fairy tale (famous characters of the world of fables such as Cinderella and Snow White live out their stories in the same forest at the same time), and the bleak **Passion** (1994), that was almost the antithesis of the "musical comedy". Sondheim always seemed morbidly attracted by happiness like a man who can only envy it in others but never personally achieve it, and thus can only speculate on how it feels without actually feeling it. Basically, Sondheim destroyed the moral certainties that Rodgers and Hammerstein had created.

Human life looked suddenly loose and undefined, awash in an ambivalent moral universe.

The influence of Sondheim and Fosse led to Michael Bennett's **A Chorus Line** (1975), mostly scored by Marvin Hamlisch, an era-defining event.

But the creative crisis of the musical was still raging, as proven by the nostalgic mood of the Seventies that prompted revivals of just about everything (musicals, burlesques, fairy tales, etc). The best manifestations of this trend were probably Charles Strouse's old-fashioned **Annie** (1976), inspired by the **Little Orphan Annie** comic strip, and Gower Champion's **42nd Street** (1980), a remake of Lloyd Bacon's film of 1933, originally choreographed by Busby Berkeley. These productions seemed to poke fun at the musical while the musical was dying.

Andrew Lloyd-Webber was the (British) composer who single-handedly resurrected the musical. As a teenager, he and lyricist Tim Rice had already envisioned a futuristic production, **Joseph and the Amazing Technicolor Dreamcoat** (1967), influenced by the psychedelic age, followed by **Jesus Christ Superstar** (1971), the first Broadway musical entirely devoted to rock music (with the anthemic title-song). Lloyd-Webber and Rice successfully transposed the traditional musical into the technological age with **Evita** (1979), a musical biography of Eva Peron that included the hit song *Don't Cry For Me Argentina* (one of the last show tunes to be able to compete in the charts with pop, soul and rock music), and then did the same to the traditional revue with **Cats** (1982), based on Thomas-Stearns Eliot's book and relying more on effects than on melodies (*Memory*) and to the operetta with **Phantom of the Opera** (1986) and to the extravaganza with the truly extravagant (but high-tech) **Starlight Express** (1984). Lloyd-Webber's light-weight spectacles were the exact opposite of (almost the antidote to, or maybe complementary to) Sondheim's brainy meditations.

A similar style was pursued in France by Claude-Michel Schonberg, who attained world-wide success with **Les Miserables** (1980) a musical adaptation of Victor Hugo's novel, and **Miss Saigon** (1989), which transposed Puccini's **Madama Butterfly** in Vietnam. He became the first French composer of musical theater since Jacques Offenbach to become a star in the USA.

Alan Menken's sci-fi spoof **Little Shop of Horrors** (1982), a musical adaptation of Roger Corman's horror film of 1960, started a vogue for animated musicals.

Veterans thrived in the new atmosphere, delivering some of the most adventurous musicals of the era, for example Jerry Herman's **Le Cage Aux Folles** (1983) and John Kander's **Kiss of the Spiderwoman** (1993).

The nostalgic element was not dead yet, as Maury Yeston's **Titanic** (1997) and Lynn Ahrens's and Stephen Flaherty's **Ragtime** (1998) proved (two musicals inspired by the styles of the early 20th century).

Hans Zimmer's **The Lion King** (1997) marked two important changes: it was the first hit scored by a former rock musician (ex Buggles), and it was the first major hit produced for a corporation (the Disney Corporation) not a traditional impresario.

Hollywood: the Post-war Musical Films

Hugh Martin scored Vincent Minnelli's nostalgic epic **Meet Me In St Louis** (1944), that included Kerry Mills' *Meet Me In St Louis* (1904) and Martin's *The Boy Next Door*, *Have Yourself a Merry Little Christmas,* and *The Trolley Song*. The musical genre was declining in Hollywood, but Vincent Minnelli dominated whatever was left of it by employing Cole Porter for **The Pirate** (1948), George Gershwin for **An American In Paris** (1951), Frederick Loewe for **Gigi** (1958).

In the 1950s, Stanley Donen managed to compete against Minnelli with **Singin' In The Rain** (1952), starring Gene Kelly and Cyd Charisse, for which Nacio Herb Brown assembled a sort of personal anthology of hits. Gene DePaul scored Donen's second classic, **Seven Brides for Seven Brothers** (1954).

George Cukor's best musical were as light as his comedies: **A Star Is Born** (1954), scored by Ray Heindorf, and **Les Girls** (1957), scored by, scored by Cole Porter.

The best of the Doris Day musicals was probably David Butler's **Calamity Jane** (1953), scored by Sammy Fain.

But rock'n'roll, launched by a soundtrack, Richard Brooks' **The Blackboard Jungle** (1955), was pervasive also in musical films, particularly Elvis Presley's numerous vehicles: **Jailhouse Rock**

(1956), **Girls Girls Girls** (1962) and **Viva Las Vegas** (1964), all based on his hits.

Robert Stevenson's **Mary Poppins** (1964), scored by Richard Sherman *Supercalifragilisticexpialidocious*, (*Chim Chim Cher-Ee*, *Feed The Birds*, *A Spoonful of Sugar*), signaled that the musical was transitioning from entertainment for adults to entertainment for children.

Martin Scorsese's **New York New York** (1977), scored by John Kander (notably the title-tune), and Blake Edwards' **Victor/Victoria** (1982), scored by Henry Mancini and Leslie Bricusse, were the only notable musicals for adults for a while, a sign of rapid decline.

It was, in fact, the Disney corporation that dominated musical films in the 1990s. Alan Menken scored several Walt Disney animated musical productions: **The Little Mermaid** (1989), Robert-Jess Roth **Beauty and the Beast** (1991), John Musker's and Ron Clements' **Aladdin** (1992), Mike Gabriel's and Eric Goldberg's **Pocahontas** (1995), **The Hunchback of Notre Dame** (1996). Elton John took over for **The Lion King** (1994).

Baz Luhrmann's futuristic **Moulin Rouge** (2001), starring Nicole Kidman and using a collage of new and old songs from differet songwriters (arranged and glued together by Craig Armstrong), was the first successful attempt at revitalizing the musical film in three decades.

POST-WAR FILM MUSIC

Hollywood: The New Wave of Film Music

By the time rock'n'roll changed the shape of the recording industry, the concept of a film soundtrack had also changed dramatically. The score was no longer mere marketing for the film, but a product on its own that could be as profitable as the movie itself. On the other hand, purely instrumental scores were still conceived of as in the old days: rarely released on record. Even that changed when two instrumental soundtracks, released on LP, climbed the sale charts: Victor Young's score for Michael Anderson's **Around the World in 90 Days** (1956) and Ernest Gold's score for Otto Preminger's **Exodus** (1961). Gold composed both for drama, such as Stanley Kramer's **On The Beach** (1959), that includes *Waltzing Matilda*, and for comedies, such as **It's A Mad Mad Mad Mad World** (1963).

Henry Mancini crafted a unique style that harked back to lounge music, Latin music and traditional jazz. After scoring Orson Welles' **Touch Of Evil** (1958), Mancini worked on the "Gunn" television series, immortalized in his most famous theme, *Peter Gunn* (1958), vaguely reminiscent of Stan Kenton's jazz sound. His longest association was with Blake Edwards, for whom he composed soundtracks that yielded other celebrated themes: *Moon River* from **Breakfast at Tiffany's** (1961), *Pink Panther Theme* (with saxophone by Plas Johnson) from **The Pink Panther** (1964) and its sequels, *Days of Wine and Roses* from the namesake film (1962), *It's Easy To Say* from **10** (1979), from **The Great Race** (1965) to **Victor/Victoria** (1982). Another famous song was *The Baby Elephant Walk* from Howard Hawks' **Hatari** (1962). He also worked for Stanley Donen on **Charade** (1963) and **Arabesque** (1966), marked by the same "sad humour" of the Edwards' scores.

Nelson Riddle (Sinatra's arranger) scored Stanley Kubrick's **Lolita** (1962).

In Italy, Nino Rota crafted the sound of Federico Fellini's masterpieces **I Vitelloni** (1953), **La Strada** (1954), **Le Notti di Cabiria** (1957), **La Dolce Vita** (1960), **8 1/2** (1963), **Giulietta degli Spiriti** (1965), **I Clown** (1971), **Amarcord** (1974), and is co-responsible for their provincial atmosphere. His scores combine

Italian folk music, circus music and jazz in warm and laid-back tones. The sense of drama was stronger in Luchino Visconti's **Rocco e i Suoi Fratelli** (1960) and **Il Gattopardo** (1963). Rota's progression towards a more aristocratic language, even if still grounded in popular music, continued with Franco Zeffirelli's **Romeo and Juliet** (1969) and Francis-Ford Coppola's **The Godfather** (1972) and its sequels.

Giovanni Fusco was to Michelangelo Antonioni as Rota was to Fellini. He scored his psychological masterpieces **L'Avventura** (1960), **L'Eclisse/ Eclipse** (1962) and **Deserto Rosso** (1964), besides Alain Resnais' **Hiroshima Mon Amour** (1959).

In France, Michel Legrand tried different avenues, first with Jacques Demy's **Les Parapluies de Cherbourg** (1964) whose entire dialogue was sung by the actors, and then with the cinematic operetta **Les Demoiselles de Rochefort** (1966). He scored several classics of the "nouvelle vague", such as Agnes Varda's **Cleo de 5 A 7** (1961) and Jean-Luc Godard's **Bande A Part** (1964). His Hollywood soundtracks yielded the hit songs *The Windmills of Your Mind*, off Norman Jewison's **The Thomas Crown Affair** (1968), *What Are you Doing the Rest of Your Life*, off Richard Brooks' **The Happy Ending** (1969), the theme from Buzz Kulik's **Brian's Song** (1971). He also worked on the soundtrack for Robert Mulligan's **Summer of '42** (1971), on Joseph Losey's **The Go-Between** (1971), perhaps the most elaborate, a veritable symphonic suite, on Richard Lester's **The Three Musketeers** (1974), that mimics baroque music, on Barbra Streisand's musical **Yentl** (1983) and on his Broadway opera bouffe **L'Amour - Le Passe-Muraille** (1997).

George Delerue, influenced by Rota, scored Alain Resnais' **Hiroshima Mon Amour** (1959) and Jean-Luc Godard's **Le Mepris** (1963), but, more importantly, crafted the ambience of most of Francois Truffaut's classics: **Jules et Jim** (1961), **Tirez sur le Pianiste** (1962), **Les Deux Anglaises** (1971), **La Nuit Americaine** (1973), **Le Dernier Metro** (1980). Each of them, as well as Mike Nichols' **The Day of the Dolphin** (1973), was a sophisticated tribute to French melodic music.

But the French "nouvelle vague" had no Morricone, so it had to improvise from film to film: Algerian jazz pianist Martial Solal scored Jean-Luc Godard's **A Bout de Souffle** (1959), singer-songwriter Jean Constantin scored Francois Truffaut's **Les**

Quatrecents Coups (1959), composer Antoine Duhamel scored Francois Truffaut's **Baisers Voles** (1968), and Miles Davis in person scored Louis Malle's **Ascenseur pour l'Echafaud** (1958).

Ingmar Bergman hired classical composers for his soundtracks: Erland Von Koch for **Fangelse** (1949), Erik Nordgren for **Glycklarnas Afton/ Sawdust and Tinsel** (1953), **Sommarnattens Leende/ Smiles of a Summer Night** (1955), **Ansiktet/ Magician** (1957), the medieval and gothic score for **Det Sjunde Inseglet/ Seventh Seal** (1956), **Smultronstallet/ Wild Strawberries** (1957), **Jungfrukallan/ Virgin Spring** (1959) and **Nattvardsgatterna/ Winter Light** (1962), Lars Johan Werle for **Persona** (1966) and **Bargtimmen/ Hour of the Wolf** (1967), while **Skammen/ Shame** (1968) has no music score.

Polish jazz composer Krzysztof Komeda was called by Roman Polanski to score his early films, from **Noz w Wodzie/ Knife in the Water** (1962) to **Rosemary's Baby** (1968), demonstrating a unique ability to mix the lyrical and the harrowing.

On the other hand, Maurice Jarre focused on pompous scores for colossal romantic productions such as David Lean's **Lawrence of Arabia** (1962) and **Doctor Zhivago** (1965), whose *Lara's Theme* was a massive hit (later reissued as *Somewhere My Love*). But he also worked on Roger Vadim's futuristic **Barbarella** (1968), John Huston's western **The Life And Times Of Judge Roy Bean** (1972), Adrian Lyne's thriller **Fatal Attraction** (1987), before becoming Peter Weir's trusted composer for **Witness** (1985), **Mosquito Coast** (1986) and **Dead Poets Society** (1989). His score for Jerry Zucker's **Ghost** (1990) was the archetype for the fusion of electronic and orchestral music.

In Greece, Mikis Theodorakis introduced a strong folk element in Michael Cacoyannis' **Zorba** (1964) and Costa-Gavras' **Z** (1969). More importantly, Eleni Karaindrou composed the soundtracks to some of Theo Angelopoulos' masterpieces: **O Thiassos/ Traveling Players** (1975) **Jaxidi sta Kithira/ Voyage to Citera** (1984), **O Melissokomos/ The Beekeeper** (1986), **To Pio Stin Omichli/ Landscape In The Mist** (1988), **The Suspended Step of the Stork** (1991), **To Vlemma tou Odyssea/ Ulysses' Gaze** (1995), **Mia Eoniotita ke Mi Mera/ Eternity And A Day** (1998).

In Britain, John Barry's bombastic, lyrical and humorous soundtracks for Terence Young's "James Bond" movies became almost synonymous with the "Swinging London": **Dr No** (1962) was the first one, but his art probably peaked with **Goldfinger** (1964). He lent a grave, serious tone to Sidney Furie's **The Ipcress File** (1965), possibly his best work (a masterful fusion of jazz and classical motifs), James Hill's **Born Free** (1966), the theme of John Schlesinger's **Midnight Cowboy** (1969), and Lawrence Kasdan's **Body Heat** (1981). More conventional soundtracks include Sidney Pollack's **Out Of Africa** (1985), Francis Ford Coppola's **Peggy Sue Got Married** (1986), Kevin Costner's **Dances with Wolves** (1990).

Italian composer Ennio Morricone was a master of ambience and suspense whose soundtracks relied on martial but slow rhythms, evocative melodies (often sung by classical voices), that mixed exotic and almost sacred overtones with a sense of nostalgia and of fatalism. His arrangements shunned the orchestra and preferred to emphasize the timbres of the individual instruments (particularly harmonica, trumpet and guitar) and the female voice. He applied this austere style to a rather trivial genre, Sergio Leone's "spaghetti westerns" **Per Un Pugno di Dollari** (1964) and **Il Buono Il Brutto Il Cattivo** (1967), as well as other westerns such as Don Siegel's **Two Mules for Sister Sara** (1969). By the time Leone upped the ante with the epic **C'Era Una Volta il West/ Once Upon a Time in the West** (1969), Morricone's style approached the classical opera. He continued to refine the metaphysical element of his music in Bernardo Bertolucci's **1900** (1976) and Terrence Malick's **Days of Heaven** (1978), achieving in Roland Joffe's **Mission** (1986) an almost liturgical peak.

Japanese classical composer Toru Takemitsu left his mark on a generation of Japanese films: Masaki Kobayashi's **Seppuku/ Hara Kiri** (1962), **Kwaidan** (1964), **Joiuchi/ Samurai Rebellion** (1967), **Nihon no Seishun/ Hymn to a Tired Man** (1968), **Kaseki/ The Fossil** (1971); Hiroshi Teshigahara's **Suna no Onna/ Woman in the Dunes** (1964), **Face Of Another** (1966) and **Rikyu** (1989); Akira Kurosawa's **Dodeskaden** (1970) and **Ran** (1985); Nagisa Oshima's **Gishiki/ Ceremony** (1971) and **Ai No Corrida/ In the Realm of the Senses** (1976); Masahiro Shinoda's **Kawaita Hana/ Pale Flower** (1964), **Double Suicide** (1969), and **Hanare-Goze Orin/ Ballad of Orin** (1977); Shohei Imamura's **Kuroi Ame/ Black Rain** (1989). His scores merge western, eastern and avantgarde sensibility in a seductive and evocative whole.

Among Hollywood's most original composers of the Sixties, David Amram scored Elia Kazan's **Splendor In The Grass** (1961) and John Frankenheimer's **The Manchurian Candidate** (1962).

Jazz great and pop arranger Quincy Jones tried his hand at the movies with Richard Brooks' terrifying **In Cold Blood** (1967) and Peter Collinson's hilarious **The Italian Job** (1969), proving adept at both psychological drama and superficial comedy. He also scored Sam Peckinpah's **The Getaway** (1972).

Frank DeVol penned the soundtracks for Robert Aldrich's two masterpieces, **Whatever Happened to Baby Jane** (1962) and **Hush Hush Sweet Charlotte** (1965), as well as Elliot Silverstein's unusual western **Cat Ballou** (1965) and Stanley Kramer's comedy **Guess Who's Coming to Dinner** (1967).

Jerry Goldsmith crafted John Guillermin's **Blue Max** (1966), which possibly remained his most adventurous soundtrack, and a handful that displayed his willingness to experiment with different formats: John Frankenheimer's **Seconds** (1966), Franklin Schaffner's **Planet of the Apes** (1968), that was pure avantgarde music, basically a concerto for sound effects, Franklin Schaffner's **Papillon** (1973), Roman Polanski's **Chinatown** (1974), Richard Donner's **The Omen** (1976), Peter Hyams' **Capricorn One** (1978). By comparison, his later scores are rather uneventful, but they nonetheless include the unreleased original score for Ridley Scott's **Legend** (1985), James Cameron's **Alien** (1986), Paul Verhoeven's **Basic Instinct** (1992) and Curtis Hanson's **L.A. Confidential** (1998).

Dave Grusin ran the gamut from "mood music", in Sidney Pollack's **Three Days of the Condor** (1975), romantic pop, in Warren Beatty's **Heaven Can Wait** (1978), solo piano, in Mark Rydell's **On Golden Pond** (1981), vaudeville, in Sydney Pollack's **Tootsie** (1982), that contains *It Might Be You*, Latin, in Sydney Pollack's **Havana** (1990), rhythm'n'blues, in Sidney Pollack's **The Firm** (1993), jazz, in Sydney Pollack's **Random Hearts** (1999), to torch song, in Steve Kloves' **The Fabulous Baker Boys** (1989).

The Sixties were also the age of tv soundtracks, that, in many ways, represented the real soundtrack of the era: Jay Livingston's **Bonanza Theme** (1959), the same man who composed some of cinema's most famous melodies: *To Each His Own* (1946), *Mona Lisa* (1950), *Silver Bells* (1951), *Que Sera Sera* (1956); Vic Mizzy's

The Addams Family Theme (1964), Alexander Courage's *Star Trek Theme* (1966), Sherwood Schwartz's *The Brady Bunch Theme* (1969), Patrick Williams' themes for **The Mary Tyler Moore Show** (1970), **The Bob Newhart Show** (1972) and **The Streets of San Francisco** (1972), all the way to Edward Shearmur's theme for the tv series **Charlie's Angels** (1976), that basically summarized the previous era.

Laurie Johnson wrote the themes for a British serial, the futuristic secret-agent thriller **The Avengers**, that debuted in 1961. He also scored Stanley Kubrick's political comedy **Dr Strangelove** (1964), but probably his most fantastic soundtrack was the one for Brian Clemens' **Captain Kronos - Vampire Hunter** (1974).

A specialist of music for farcical comedy, Ira Newborn wrote the themes for the tv series **Dragnet** (1967) and **Police Squad** (1982), that sound like parodies of Henry Mancini soundtracks, and then the series begun with David Zucker's **Naked Gun** (1988).

Classical and jazz composer Lalo Schifrin wrote the theme for the tv series **Mission Impossible** (1966) and **Mannix** (1967) but also became a specialist in soundtracks for action movies, such as Stuart Rosenberg's **Cool Hand Luke** (1967), Peter Yates' **Bullitt** (1968), Don Siegel's **Coogan's Bluff** (1968), **Dirty Harry** (1971) and **Charley Varrick** (1973), all the way to Brett Ratner's **Rush Hour** (1998).

Rock music became a major source of film music after the international success of a few scores that were mere collages of pre-existing hits by various rock artists: Mike Nichols' **The Graduate** (1967), Dennis Hopper's **Easy Rider** (1969), John Schlesinger's **Midnight Cowboy** (1969), Michelangelo Antonioni's **Zabriskie Point** (1970), Nicolas Roeg's **Performance** (1970), Stuart Hagmann's **The Strawberry Statement** (1970), culminating with Michael Wadleigh's documentary on **Woodstock** (1970). Rock music dramatically changed the style of Hollywood soundtracks (even when they were not directly using rock songs). In the 1970s, Hollywood discovered soul music as well, starting with Gordon Parks' films **Shaft** (1971), scored by Isaac Hayes, and **Superfly** (1972), a vehicle for Curtis Mayfield's music. Gato Barbieri scored Bernardo Bertolucci's **Last Tango In Paris/ Ultimo Tango a Parigi** (1972), Bob Dylan scored Sam Peckinpah's **Pat Garret and Billy the Kid** (1973), Herbie Hancock scored Michael Winner's **Death**

Wish (1974). This crescendo eventually led to George Lucas' **American Graffiti** (1973), whose score not only included rock songs but rock songs from twenty years earlier ("oldies").

Rock musician Vangelis Papathanassiou entered cinema with several groundbreaking works, such as the two scores for Frederic Rossif, **L'Apocalypse Des Animaux** (1973) and **Opera Sauvage** (1979), but then veered towards the synthesizer-based symphonic opulence of Hugh Hudson's **Chariots Of Fire** (1981), Koreyoshi Kurahara's **Antarctica** (1985), and Ridley Scott's **1492 Conquest of Paradise** (1995), as well as the ultimate futuristic thriller, Ridley Scott's **Blade Runner** (1982).

Despite Francis Lai's theme for Arthur Hiller's **Love Story** (1971) and Fred Karlin's *For All We Know*, off Cy Howard's **Love And Other Strangers** (1970), the dominant theme of the 1970s was alienation, best represented by Roy Budd's calculated score for the Mike Hodges' thriller **Get Carter** (1971), George Aliceson Tipton's subdued score for Terrence Malick's **Badlands** (1973), Bill Conti's vibrant theme for John Avildsen's **Rocky** (1976).

Polish composer Wojciech Kilar created the haunting atmospheres of Andrzej Wajda's **Ziemia Obiecana/ The Promised Land** (1975), Paul Grimault's **Le Roi Et L'Oiseau** (1980) and Francis Ford Coppola's **Dracula** (1992).

French composer Philippe Sarde scored Claude Sautet's **Cesar et Rosalie** (1972), Roman Polanski's **Le Locataire/ The Tenant** (1976), Jean-Jacques Annaud's **La Guerre du Feu/ Quest for Fire** (1981), Bernard Tavernier's **Coup de Torchon** (1982) and **Une Dimanche Dans la Campagne** (1984).

French musician Francis Lai, Edith Piaf's accordionist, became Claude Lelouch's trusted composer after **Un Homme et Une Femme** (1966) and **L'Homme qui me Plait** (1969), that mixed a tenderly romantic sensibility with neoclassical ambitions, an approach also found in Lai's ambitious score for Edouard Logereau's **Louve Solitaire** (1968).

David Shire's solo-piano score for Francis Ford Coppola's political thriller **The Conversation**(1974), and his complex and dissonant suite for Joseph Sargent's **The Taking of Pelham One-Two-Three** (1974), belonged to the cinema of alienation, but his revivalist scores for David Zelag Goodman's **Farewell My Lovely** (1975), Robert Wise's **The Hindenburg** (1975), John Badham's **Saturday**

Night Fever (1977), that he only partially composed but that launched disco-music in Hollywood (and in the world), and Randal Kleiser's **Grease** (1978), a compilation of rock songs inspired by the style of the 1950s, were the quintessential artifacts of the nostalgic cinema that came afterwards.

Marvin Hamlish's score for George Roy Hill's **The Sting** (1973) was instrumental in launching a revival of ragtime music. He also scored Woody Allen's **Take the Money and Run** (1969) and **Bananas** (1971).

Another nostalgic score was Richard-Rodney Bennett's **Murder On The Orient Express** (1974).

At the other end of the spectrum, the Seventies also witnessed the full-fledged introduction of electronics into film music, starting with Gil Melle's soundtrack for **The Andromeda Strain** (1971), performed on an electronic instrument called "Percussotron III" (possibly the first and only instrument ever built specifically for a film soundtrack) and with Wendy Carlos's score for Stanley Kubrick's **A Clockwork Orange** (1971), that recycled Beethoven, Rossini and Purcell played on synthesizers, followed by Fred Karlin's electronic and orchestral soundscape for Michael Crichton's sci-fi fantasy **Westworld** (1973).

Giorgio Moroder brought the electronic arrangements of disco music to film soundtracks such as Alan Parker's **Midnight Express** (1978), Paul Schrader's **American Gigolo** (1980) and **Cat People** (1982), perhaps his best, Adrian Lyne's **Flash Dance** (1983), that feels like one long music video (both in the film-making style and in the interaction between sounds and images), Wolfgang Petersen's **The Never Ending Story** (1984), Tony Scott's **Top Gun** (1986).

John Carpenter was a rarity: a filmmaker who also composed his own scores, often with help from Alan Howarth. They coined a new genre of electronic rock-influenced music on **Assault On Precinct 13** (1976), **Halloween** (1978), **The Fog** (1980), **Escape from New York** (1981), **Dark Star** (1982), **Christine** (1983), etc.

Howard Shore was horror master David Cronenberg's composer for many years, through **Shivers** (1974), **Scanners** (1981), **Videodrome** (1983), **Dead Ringers** (1988), **Naked Lunch** (1991) and **Crash** (1996), but he proved his versatility with Jonathan Demme's **The Silence of the Lambs** (1991), Chris Columbus' **Mrs Doubtfire** (1993), David Fincher's **Game** (1998) and **7even** (1999) and Kevin Smith's **Dogma** (1999), that led him to the task of scoring the big-budget productions of Peter Jackson's **The Lord Of The Rings** (2001) and its sequels.

On the other hand, John Williams was perhaps the most neo-classical of cinema's composers, a faithful disciple of Gustav Mahler and Richard Strauss. He scored Steven Spielberg's **Jaws** (1975), **Close Encounters of the Third Kind** (1977), the "Indiana Jones" series, starting with **Raiders of the Lost Ark** (1981), **E.T.**(1982) and **Schindler's List** (1993), but made history (although backwards) with George Lucas' "Star Wars" series, starting with **Star Wars** (1977), one of the most popular soundtracks ever, that resurrected the orchestral score a` la Steiner/Korngold. Williams' later soundtracks included commercial comedies, such as Chris Columbus' **Home Alone** (1990), that he scored in an equally trivial manner but that were all very popular, and the "Harry Potter" series, starting with Chris Columbus' **Harry Potter and the Philosopher's Stone** (2001).

During the 1980s, rock music was impossible to contain. Soundtracks that were basically compilations of rock, soul and disco hits continued to proliferate: James Bridges' **Urban Cowboy** (1980), Lawrence Kasdan's **The Big Chill** (1983), a collection of old Motown tunes and one of the best-selling soundtrack albums of all times, Herbert Ross' **Footloose** (1984), Martin Brest's **Beverly Hills Cop** (1984), Ivan Reitman's **Ghostbusters** (1984), Taylor Hackford's **White Nights** (1985), Emile Ardolino's **Dirty Dancing** (1987), Lawrence Kasdan's **The Bodyguard** (1992), peaking perhaps with Robert Zemeckis' **Forrest Gump** (1994), a classic compilation of oldies that accompany the hero through the ages of his life. Designing the sequence of songs became as important as designing the scenes of the film. At the same time, the relationship between the song and the scene became looser and looser. Soundtrack composers often seemed to ignore the film they were "soundtracking". (In the 1990s it even became fashionable to release albums titled after a film that were actually not the soundtrack of the film, or contained only a few songs from the real soundtrack).

Bollywood

The musical in India was more than just one genre: it was "the" genre. The film industry relied on the music (and the dancing) more than on the story and on the acting to sell a film.

The main language of poetry in India was actually Urdu, not Hindi and certainly not English. Therefore Muslim songwriters were in high demand in the Mumbai film industry. They would write in a language that was not quite the literate Hindi of novelists but a colloquial Hindustani that ordinary people could identify with.

The typical melody of those songs was trivial. What made the song stick was the lyrics. Nothing made songs more popular than films.

The arrangements, however, could be very creative, drawing from Indian classical and folk music as well as from Western sources. Western instruments were common in Indian film soundtracks long before Indian instruments became common in Western music. The "East-West fusion" popularized in the 1960s by US and British musicians was actually déjà vu in India.

In fact, it was a multi-layered kind of fusion. Bollywood was ethnically promiscuous in a way that Indian society never was. The same film could feature Hindu, Muslim, Christian, Jewish and Parsi actors, and the Hindus could come from any corner of the subcontinent.

Note that, with the exception of Hindi superstar Amitabh Bachchan, the biggest Bollywood actors have consistently been Muslim, starting with Dilip Kumar (real name Yusuf Khan) and Nargis (Fatima Rashid) to the triad of the 1990s (Shahrukh Khan, Salman Khan, Aamir Khan).

Composers of film music include many who scored national hits: Anil Biswas, Shankar Jaikishan, Naushad Ali, Sachin Dev Burman, Pandit Husan Lal Bhagat Ram, Ramchandra Narhar Chitalkar, Hemant Kumar, Salil Chowdhury, Mohammed Zahur Khayyam, Shankar Sharma, Sajjad Hussain, Roshan (Roshanlal Nagrath), Kalyanji-Anandji (the duo of Kalyanji Virji Shah and Anandji Virji Shah), Vasant Desai, Sudhir Phadke, Hansraj Behl, Madan Mohan, and Usha Khanna. For example, Raj Kapoor's "Awaara" (1951), composed by Shankar (Raghuvanshi Singh) & Jaikishan (Dayabhai Panchal).

Indian movies came to be characterized by shrill female singers after the success in the 1950s of playback singer Lata Mangeshkar, who eventually held the dubious honor of having released more records than any other musician in history, the daughter of Hindustani classical vocalist Dinanath Mangeshkar. Her hits include Khemchand Prakash's "Aayega Aanewaala,"from the movie Mahal (1949), Naushad's "Pyar Kiya To Darna Kya", from Mughal-e-Azam (1960), and Shankar Jaikishan's "Ajeeb Dastaan Hai Yeh", from Dil Apna Aur Preet Parai (1960).

In the 1990s Bollywood music expanded beyond India thanks to composers such as Allah-Rakha Rahman, who scored Mani Ratnam's films Roja (1992) and Bombay (1995) and then Danny Boyle's Slumdog Millionaire (2008).

Film Music as Ambience

As they got older, rock musicians came to the forefront of the soundtrack business: Pino Donaggio's suspense scores for Brian DePalma's **Dressed to Kill** (1980), **Blow Out** (1981) and **Body Double** (1984); Ry Cooder's stylized folk music for Walter Hill's **Long Riders** (1980) and Wim Wenders' **Paris Texas** (1983); Prince's personal statements for Albert Magnoli's **Purple Rain** (1984); Ryuichi Sakamoto's sophisticated electronic languor for Nagisa Oshima's **Merry Christmas Mr Lawrence** (1984), Bernardo Bertolucci's **The Last Emperor** (1986) and **The Sheltering Sky** (1990), Pedro Almodovar's **High Heels** (1992); and, best of all, Peter Gabriel's soundtrack for Martin Scorsese's **The Last Temptation of Christ** (1989), a spiritual suite of ethnic music that set a new standard for scoring films.

Stewart Copeland (of the Police) created a style heavy on rhythm and electronica for Francis-Ford Coppola's **Rumble Fish** (1983), and especially for Oliver Stone's **Wall Street** (1987) and **Talk Radio** (1988). His most surreal score was for Kevin Reynolds' **Rapa Nui** (1994), that employs percussion, synthesizer, ethnic instruments, choir and orchestra.

Singer-songwriter Randy Newman used a witty and nostalgic sense of his nation's roots-music to pen Milos Forman's **Ragtime** (1981), Barry Levinson's **The Natural** (1984), Ron Howard's **Parenthood** (1989), that contains *I Love To See You Smile*, Barry

Levinson's **Avalon** (1990), Richard Donner's **Maverick** (1994), John Lasseter's **Toy Story** (1995), Gary Ross' **Pleasantville** (1998).

Hans Zimmer (ex Buggles) blended electronic, classical, popular and world music in his scores for Barry Levinson's **Rain Man** (1988), Ridley Scott's **Thelma and Louise** (1991), Terrence Malick's **The Thin Red Line** (1998).

Mark Knopfler (of Dire Straits) penned the electronic score for Uli Edel's **Last Exit to Brooklyn** (1990) and the haunting Morricone-style atmosphere of Barry Levinson's **Wag the Dog** (1997).

Danny Elfman (of Oingo Boingo) composed some of the most imaginative soundtracks of his time: Tim Burton's **Beetlejuice** (1988), **Edward Scissorhands** (1990), **Batman Returns** (1992) and especially **Mars Attack** (1996); Martin Brest's **Midnight Run** (1988), Warren Beatty's **Dick Tracy** (1990), Henry Selick's **Nightmare Before Christmas** (1993), Guy Van Sant's **To Die For** (1995) and **Good Will Hunting** (1997), Taylor Hackford's **Dolores Claiborne** (1994), Brian DePalma's **Mission Impossible** (1996), Sam Raimi's **A Simple Plan** (1998). Elfman specialized in unsettling music that draws from a multiplicity of styles, from roots-music to the avantgarde. He also composed themes for two tv series, **The Simpsons** and **Tales From The Crypt**.

Anne Dudley (of Art Of Noise) scored several dramas, in particular Neil Jordan's **The Crying Game** (1992), Peter Cattaneo's **The Full Monty** (1997), and Tony Kaye's **American History X** (1998), possibly her best.

Hip-hop producer Kenneth "Babyface" Edmonds scored Forest Whitaker's **Waiting To Exhale** (1995) with songs delivered by some of the top black vocalists of the time.

New Zealand's industrial rocker Graeme Revell (of SPK) coined a disturbing style that employs rock music, orchestra, ethnic instruments and found sounds: Philip Noyce's **Dead Calm** (1989), Wim Wenders' **Until The End Of The World** (1991), John Woo's **Hard Target** (1993), Alex Proyas' **The Crow** (1994), Kathryn Bigelow's **Strange Days** (1995), Wayne Wang's **Chinese Box** (1998).

Ditto for avantgarde musicians, who renounced some of their harsher tones and focused on the "ambience" of their styles.

Michael Nyman became one of the most prestigious composers of film soundtracks thanks to his collaboration with director Peter

Greenaway: **The Draughtsman's Contract** (1982), **A Zed & Two Noughts** (1985), **Drowning By Numbers** (1988), **The Cook, The Thief, His Wife & Her Lover** (1989) and **Prospero's Books** (1991). But he also scored Jane Campion's **The Piano** (1993) and Andrew Niccol's **Gattaca** (1997) in a more traditional style.

Minimalist composer Philip Glass revolutionized the genre with Godfrey Reggio's trilogy **Koyaanisqatsi** (1983), **Powaqaatsi** (1988) and **Naqoyqatsi** (2003), an experiment in audio-visual fusion, and with the ethereal scores of Paul Schrader's **Mishima** (1985) and Martin Scorcese's **Kundun** (1998).

Mark Isham fused Miles Davis-ian jazz-rock and new-age music for Alan Rudolph's **Trouble In Mind** (1985) and **The Moderns** (1988), as well as for Robert Redford's **A River Runs Through It** (1992).

Angelo Badalamenti concocted a mysterious, sensual and subliminal country-pop-jazz fusion in his soundtracks for David Lynch's **Blue Velvet** (1986), **Twin Peaks** (1990), **Wild At Heart** (1990), **Mulholland Drive** (2001). Another major achievement was the music for Jean-Pierre Jeunet's surreal **La Cité des Enfants Perdus** (1995).

Michael Galasso fused his background in minimalist and world music to create the score for Kar-wai Wong 's **In the Mood for Love** (2000).

Goran Bregovic created the effervescent musical parade for Emil Kusturica's **Time of the Gypsies** (1989), **Underground** (1995) and **Black Cat White Cat** (1998), as well as Patrice Chereau's **La Reine Margot** (1994).

Among prolific all-purpose Hollywood composers, and a master of soaring apotheoses, James Horner scored Walter Hill's **48 Hrs** (1982), James Cameron's **Aliens** (1986), Mel Gibson's **Braveheart** 1995), and James Cameron's **Titanic** (1997), that included *My Heart Will Go On* and became the best-selling soundtrack album of all times; etc. His post-Wagnerian symphonies merged with the sounds of nature in **Terence Malick's The New World** (2005).

Harold Faltermeyer worked on Martin Brest's **Beverly Hills Cop** (1984).

George Fenton scored Richard Attenborough's moving dramas **Gandhi** (1982) and **Cry Freedom** (1987), as well as Marshall Herskovitz's **Dangerous Beauty** (1998).

Michael Kamen proved to be a virtuoso of cinematic music with the soundtrack for Terry Gilliam's **Brazil** (1985), built from variations on the eponymous song, Gilliam's **The Adventures of Baron Munchausen** (1989), that mixed vaudeville and classical music, and then he applied the lesson to action movies such as Richard Donner's **Lethal Weapon** (1987), that uses Eric Clapton's guitar and David Sanborn's saxophone to complement the lines of the two protagonists, and John McTiernan's **Die Hard** (1988). Despite the very low quality of some of the movies he scored, his style that borders on rock and pop yielded a number of hits: *Everything I Do*, off John Irvin's **Robin Hood** (1991), *It's Probably Me*, off John McTiernan's **Lethal Weapon 3** (1992), *All For Love*, off Stephen Herek's **The Three Musketeers** (1993), *Have You Really Ever Loved A Woman*, off Jeremy Leven's **Don Juan DeMarco** (1994), *Rowena*, off Stephen Herek's **Mr Holland's Opus** (1995), that also contains Kamen's tour de force, *American Symphony*.

Trevor Jones penned two very different scores (one classical, one rock) for Jim Henson's **The Dark Crystal** (1982) and **Labyrinth** (1986).

Carter Burwell specialized in scores for unconventional movies. He penned the subdued chamber soundtracks for Joel Coen's **Blood Simple** (1984), **Raising Arizona** (1987), **Miller's Crossing** (1990), **Barton Fink** (1991), **The Hudsucker Proxy** (1993), for soprano and choir, and **Fargo** (1996), as well as for Bill Condon's **Gods and Monsters** (1998), for chamber ensemble, Richard Donner's **Conspiracy Theory** (1997) and Spike Jonze's **Being John Malkovich** (1999), each of them characterized by discontinuity of style.

A similar talent, Mason Daring, specialized in scores for John Sayles, that usually reflect the location of the story and create its ambience: **Matewan** (1987), **The Secret of Roan Inish** (1994), **Lone Star** (1996), **Men With Guns** (1997).

The US composer John Corigliano scored two of the most daring soundtracks of the era: Ken Russell's **Altered States** (1980) and Francois Girard's **Le Violon Rouge** (1998).

Another classical composer, Lee Holdridge, penned the melodies for Don Coscarelli's **The Beastmaster** (1982) and Ron Howard's

Splash (1984), as well as the theme song for the tv series **Moonlighting** (1985).

Brad Fiedel became famous with the menacing, futuristic electronic score of James Cameron's **The Terminator** (1984), but also scored the horror soundtrack for Wes Craven's **The Serpent and the Rainbow** (1988) and the romantic soundtrack for Donald Petrie's **Mystic Pizza** (1988).

Alan Silvestri, a master of quotation from the past, was Robert Zemeckis' trusted composer for his blockbuster movies: **Romancing the Stone** (1984), **Back to the Future** (1985), **Who Framed Roger Rabbit** (1988). He also composed the theme for Lawrence Kasdan's **The Bodyguard** (1992).

Thomas Newman made his reputation with the pop/rock pastiche of Susan Seidelman's **Desperately Seeking Susan** (1985), but became a staple of Hollywood blockbusters with the more conventional albeit highly evocative style that he applied to Martin Brest's **Scent Of A Woman** (1992), Frank Darabont's **The Shawshank Redemption** (1994), Jocelyn Moorhouse's **How to Make an American Quilt** (1995), Gillian Armstrong's **Oscar and Lucinda** (1997), Robert Redford's **The Horse Whisperer** (1998), Sam Mendes' **American Beauty** (1999), Steven Soderbergh's **Erin Brockovich** (2000).

Basil Poledouris created the eerie soundscape for John Milius' **Conan the Barbarian** (1982), basically a collage of sound effects, and then applied that lesson to the field of action movies, for example Paul Verhoeven's **Starship Troopers** (1997).

Christopher Young specialized in horror movies, such as Clive Barker's **Hellraiser** (1987), Bruce Robinson's **Jennifer 8** (1992) and Roger Donaldson's **Species** (1995).

Bruce Broughton established himself as a new master of the western soundtrack with Lawrence Kasdan's **Silverado** (1985) and George Cosmatos' **Tombstone** (1993).

Cliff Eidelman debuted with terrifying masses of symphonic and choral sounds, such as for Monica Teuber's **Magdalene** (1988) and Robert Young's **Triumph of the Spirit** (1989).

Randy Edelman penned melodic fantasias for light comedies such as Jonathan Lynn's **My Cousin Vinny** (1992) and Jon Turteltaub's **While You Were Sleeping** (1995). But his more serious style surfaced on dramatic scores that employed a combination of synthesizers and orchestra, such as Alan Parker's **Come See the Paradise** (1990), Ronald Maxwell's **Gettysburg** (1993), Rob Cohen's **Dragonheart** (1996).

Among themes for tv series, Gary Portnoy's *Where Everybody Knows Your Name* (1982) for **Cheers**, and Mark Snow's **X Files Themes** (1993), became very popular.

Videogame Music

The first videogames were invented in the 1970s, and the first blockbuster videogame was Toshihiro Nishikado's "Space Invaders" in 1978 but it wasn't until Masayuki Uemura's "Nintendo Entertainment System" in 1985 that the videogame became a complex multimedia experience. Initially the music for a videogame was composed by the author himself, as in the case of Shigeru Miyamoto's "Donkey Kong Ditty" (1981) and Alex Pajitnov's "The Tetris Syndrome" (1985). Videogame music came of age between 1984 and 1989, when pioneers such as Koji Kondo ("Supermario Bros", 1985), Jeroen Tel and Rob Hubbard began to compose music for games. It was, by definition, a digital form of music, that had to play using the limited electronic chips implanted in the computer. Nonetheless, those were the humble beginnings of digital popular music. As the videogame entered its renaissance period in the early 1990s, and 16-bit and 32-bit microprocessors allowed for superior sonic fidelity, its soundtracks emancipated themselves from the cliches of the old game arcades and became more and more "musical".

Film Music of the 1990s

At the end of the century, the main disciples of Morricone and Rota were Luis Bacalov, with Michael Radford's **Il Postino** (1995), and Nicola Piovani, with Roberto Benigni's **La Vita E` Bella/ Life Is Beautiful** (1998).

French composer Yann Tiersen grafted childish minimalist music into disjointed folk music for Jean-Pierre Jeunet's **Amelie** (2001) and Wolfgang Becker's **Goodbye Lenin** (2003).

In Spain, Alberto Iglesias was Pedro Almodovar's trusted composer for **Hable con Ella/ Talk To Her** (2002) and **Mala Educacion/ Bad Education** (2004), colorful fusions of Spanish folk music (such as flamenco) and classical music.

Scottish rock producer Craig Armstrong coined a personal style relying on synthesized strings, piano and percussion for Baz Luhrmann's **Romeo And Juliet** (1998), Jake Scott's **Plunkett And Macleane** (1999), Roger Kumble's **Cruel Intentions** (1999), Mike Barker's **Best Laid Plans** (1999), Phillip Noyce's **Bone Collector** (1999), and Baz Luhrmann's **Moulin Rouge** (2001).

Canadian new-age music composer Mychael Danna crafted some of the most delicate and evocative soundtracks of the 1990s, particularly for Atom Egoyan's **Exotica** (1994), **Sweet Hereafter** (1997), **Kama Sutra** (1996) and **Felicia's Journey** (1999), but also for Ang Lee's **The Ice Storm** (1997) and Mira Nair's **Monsoon Wedding** (2002).

Former Dead Can Dance's vocalist Lisa Gerrard composed the mostly-instrumental soundtrack for Niki Caro's **The Whale Rider** (2003).

Eric Serra scored Luc Besson's **La Femme Nikita** (1991), **Leon/ The Professional** (1994) and **The Fifth Element** (1996).

James Newton Howard emerged as a prolific and eclectic composer with Garry Marshall's **Pretty Woman** (1990), Barbra Streisand's **The Prince of Tides** (1991), Andrew Davis' **The Fugitive** (1993), Wolfgang Petersen's **Outbreak** (1995), Kevin Reynolds' **Waterworld** (1995), PJ Hogan's **My Best Friend's Wedding** (1997), Taylor Hackford's **Devil's Advocate** (1998), Night Shyamalan's **Sixth Sense** (1999), as well as the theme for the tv series **ER** (1994).

Classical composer Elliot Goldenthal created the hallucinated ambience of Gus VanSant's **Drugstore Cowboy** (1989), then the neurotic orchestral suite of David Fincher's **Alien 3** (1992), the madcap stylistic romp of Joel Schumacher's **Batman Forever** (1995), Barry Levinson's **Sphere** (1998), July Taymor's **Titus** (1999).

Jon Brion specialized in eerie and sometimes suspenseful soundscapes, such as the ones assembled for Paul Thomas Anderson's **Magnolia** (1999) and **Punch-Drunk Love** (2002), and Michel Gondry's **Eternal Sunshine of the Spotless Mind** (2004).

Other films with innovative soundtracks at the turn of the centuries included: Regis Warnier's **Indochine** (1992) by Patrick Doyle, Wayne Wang's **The Joy Luck Club** (1993) by Rachel Portman, Renny Harlin's **Cutthroat Island** (1995) by John Debney, Rob

Reiner's **The American President** (1995) by Marc Shaiman, Jim Jarmusch's **Dead Man** (1996) by Neil Young, Roland Emmerich's **Independence Day** (1996) by David Arnold, Jan DeBont's **Twister** (1996) by Mark Mancina, Anthony Minghella's **The English Patient** (1996) by Gabriel Yared, Larry Wachowski 's **The Matrix** (1999) by Don Davis, Ang Lee's **Crouching Tiger Hidden Dragon** (2000), by Chinese classical composer Tan Dun; Philip Kaufman's **Quills** (2000), by Stephen Warbeck, influenced by Michael Nyman; Alex Proyas' **I Robot** (2004) by Marco Beltrami, Mel Gibson's **The Passion of the Christ** (2004) by John Debney.

Chronology of Events

1867:
The first collection of "Slave Songs of the United States" is published

1877:
Thomas Edison invents sound recording, and a phonograph to play sound recorded on cylinders

1880:
The tango is born in Buenos Aires

1885:
Benjamin Franklin Keith and Edward Franklin Albee set up a nation-wide chain of vaudeville theaters

1887:
Emile Berliner builds the first gramophone, that plays sound recorded at 78 RPM on a flat record

1889:
Columbia is founded by Edward Easton

1892:
Popular music becomes big business and music publishers rent offices around Union Square in New York City, an area that is renamed "Tin Pan Alley" (sheet music is the primary "product" of popular music and the industry is dominated by music publishing houses)

1893:
Kerry Mills's *Rastus On Parade* is the first published cakewalk

1894:
Hawaiian guitarist Joseph Kekeku invents the slide guitar (by fretting the guitar with a comb)
The weekly Billboard magazine begins publication, offering "charts" of music sales

1895:
Ben Harney's *You've Been a Good Old Wagon* is the first ragtime piece to be published
The first jazz band, the Spasm Band, first performs in New Orleans
Gugliemo Marconi invents the radio

1897:
Edwin Votey invents the player piano

1898:
Emile Berliner sells the European rights to the gramophone to the Gramophone Company or HMV (His Master's Voice)

1899:
Scott Joplin's *Maple Leaf Rag* (1899) starts the ragtime craze

1901:
Emile Berliner founds the record label Victor Talking Machines
Melville Clark builds the first full 88-key player piano

1903:
Will-Marion Cook's musical revue **In Dahomey** exports cakewalk to Britain

1907:
Fred Barrasso creates a chain of vaudeville theaters that evolves into the Theater Owners's Booking Association (T.O.B.A.).

1909:
The term "jazz" is used for the first time in the song *Uncle Josh in Society* (but it refers to ragtime)

1910:
John Lomax publishes "Cowboy Songs and Other Frontier Ballads"
350,000 pianos are manufactured in the USA

1912:
William Spiller's band, the Musical Spillers, export ragtime to Britain
The incidental music to Richard Walton Tully's play **Bird of Paradise** popularizes the ukulele and the steel guitar
The first blues is published, Hart Wand's *Dallas Blues*

1914:
Jerome Kern invents the "musical" by integrating music, drama and ballet and setting it into the present
The American Society for Composers (ASCAP) is founded to protect songwriters

1916:
The first record to be advertised as "samba" is Ernesto Joaquim Maria dos Santos, better known as "Donga", *Pelo Telefone*
Piano makers Brunswick start a record label
Cecil Sharp publishes a collection of folk music from the Appalachian mountains

1917:
The first jazz record is cut in New York

1918:
James Europe's Hellfighters export jazz to France

1919:
General Electric absorbs the US branch of Marconi Wireless Telegraph and renames it Radio Corporation of America (RCA)
Will Marion Cook's syncopated orchestra plays jazz for King George V in Britain

1920:
Mamie Smith's *Crazy Blues* is the first blues by a black singer to become a nation-wide hit
Westinghouse Electric starts the first commercial radio station, "KDKA"

1921:
106 million records are sold in the USA, mostly published on "Tin Pan Alley", but control of the market is shifting to the record companies
Okeh introduces a "Colored Catalog" targeting the black community, the first series of "race records"

1922:
Trixie Smith cuts *My Man Rocks Me With One Steady Roll*
Texan fiddler Eck Robertson cuts the first record of "old-time music"
James Sterling buys out the British division of Columbia

1923:
Bessie Smith cuts her first blues record
John Carson records two "hillbilly" songs and thus founds country music

1924:
The Music Corporation of America (MCA) is founded in Chicago as a talent agency
German record company Deutsche Grammophon (DG) founds the Polydor company to distribute records abroad
Riley Puckett introduces the "yodeling" style of singing into country music

1925:
The Mills Brothers popularize the "barbershop harmonies"
Carl Sprague is the first musician to record cowboy songs (the first "singing cowboy" of country music)
The electrical recording process is commercially introduced, quickly replacing the mechanical one
78.26 RPM is chosen as a standard for phonographic records because phonographs at that speed could use a standard 3600-rpm motor and 46-tooth gear (78.26 = 3600/46).
Nashville's first radio station is founded (WSM) and begins broadcasting a program that will change name to "Grand Ole Opry"

1926:
Bing Crosby cuts his first record and invents the "crooning" style of singing
thanks to a new kind of microphone
Blind Lemon Jefferson is the first bluesman to enter e major recording studio
Will Shade founds the first "jug band" in Memphis, inspired by Louisville's first
jug bands
The magazine "Phonograph Monthly Review" is founded
Vitaphone introduces 16-inch acetate-coated shellac discs playing at 33 1/3 RPM
(a size and speed calculated to be the equivalent of a reel of film)
The British magazine "Melody Maker" is founded
General Electric founds the "National Broadcasting Company" (NBC)

1927:
Meade Lux Lewis cuts *Honky Tonk Train*, the most famous boogie woogie
 Jimmie Rodgers, the first star of country music, adopts "yodeling" style of
singing, the blues style of black music, and the Hawaian slide guitar
Classical composer Kurt Weill begins a collaboration with playwright Bertold
Brecht, incorportating jazz, folk and pop elements in his soundtracks
Sales of "race records" reach $100 million

1928:
The United Independent Broadcasters (later renamed Columbia Broadcasting
System, or CBS) of 47 affiliate stations is founded
Clarence "Pinetop" Smith cuts *Pinetop's Boogie Woogie*

1929:
Decca is founded in Britain by Edward Lewis as a classical music company
RCA buys Victor Talking Machines
The "Great Depression" destroys the record industry
Blind Lemon Jefferson dies

1930:
Warner Brothers buys Brunswick

1931:
EMI (Electrical and Musical Industries), formed by the merger of Gramophone
and the British subsidiary of Columbia, opens the largest recording studio in the
world at Abbey Road in London, while the US division of Columbia is sold
 George Beauchamp invents the electric guitar (the Rickenbacker)
Gene Autry's *Silver Hairde Daddy Of Mine* popularizes the "honky-tonk" style of
country music

1932:
Thomas Dorsey's *Precious Lord* invents gospel music in Chicago
Milton Brown and Bob Wills invent "western swing"

1933:
Cuban bandleader Ignacio Pineiro releases *Echale Salsita*, the song that gives the name "salsa" to Cuba's dance music
Only six million records are sold in the USA
Jimmie Rodgers dies
Sales of "race records" drop to $6 million

1934:
John Lomax and his son Alan begin recording black music of the southern states, and discover the gospel genre of "rocking and reeling"
Laurens Hammond invents the Hammond organ
The first magazine devoted to jazz music, Down Beat, is published

1935:
The radio program "Hit Parade" is launched
Woody Guthrie writes the *Dust Bowl Ballads* and becomes the first major singer-songwriter
Max Gordon founds the jazz club "Village Vanguard" in New York

1936:
Roy Acuff becomes the first star of Nashville's country music
Bluesman Robert Johnson cuts his first record
Carl Stalling begins scoring the soundtracks for Warner Brothers' cartoons
The Gibson company produces its first electric guitar, the ES-150

1937:
Records by the "big bands" are the best sellers
The mambo is born in Cuba

1938:
A Carnegie Hall concert by the piano trio of Albert Hammons, Meade Lux Lewis and Pete Johnson launches the boogie-woogie craze
CBS buys USA's Columbia

1939:
Leo Mintz founds a record store in Cleveland, the "Record Rendezvous", specializing in black music
John Cage composes *Imaginary Landascape N.1* for magnetic tape
The "Grand Ole Opry" moves to Nashville's "Ryman Auditorium" and is broadcasted by the national networks

1940:
Disney's "Fantasia" introduces stereo sound
Pete Seeger forms the Almanac Singers to sing protest songs with communist overtones
Keynote is founded by Eric Bernay

1941:
Arkansas' radio station KFFA hires Sonny Boy Williamson to advertise groceries, the first case of mass exposure by blues singers
"La Discotheque" a club devoted to jazz music, opens in Paris

1942:
Bing Crosby's *White Christmas* becomes the best-selling song of all times (and will remain so for 50 years)
Los Angeles bluesman T-Bone Walker incorporates jazz chords into the blues guitar with *I Got A Break Baby*

Capitol is founded in Hollywood, the first major music company which is not based in New York
Savoy is founded in Newark (NJ) by by Herman Lubinsky to promote black music

1943:
The first "disc jockeys" follow the US troops abroad
The USA army introduces V-Discs that play six minutes of music per side
Richard Rodgers and Oscar Hammerstein produce the musical *Oklahoma* that uses choreographer Agnes de Mille to design the ballets
King is founded in Cincinnati by Sydney Nathan to promote black music

1945:
Les Paul invents "echo delay", "multi-tracking" and many other studio techniques
White bluesman Johnny Otis assembles a combo for *Harlem Nocturne* that is basically a shrunk-down version of the big-bands of swing
Mercury is founded in Chicago
Jules Bihari founds Modern Records in Los Angeles, specializing in black music
Bill Monroe's *Kentucky Waltz* popularizes the "bluegrass" style

1946:
Louis Jordan launches "jump blues" with *Choo Choo Ch'Boogie*
Muddy Waters cuts the first records of Chicago's electric blues (rhythm and blues)
Carl Hogan plays a powerful guitar riff on Louis Jordan's *Ain't That Just Like a Woman*
Lew Chudd founds Imperial Records in Los Angeles, specializing in black music
The Metro-Goldwyn-Mayer (MGM) film company opens a recording business to sell their movie soundtracks
Specialty Records is founded by Art Rupe in Los Angeles to specialize in black popular music

1947:
Billboard's writer Jerry Wexler coins the term "rhythm and blues" for Chicago's electric blues
Roy Brown writes and cuts *Good Rockin' Tonight* in Texas
Six majors control the music market: Columbia, RCA Victor, Decca, Capitol, MGM, Mercury

The Hollywood-based tv program of Korla Pandit (John Red), pretending to be an Indian guru and playing a Hammond organ, publicizes exotic sounds
Chess Records is founded in Chicago by two Polish-born Jews to promote rhythm and blues
Ahmet Ertegun founds Atlantic in New York to promote black music at the border between jazz, rhythm and blues and pop

1948:
Pete Seeger forms the Weavers, which start the "folk revival"
Detroit rhythm'n'blues saxophonist Wild Bill Moore releases *We're Gonna Rock We're Gonna Roll*
Columbia introduces the 12-inch 33-1/3 RPM long-playing vinyl record
Rodgers & Hammerstein's **Tale Of The South Pacific** introduces exotic sounds to Broadway
Leo Fender introduces its electric guitar (later renamed Telecaster)
Moe Asch founds Folkways, devoted to folk music
Ed Sullivan starts a variety show on national television (later renamed "Ed Sullivan Show")
Memphis' radio station WDIA hires Nat Williams, the first black disc jockey
The magazine "Billboard" introduces charts for "folk" and "race" records

1949:
Fats Domino cuts *The Fat Man*, a new kind of boogie
Hank Williams' *Lovesick Blues* reaches the top of the country charts
Scatman Crothers cuts *I Want To Rock And Roll* (1949), with Wild Bill Moore on saxophone
RCA Victor introduces the 45 RPM vinyl record
Fantasy is founded
Todd Storz of the KOWH radio station starts the "Top 40" radio program
The "Billboard" chart for "race" records becomes the chart for "rhythm and blues" records
Aristocrat changes its name to Chess

1950:
Jac Holzman founds Elektra in New York to promote new folk and jazz musicians
Les Baxter's **Music Out of the Moon** incorporates exotic themes in instrumental music
The first major rhythm'n'blues festival is held in Los Angeles (the "Blues & Rhythm Jubilee")
Dutch electronics giant Philips enters the recording business

1951:
The white Cleveland disc jockey Alan Freed decides to speculate on the success of Leo Mintz's store and starts a radio program, "Moondog Rock'n'Roll Party", that broadcasts black music to an audience of white teenagers
The first rock and roll record, Ike Turner's *Rocket 88*, is released
The first juke-box that plays 45 RPM records is introduced

Howlin Wolf and Joe Turner popularize the "shouters"
Victor and Columbia agree to split the record market: Victor sells 33 RPM long-playing records and Columbia sells 45 RPM records
Gunter Lee Carr cuts the dance novelty *We're Gonna Rock*
The first Jamaican studio opens and begins recording "mento" music

1952:
Bill Haley forms the Comets, the first rock and roll band
The Weavers, accused of being communists, are forced to dissolve
Bob Horn's "Bandstand" tv program airs from Philadeplhia every weekday afternoon
The Cleveland disc jockey Alan Freed (aka Moondog) organizes the first rock and roll concert, the "Moondog Coronation Ball"
Gibson introduces its solid-body electric guitar, invented by Les Paul a few years earlier
Roscoe Gordon, a Memphis pianist, invents the "ska" beat with *No More Doggin'*
Sam Phillips founds Sun Records and declares "If I could find a white man who sings with the Negro feel, I'll make a million dollars"
Charles Brown's *Hard Times* is the first hit by Jerry Leiber and Mike Stoller to enter the charts

1953:
Bill Haley's *Crazy Man Crazy* is the first rock and roll song to enter the Billboard charts
The Orioles' *Crying in the Chapel* is the first black hit to top the white pop charts
Todd Matshikiza's musical *Makhaliphile* fuses classical, jazz and African music
Sam Phillips records the first Elvis Presley record in his Sun studio of Memphis using two recorders to produce an effect of "slapback" audio delay
Hank Williams dies at 30
CBS launches a sub-label, Epic
Delmark is founded by Bob Koester
The black market constitutes 5.7% of the total US market for records
Vee-Jay is founded in Indiana, owned by a black couple and specializing in black music

1954:
Boom of doo-wop
Bill Haley's version of "Rock Around The clock" is the first rock song used in a movie soundtrack
Joe Turner cuts the blues novelty *Shake Rattle And Roll*
The record companies switch from 78 RPMs to 45 RPMs
EMI (Electrical and Musical Industries) buys Capitol
The Country Music Disc Jockeys' Association (CMA) is founded in Nashville
Japanese electronic company TTK (later Sony) introduces the world's first transistor radio
The first Newport Jazz Festival is held, the first hazz festival in the world

1955:
Frank Sinatra's **In The Wee Small Hours** (1955) is the first concept album of pop music
Pete Seeger releases the first album of African music by a white musician, **Bantu Choral Folk Songs**
Lonnie Donegan's *Rock Island Line* launches a new genre in Britain, "skiffle"
Chuck Berry cuts his first rock and roll records, the first ones to have the guitar as the main instrument, and invents the descending pentatonic double-stops (the essence of rock guitar)
Bo Diddley invents the "hambone" rhythm
The Chordettes and the Chantels are the first girl-groups
Ray Charles invents "soul" music with *I Got A Woman*, a secular adaptation of an old gospel
Indian sarod player Ali Akbar Khan performs at the Museum of Modern Art of
ABC-Paramount is founded in New York New York
The magazine "Village Voice" is founded by Dan Wolf, Ed Fancher and Norman Mailer
Ace Records is formed by Johnny Vincent in New Orleans, specializing in black music

1956:
The popularity of rock and roll causes the record industry to boom and allows independent labels to flourish
Ska develops in Jamaica
Martin Denny's **Exotica** invents a new genre
Norman Granz founds Verve to promote alternative jazz musicians
Elektra pioneers the "compilation" record, containing songs by different musicians

1957:
Golden age of the teen-idols
Link Wray's *Rumble* invents the "fuzz-tone" guitar sound
Harry Belafonte's *Banana Boat* launches "calypso"

1958:
Golden age of instrumental rock
The Kingstone Trio's *Tom Dooley* launches the folk revival
Lowman Pauling uses guitar distortion and feedback on the Five Royales' *The Slummer The Slum*
The film company Warner Brothers enters the recording business
Big Bill Broonzy dies at 65
RCA introduces the first stereo long-playing records
Don Kirshner opens offices at the Brill Building
David Seville's *The Witch Doctor* and the Tokens' *Tonite I Fell In Love* are the first novelty hits
Bobby Freeman's *Do You Wanna Dance* begins the "dance craze"
Antonio Carlos Jobim's *Chega de Saudade* coins bossanova
The Columbia-Princeton studio is established in New York for avantgarde

composers, with an RCA Mark II synthesizer
Stax is founded in Memphis to promote black music

1959:
In Jamaica Theophilus Beckford cuts the first "ska" song, *Easy Snapping*
Rick Hall founds the FAME studios in Muscle Shoals, Alabama
The Drifters' *There Goes My Baby* introduces Latin rhythm into pop music
Babatunde Olatunji's **Drums of Passion** introduces the USA to African polyrhythms
The first Newport Folk Festival is held
 Barry Gordy founds Tamla Motown in Detroit to release party-oriented soul records
Chris Blackwell founds Island in Jamaica
Puertorican dj Polito Vega begins broadcasting Latin music in New York
 600 million records are sold in the USA
 Since 1955, the US market share of the four "majors" has dropped from 78% to 44%, while the market share of independent record companies increased from 22% to 56%
Since 1955, the US market has increased from 213 million dollars to 603 million, and the market share of rock and roll has increased from 15.7% to 42.7%

1960:
Twist is the biggest dance-craze in the year of the dance-crazes
 The Shirelles' *Will You Love Me Tomorrow* coins a form of romantic multi-part vocal harmonies
 The word "reggae" is coined in Jamaica to identify a "ragged" style of dance music, with its roots in New Orleans rhythm and blues
Philips buys Mercury
Frank Sinatra founds Reprise Records

1961:
Dick Dale uses the term "surfing" to describe his instrumental rock and roll
Bob Dylan arrives at New York's Greenwich Village
British bluesman Alexis Korner forms the Blues Incorporated, with a rotating cast that will include Charlie Watts, John Surman, John McLaughlin, Mick Jagger, Brian Jones, Keith Richard, Eric Burdon, Jack Bruce, Ginger Baker, etc
Howlin Wolf cuts the **Rocking Chair** album, the masterpiece of rhythm'n'blues
The magazine "Mersey Beat" is founded in Liverpool
The Tokens' *The Lion Sleeps Tonight* uses operatic singing, Neapolitan choir, yodel, proto-electronics
Stax begins to produce soul records in Memphis
Kenny Gamble and Leon Huff found Philadelphia International to produce soul records with orchestral arrangements
 MGM buys Verve
ABC-Paramount starts a sub-label for jazz, Impulse
The "Peppermint Lounge" opens in New York

1962:

The Beach Boys' *Surfin* (released in december 1961) launches surf-music in the charts

The US producer Phil Spector creates a style of production named "wall of sound"

Most pop hits are written and produced at the Brill Building

The bishop of New York forbids Catholic students from dancing the Twist

Golden age of the girl-groups

Herb Alpert founds A&M in Los Angeles

Boom of the Tamla Motown record label

MCA buys the US recording company Decca

The US market share of the four "majors" drops to 26%

1963:

"Beatlesmania" hits Britain

Davy Graham in Britain and Sandy Bull in the USA fuse folk, blues, jazz and Indian raga

A soul record, Marvin Gaye's *Can I Get A Witness*, becomes the anthem of British mods

50% of US recordings are made in Nashville

Elmore James dies at 45

The FBI spies on folksingers such as Bob Dylan and Phil Ochs.

Warner buys Reprise

1964:

James Brown coins a percussive style of soul, the predecessor of "funk"

Millie Small's *My Boy Lollipop* is the first worldwide ska hit

Wilson Pickett creates an evil, ferocious kind of soul music with with *In The Midnight Hour*

Fania is founded to record Latin music

1965:

The Supremes have four number-one hits and the Four Tops have two, all of them written by Tamla's team of Brian Holland, Lamond Dozier and Eddie Holland

Robbie Basho's **Seal Of The Blue Lotus** fuses raga, jazz, blues and pop music

Otis Redding's *I've Been Lovin' You Too Long* is soul music in which the instrumental backing has de facto replaced the gospel choir

The "Whiskey-A-Go-Go" opens on Sunset Blvd in Hollywood

1966:

Boom of the blues revival in the USA and Britain

Sire is founded in London

1967:

Ralph Gleason founds the magazine "Rolling Stone"

Dyke And The Blazers cut *Funky Broadway*, the song that gives a genre its name

Otis Redding dies at 26

Woody Guthrie dies at 55

Warner Brothers purchases Atlantic
Byg is founded in France
Chrysalis is founded in London
In Jamaica, disc jockey Ruddy Redwood makes instrumental versions of reggae hits
Neil Diamond's *Red Red Wine* is the first reggae hit by a pop musician
Caetano Veloso and Gilberto Gil found the "tropicalismo" movement in Brazil

1968:
Toots And The Maytals' *Do The Reggae* launches reggae in the USA

1969:
The world's music market is worth two billion dollars

1970:
King Tubby invents "dub" in Jamaica using the recording console like an instrument
Smokey Robinson's *The Tears Of A Clown* fuses vaudeville, classical music and soul music

1971:
Marvin Gaye, Isaac Hayes, Curtis Mayfield and Stevie Wonder begin producing artsy soul records
Marvin Gaye's *Mercy Mercy Me* is the first ecological song

1972:
Cameroon-born and Paris-based musician Manu Dibango invents "disco music" with *Soul Makossa*

1973:
The film **The Harder They Come** brings reggae to the West
A tv special uses the term "salsa" for Latin music

1974:
Barry White plays orchestral soul for the discos

1975:
Boom of funk music
Calhoun's *Dance Dance Dance* is the first 12" single
Jamaican disc-jockey Clive "Hercules" Campbell re-invents the breakbeat in New York, thereby inventing "rap music" and "hip hop"

Alphabetical Index of Names

www.ingramcontent.com/pod-product-compliance
Lightning Source LLC
Chambersburg PA
CBHW051820090426
42736CB00011B/1570